THE
SUPREME
COURT

THE
SUPREME
COURT

THE PERSONALITIES
AND RIVALRIES
THAT DEFINED
AMERICA

Jeffrey Rosen

Times Books
Henry Holt and Company
New York

Times Books
Henry Holt and Company, LLC
Publishers since 1866
175 Fifth Avenue
New York, New York 10010
www.henryholt.com

Henry Holt® *is a registered trademark of Henry Holt and Company, LLC.*

Distributed in Canada by H. B. Fenn and Company Ltd.

Library of Congress Cataloging-in-Publication Data

Rosen, Jeffrey, date.
   The Supreme Court : the personalities and rivalries that defined America / Jeffrey Rosen.
      p. cm.
   ISBN-13: 978-0-8050-8182-4
   ISBN-10: 0-8050-8182-8
      1. United States. Supreme Court—History.   2. Judges—United States—Biography.
3. Judges—United States—History.   4. Judges—United States—Psychology.
5. Judges—United States—Biography.   I. Title.

KF8744.R67 2006
347.73'2634—dc22   *2006050941*

Henry Holt books are available for special promotions and premiums.
For details contact: Director, Special Markets.

First Edition 2007

Designed by Meryl Sussman Levavi

Printed in the United States of America

10 9 8 7 6 5 4 3 2 1

For Hugo and Sebastian,
with appreciation for their judicious temperaments

Contents

THE
SUPREME
COURT

A Question
of Temperament

———

On April 8, 1952, to prevent an imminent steelworkers' strike that he thought would cut off the flow of guns to U.S. troops in the middle of the Korean War, President Harry S. Truman decided to use his authority as commander in chief to seize the nation's steel mills. His decision would provoke more criticism than any other in his presidency. But Truman had been emboldened to act in part because of confidential advice from Chief Justice Fred Vinson, whom Truman had appointed to the Supreme Court in 1946. When Truman informed Vinson in advance of his intention to seize the steel mills, the chief justice assured his friend the president that the seizure would be legal under his executive powers and that a majority of the Court would support it. Vinson's advice turned out to be wrong. In June, two months after the president issued his executive order, the Supreme Court declared in *Youngstown Sheet & Tube v. Sawyer* that Truman had acted unconstitutionally. Writing for a 6–3 majority, Justice Hugo Black declared that the Constitution gives Congress, not the president, the power to make laws, and Congress had refused to authorize this heavy-handed approach to settling labor disputes. Black read his opinion for the Court from the bench. "Even though 'theater of war' be an expanding concept," he drawled in his calm and deliberate southern accent, "we cannot with faithfulness to our constitutional system hold that the Commander in Chief of the Armed Forces has the ultimate power as such to take possession of private property in order to keep labor disputes from stopping production." Although an ardent Democrat as well as a former senator, Black revered the institution of the Supreme Court as something larger than the individual justices who composed it, and masterfully persuaded a majority of his colleagues to enforce the limits that the Constitution places on the president's power. Vinson filed a sputtering dissent insisting that any president worthy of the office should be free to take emergency measures necessary to ensure the "survival of the nation." Truman was understandably livid at his rebuke by a Court that had been appointed entirely by him or by his Democratic predecessor, Franklin D. Roosevelt. But Black soon made amends by inviting the aggrieved president and the entire Court over to his house in Alexandria, Virginia, for bourbon and a barbecue. As the canapés were passed around, the mollified Truman declared, "Hugo, I don't much care for your law, but, by golly, this bourbon is good."[1]

Fifty-four years later, a similar drama unfolded at the Supreme Court. President George W. Bush, seeking to protect the nation after the terrorist attacks of September 11, 2001, issued an executive order creating special military commissions to try suspected enemy combatants who were being held at Guantánamo Bay. His decision, combined with other assertions of unilateral presidential power to authorize something close to torture or indefinite detention of suspected terrorists, provoked more criticism than any other in his presidency. Bush had been emboldened to act in part because his legal advisers had as-

sured him that unilateral action would be upheld as constitutional under his powers as commander in chief, and also, perhaps, because the
chief justice he had recently appointed, John G. Roberts, Jr., had sustained Bush's action as an appellate judge. When the Supreme Court
heard the case in 2006, Roberts properly recused himself because of
his earlier participation in the case, but Bush still had reason for optimism: seven of the nine justices were Republican appointees, including an associate justice appointed by Bush, Samuel A. Alito. In
Hamdan v. Rumsfeld, however, by a vote of 5–3, the Supreme Court
held that the president's military commissions were illegal. In his
opinion for the Court, Justice John Paul Stevens emphasized that the
president could create military commissions only with congressional
support, and Congress had refused to give Bush the power to create
the military commissions at issue in the case. In an emotional dissenting opinion, which he read aloud from the bench (only the second
time he has done so in his fifteen years on the Court), Justice Clarence
Thomas declared that the majority had endangered the nation by
"sorely hamper[ing] the President's ability to confront and defeat a
new and deadly enemy." Thomas, like Vinson, insisted that the president's inherent authority as commander in chief was broad enough to
allow him to act unilaterally in times of war.

The impassioned performances by two justices—Black in 1952,
Thomas in 2006—open a window onto the Supreme Court. In many
respects, the similarities between Black and Thomas are striking.
Both were appointed to the Court in their forties by a president who
relished the opportunity to put a stick in the eye of his congressional
opponents. Black, a southern white liberal, was Franklin D. Roosevelt's first appointment after his bitter defeat over expanding the
Court's membership in 1937; Thomas, a southern black conservative,
was George H. W. Bush's choice to replace the civil rights icon Thurgood Marshall in 1991. Both had been on the Court for exactly fifteen

years when these cases about presidential power in wartime came before them—long enough to accustom themselves to the Court's peculiar rituals and to find their jurisprudential voices. And both men considered themselves strict constructionists and constitutional fundamentalists who refused to enforce rights that did not appear explicitly in the Constitution and believed that the constitutional text should be construed in light of the original understanding of its framers and ratifiers.

Despite these similarities in background and judicial philosophy, Black and Thomas differed in one crucial respect: judicial temperament. Black revered the institution of the Court so passionately that when he proposed marriage to his secretary, Elizabeth (six years after the death of his first wife), he made a little speech about how he had been having a love affair with the Court for almost twenty years, and therefore she had to be, like Caesar's wife, above reproach: "I have to know that the woman I marry is a one-man woman," he declared.[2] This reverence led him to moderate or to rein in his strict constructionist ideology when he thought the good of the Court and the country required it. As a result, he became one of the most influential justices of his era, redefining large areas of American law in his own image. Thomas, by contrast, is an ideological purist, more interested in being philosophically consistent than in persuading colleagues to embrace his vision. He is so zealous in his devotion to carrying every principal to its logical conclusion that his ideological ally Justice Antonin Scalia told Thomas's biographer that Thomas would overturn any judicial precedent with which he disagreed, whereas he, Scalia, wouldn't do that.[3] Thomas is underrated as a constitutional lawyer in the popular imagination: his *Hamdan* opinion, like much of his work, was exhaustively researched, and his colleagues have praised his technical ability in complicated regulatory cases. But because Thomas approaches the law as an essentially academic enterprise, he is content, after fifteen years on the Court, to marginalize himself in lonely dissenting opinions, without any immediate prospect of winning majorities. Even if Thomas had the option of ruling against the president and then inviting him over for drinks in the interest of the Court—a form of interbranch socializing that is no longer thinkable in a post-Watergate age—it seems unlikely he would have the inclination to do so.

The difference between Black and Thomas shows the importance of judicial temperament on the Supreme Court. Those who have it find that the Court is their oyster; those who do not are often condemned to grumbling on the sidelines. And this has been the story of the Supreme Court from the beginning.

———

In an age of tell-all memoirs and reality television, the Supreme Court remains the last institution of government to sustain an Olympian sense of mystery. The justices have declined to allow cameras in the courtroom; they rarely release audio recordings of their arguments; and their deliberations are secret. Operating according to traditions and rules that have remained remarkably consistent since the nineteenth century, they meet twice a week in a private conference room to which no clerks or visitors are admitted. (The most junior justice answers the door if an assistant knocks with an urgent message.) Speaking in order of seniority, the nine justices announce their tentative votes on each case, and with five votes, a majority can rewrite the law in whatever way it likes. A few months after holding public arguments, the justices emerge to issue their opinions and dissents, and then they disappear behind the red velvet curtains without offering further comment. Everything about the Court's majestic rituals— from the white marble palace to the black robes—is designed to minimize the human element and to convey the impression that the

Court's opinions are, if not the word of God, the impersonal pronouncements of a Delphic oracle.

The Court's resistance to publicity may or may not increase the public's understanding of how it goes about its business, but it hasn't hurt the Court's legitimacy. On the contrary, the justices understand that familiarity breeds contempt and inaccessibility promotes authority. (When the Court first allowed audio recordings of oral arguments to be broadcast on the radio not long ago, some of those who tuned in had the sense of listening to a prewar British king delivering a wireless address to the Empire.) Unlike the president and members of Congress, who increasingly govern by personality, leaks, and the illusion of intimacy, the justices of the Supreme Court have generally resisted the relentless public demands for personal exposure. As a result, few citizens can identify the justices by name. At the same time, the Supreme Court has maintained relatively high approval ratings in a polarized age.

The ideal of the justices as impersonal oracles, of course, is something of a myth. Like any small group, the Court is a deeply human institution, where quirks of personality and temperament can mean as much as ideology in shaping the law. Justice Oliver Wendell Holmes, Jr., famously described his colleagues as "nine scorpions in a bottle"; they might also be compared to nine prima donnas in a long-running soap opera, where the backstage dramas—the rivalries, courtships, flings, and breakups—can be as important as what takes place in front of the spotlights. Although most of the justices have strongly held views and preconceptions when they join the Court, most are changed in important ways by their interactions with their colleagues. And some prove more successful on the bench than others, not only because of their judicial philosophies but also because of their judicial temperaments.

Elusive as it is important, judicial temperament is notoriously hard to define. One of the best definitions was offered by Chief Justice John Roberts. "I think judicial temperament is a willingness to step back from your own committed views of the correct jurisprudential approach and evaluate those views in terms of your role as a judge," Roberts told me in an interview at the end of his first term on the Court. "It's the difference between being a judge and being a law professor, and appreciating that it's not so much a question of analytical coherence or overview, it's more a question of where this fits in with the Court's established body of law. And how it's going to be received as law." In other words, judicial temperament involves a judge's willingness to "factor in the Court's institutional role," to suppress his or her ideological agenda or desire for personal attention in the interest of achieving consensus and stability.

The question of judicial temperament was much on Roberts's mind in his first term, as he made it his priority to promote unanimity and collegiality on the Court. He was surprisingly successful in this goal: under his leadership the Court issued more consecutive unanimous opinions than at any other time in recent history. But Roberts was frustrated by the degree to which his colleagues were inclined to act more like law professors than members of a collegial court: his first term had ended in what Justice John Paul Stevens called a "cacophony" of discordant voices, with opposing justices addressing each other in unusually personal terms. As a result, Roberts looked to the example of his greatest predecessor—Chief Justice John Marshall, who served from 1801 to 1835, for a model of how to rein in a group of unruly prima donnas. "If the Court in Marshall's era had issued decisions in important cases the way this Court has over the past thirty years, we would not have a Supreme Court today of the sort that we have," he said. "That suggests that what the Court's been doing over the past thirty years has been eroding, to some extent, the capital that Marshall built up." Roberts added, "I think the Court is also ripe for

7

a similar refocus on functioning as an institution, because if it doesn't, it's going to lose its credibility and legitimacy as an institution." In particular, Roberts declared, he would make it his priority, as Marshall did, to discourage his colleagues from issuing separate opinions. "I think that every justice should be worried about the Court acting as a Court and functioning as a Court, and they should all be worried, when they're writing separately, about the effect on the Court as an institution."[4]

Judicial temperament, in other words, encompasses a range of qualities: personality, character, upbringing and education, formative career experiences, work habits, and behavior when interacting with others. Temperament conforms to no political litmus test and crosses ideological lines: there are liberal and conservative loners who are more interested in attracting attention to themselves than in persuading their colleagues; and there are liberal and conservative institutionalists who are more concerned about the long-term legitimacy of the Court than about pursuing their own ideological agendas. A pragmatic disposition, a degree of humility and common sense, and the ability to interact well in groups—these have proved over time to be more important qualities than academic brilliance or rigid philosophical consistency in determining a justice's long-term influence. And those justices who have put the Court's interest before their own have contributed most to the Court's remarkable evolution from one of the most embattled and weakest institutions of government to one of the strongest and most self-confident.

One way of exploring the influence of judicial temperament on the Court is to compare the experiences of justices with very different temperaments. Consider Fred Vinson and Earl Warren, the two chief justices who presided over the Court's deliberations in *Brown v. Board of Education*. When the justices first met in 1952 to consider the case, there were, at most, only four confident votes to strike down segregation in the public schools.[5] The leader of those who were inclined to maintain the status quo was Chief Justice Vinson, a former senator with a hound dog face and deep circles under his eyes, who had impressed President Truman as a canny poker player and competent secretary of the treasury. Truman hoped that Vinson would resolve the battles of personality that were then raging on the Court. But he failed in this effort largely because his colleagues perceived him as a heavy-handed politician who was an unsubtle advocate rather than a skilled mediator. The intellectually arrogant Justice Felix Frankfurter openly belittled him as a mediocrity, prompting Vinson at one conference to threaten to punch Frankfurter in the nose.

Under Vinson's desultory and ineffective leadership, the Court was unable to reach a consensus in *Brown*, and the justices ordered new arguments to be held in the fall of 1953. But Vinson died unexpectedly from a heart attack in September, before the term began. (On the train home from the chief justice's funeral, Frankfurter remarked, "This is the first indication I have ever had that there is a God.") Vinson was succeeded by Governor Earl Warren of California, who also had a background in politics—he had been the Republican nominee for vice president in 1948—but had a far more appealing personality, and was far more adept at persuading skeptics and winning votes.

Although he never pretended to be a legal scholar, Warren was thoughtful, considerate, deferential, and unpretentious on the Court, and he sought out his new colleagues for advice rather than trying high-handedly to impose his will. Within weeks, he began to soothe the roiling tempers that had divided the justices during the Vinson years. And after the Court heard new arguments in *Brown*, Warren made clear at the justices' private conference that he believed segregation was immoral and rested on the "basic premise that the Negro race is inferior."[6] This put him at the head of a new five-justice majority for repudiating segregation. Warren also understood that the

Considerate and unpretentious, Chief Justice Earl Warren, who served from 1953 to 1969, sought out his colleagues for advice rather than trying to impose his will.

Court needed to speak with one voice on this contentious issue, so he privately visited the skeptical justices, urging them one by one to make the decision unanimous. Warren's greatest lobbying triumph came with the last holdout, the southerner Stanley Reed; after several lunches at which he encouraged Reed to do what was best for the country, Warren asked whether he really wanted to file a lone dissent, which could only encourage resistance in the South and undermine the Court's authority. Bowing to the inevitable, Reed agreed to join Warren's unanimous opinion, which the chief justice read aloud to a spellbound courtroom on May 17, 1954.

Judicial temperament is especially important for a chief justice, because of the unique demands of the job. The chief, like each of his colleagues, has one vote, and his duties are mostly procedural and

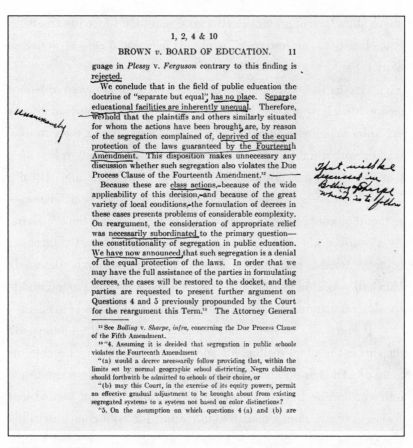

Chief Justice Warren's marginal notes on a draft of the *Brown v. Board of Education* opinion, with the notation "unanimously" prominent on the left.

organizational. It is his prerogative, when he is in the majority, to write the opinion for the Court himself or to assign the opinion to a justice he believes will reflect his legal views, as part of his broader efforts to build consensus behind the scenes. John Marshall, who is widely considered the greatest chief justice in American history, was especially deft in exercising these powers. Marshall, like most chief justices, was appointed to the Court without having previously served on it; like Warren, he had a reputation for bipartisan friendships and, above all, a lack of pretense and a good nature. ("I love his laugh—it is too hearty for an intriguer," wrote his friend and colleague Joseph Story.)

Marshall's skill in establishing convivial personal relations among his fellow justices helped him to cement the Court's authority at a vulnerable moment in its early history. Recognizing the virtues of leading with a light touch, Marshall wore a simple black robe rather than the scarlet and ermine that were traditional at the time. He also insisted that his colleagues room together in the same boardinghouse, so that they could discuss cases over glasses of his excellent Madeira. As a result of his sensitivity to the views of his political antagonists (with the notable exception of Thomas Jefferson, whom he detested), Marshall was able to steer the Court toward a middle ground and to speak for a unanimous court on the most divisive issues of his age.

If Marshall's modesty and geniality made him the prototype of the successful chief justice, his successor, Roger Taney, became the antitype. Though an able lawyer, Taney was shy, austere, frail, and reticent, and preferred to lead through indirection and behind-the-scenes intrigue rather than by cultivating sociable companionship. Under Taney, the collegial and unanimous Court fragmented. Unlike his gregarious predecessor, Taney was stubborn and had an inflated sense of judicial power. These qualities were reflected in his infamous and widely reviled opinion in *Dred Scott v. Sandford,* in which the Court ruled in 1857 that Congress had no power to ban slavery in federal territories. In a later case, after holding that President Abraham Lincoln could not suspend the writ of habeas corpus without Congress's approval, Taney went out of his way to mock the president, circulating his opinion as widely as possible to embarrass the administration. (Lincoln responded to Taney's arrogance by simply ignoring him.) Taney's overreaching destroyed his reputation.

The most successful chief justices, in other words, have shared a particular style of judicial temperament. They have been modest, likable, efficient, deft at finding common ground, and at least as smart as their colleagues without being overtly brilliant or intensely academic. Some of the most effective chiefs have been former politicians or politically minded executive officials who had a knack for bringing together colleagues of different minds. By contrast, the less successful chiefs have been insecure, heavy-handed, and more concerned with being recognized as the symbolic head of the Court than providing leadership behind the scenes.

Along with Vinson, one of the least successful chief justices in the modern era, by all accounts, was Warren E. Burger, who was appointed by President Richard Nixon to replace Earl Warren and served from 1969 to 1986. Burger fancied himself a statesman but was not smart enough to win the respect of his colleagues. His insecurity, vanity, and pomposity were openly ridiculed by liberal and conservative justices alike. Burger fussed over the placement of ceremonial silverware for private receptions while misunderstanding basic legal arguments. He also had a maddening habit of changing his vote at the last minute in order to ensure that he could write the most important opinions himself; this practice so infuriated his fellow justices that some of them eventually vented their frustrations to the journalists Bob Woodward and Scott Armstrong. The bestselling book that resulted, *The Brethren*, exposed Burger and the court to public ridicule.

An insecure associate justice can be just as handicapped as an insecure chief when interacting with colleagues. For example, Harry Blackmun, like his childhood friend Burger, was hampered by his temperamental indecisiveness and intellectual insecurity. But instead of trying to shore up Blackmun's confidence, Burger passive-aggressively needled him. Notoriously slow in producing opinions, Blackmun felt humiliated when Burger assigned him fewer majority opinions than all of his colleagues. And Blackmun's diary recording the deterioration of his relationship with Chief Justice Burger reads like that of an emotionally needy high school student ("CJ for the first time very cool," he wrote in 1980. Five years later: "CJ picks on me at conference.")[7] Although Justice Hugo Black advised him early in his tenure, "Always go for the jugular. Never agonize in an opinion," Blackmun was unable to follow his hero's advice.[8] He agonized endlessly, publicly lamenting having become emotionally involved in case after case. And he apologized for his decisions, calling them "inadequate and hesitant."[9]

The recent battles on the Court under Chief Justice William H. Rehnquist illustrate the ways in which indecisive justices are usually less effective than confident ones. Consider the pairing of Anthony Kennedy and Sandra Day O'Connor. Kennedy, like Blackmun, is noted for publicly agonizing over his decisions. In the 1992 abortion case *Planned Parenthood v. Casey*, Kennedy changed his position unexpectedly and ended up casting a crucial vote to uphold the core of *Roe v. Wade*. Kennedy's critics were especially exercised by a theatrical interview that Kennedy granted on the morning the *Casey* decision was handed down. "He stands at the window of his high-ceilinged chambers, waiting to go on the bench, looking down at the crowd of competing protesters in the plaza below," observed a reporter from the magazine *California Lawyer*. "'Sometimes you don't know if you're Caesar about to cross the Rubicon,' he says, his voice becoming almost inaudible, 'or Captain Queeg cutting your own tow line.'" Ten minutes before entering the courtroom, Kennedy announced that he wanted to be alone. "I need to brood," he murmured.

The qualities that Justice Kennedy displayed before handing down the abortion decision are the same qualities he displayed in the opinion itself and has shown throughout his tenure on the Court. He has a self-dramatizing tendency that leads him to agonize about cases, in public and private, often changing his positions after casting his votes. He makes a sincere and genuinely admirable effort to separate

his own conservative moral views from his more libertarian jurisprudential conclusions. He possesses an idealistic faith in the citizens of
the United States, expressed with the earnestness of Jimmy Stewart,
while also betraying an affinity for the grand style, a weakness for
sweeping gestures, magisterially expressed. Kennedy's opinions, as a
result, sometimes call to mind a high school civics lesson that aspires
to be chiseled on a monument. In this sense, his performance on the
Court resembles that of another even-tempered, goodhearted, moderate Republican from Sacramento: Earl Warren, a family friend at
whose feet Kennedy played as a toddler. Warren had a similar impatience for the niceties of legal doctrine, a similar penchant for expressing simple constitutional principles in ringing terms, and a
similar lack of concern for the costs of short-circuiting political debates with extravagant demonstrations of judicial power.

Kennedy's earnest temperament and idealistic view of government seem to have been shaped by his early experiences in California. He began his career as a lawyer and lobbyist, after inheriting the
family lobbying business of his father. But Kennedy always felt un-
comfortable with the messy realities of retail politics, displaying a
tendency to romanticize the ideals of American government, and expressing disappointment when citizens or colleagues in any way fall
short. Perhaps because of his impatience with politics, Kennedy has
been less successful at building consensus on the Court than Earl
Warren was: although he has been a swing vote, he has encouraged
the other justices to court him, rather than the other way around. He
seems to relish his unique status as swing justice and has resisted efforts by Chief Justices Rehnquist and Roberts to obtain broader consensus by deciding cases on narrower grounds that more justices
could accept, since this would deprive him of the ability to control the
outcome of closely divided cases. In this sense, he is outer-directed
rather than inner-directed, prefers magisterial pronouncements to

As a swing vote on the Rehnquist Court, Anthony Kennedy (left) tended to call attention to himself through sweeping pronouncements; Sandra Day O'Connor, on the other hand, used the skills she developed as a legislator in Arizona to forge coalitions, and her narrowly written opinions served to max-imize her influence.

lawyerly restraint, seems not to know precisely who he is, and puts his own interests above those of the Court.

Kennedy's effectiveness as a leader has also been hampered by his Hamlet-like indecision. He has a habit of trying on competing posi-tions, like hats in a fitting room, and wearing them for a while to see whether they feel comfortable. The agonizing can be harrowing for Kennedy's clerks and colleagues, especially in cases where the fate of abortion or school prayer or a presidential election hangs in the bal-ance. When the Court decided *Bush v. Gore* in 2000, Kennedy ago-nized until the last minute, always reserving the possibility of changing his mind.

Kennedy's temperament—earnest, emotional, given to theatri-cal displays of indecision, and comfortable with sweeping exercises of judicial power—made him the most activist justice on the Rehnquist

Court, that is, the justice who voted to strike down more federal and state laws than any other justice.[10] The second-most-activist justice was Sandra Day O'Connor, but she had a very different temperament and approach to her job. O'Connor's formative experiences were in the retail politics that so unnerved Kennedy: she was the first woman to be elected majority leader of the Arizona State Senate (or of any state senate) and the first former legislator to be appointed to the Court since 1949. O'Connor's legislative service was one of the central experiences of her life, and it is remarkable how much her performance as majority leader anticipated the role that she would come to play on the Supreme Court. In case after case, she would join the opinion of the Court and then write a concurring opinion that seemed to drain the majority opinion of its more general implications, confining her vote to the case at hand. These constant qualifications had the effect of preserving the option for O'Connor to change her mind in future cases: by ensuring that her vote was always up for grabs, she maximized her influence. Her reluctance to constrain her own discretion by following consistent principles was more characteristic of a legislator than a judge.

Unlike Kennedy, however, O'Connor was one of the most decisive justices on the Court. Although she liked to keep her options open for as long as possible, once she made up her mind, she refused to be budged. In her chambers, she sat on a hand-stitched pillow, embroidered with the motto: MAYBE IN ERROR BUT NEVER IN DOUBT.

By O'Connor's own account, the roots of her self-confidence came from her upbringing on the Lazy B cattle ranch, a 260-square-mile tract on the Arizona–New Mexico border, thirty-five miles from the nearest town and twelve miles from the nearest neighbor. On the ranch she learned to change tires, rope steer, and tend to the needs of her demanding father, a fervent Republican who hated the New Deal with a passion. At Stanford Law School, where she excelled, she dated her classmate William Rehnquist and met her future husband and fellow law review editor, John O'Connor. She then raised a family and spent four years as an assistant attorney general in Arizona, where she developed a reputation for attention to detail. Appointed in 1969 to fill a vacancy as an Arizona state senator, she was reelected in her own right the following year and in 1972 became majority leader. Six years later, she was appointed to the Arizona Court of Appeals, and in 1981, President Ronald Reagan chose her to be the first woman to serve on the Supreme Court.

O'Connor's performance in the 1992 abortion case was characteristically self-assured. While Kennedy agonized endlessly about the decision in *Casey*—wavering until the final days before the opinion circulated and musing openly about writing a brief opinion that would sidestep the question of whether abortion is a fundamental right—O'Connor made her decision to reaffirm the core of *Roe v. Wade* and never looked back. Using the same reasoning she would return to in *Bush v. Gore*, she justified her aggressive decision to short-circuit the political debate about abortion on the grounds that the Court had to save the nation from legislative battles that could only polarize and divide American citizens.

O'Connor was even more influential than Kennedy, partly because she built strong personal relationships with her more liberal colleagues, even though she disagreed with them on many issues that came before the Court. She was close to David Souter, whom she invited to her house for Thanksgiving dinner with her clerks, showing grandmotherly concern that the bachelor justice not be alone during the holidays. And Ruth Bader Ginsburg was especially grateful to O'Connor for being the first person to call her in the hospital after she was diagnosed with colon cancer. Ginsburg has said that she appreciated O'Connor's support after she joined the Court as the second female justice in 1993, and their common experience in battling cancer brought them even closer.

Although it is too soon to evaluate the ultimate influence of O'Connor and Kennedy, the evidence suggests that O'Connor's institutionally minded pragmatism has been more influential than Kennedy's more theoretically minded civics lessons. We are all still living in Sandra Day O'Connor's America, and for twenty-five years her vision came to define the Court's vision on the most divisive questions of American life—from affirmative action, religion, and abortion to the ground rules of American politics. Kennedy, by contrast, also cast many tie-breaking votes, but he has been less successful in remaking the Court in his own image. And the conflict between the pragmatic, politically confident O'Connor and the abstracted, indecisive Kennedy is not unique to the Rehnquist Court. On the contrary, it has been played out from the very beginning of the Court's existence.

This book tells the story of the Supreme Court by telling the stories of some of the conflicts of judicial temperament that shaped it. Exploring the Court as a human institution, I have chosen four pairs of personalities whose clashes have influenced the development of the Court with special force. The story begins with the great Chief Justice John Marshall and President Thomas Jefferson, cousins from the Virginia elite, whose differing visions of America set the tone for the Court's first half-century. While Marshall insisted that independent judges should be free to strike down laws that violated the Constitution, Jefferson believed just as strongly that judges should reflect public opinion. While Marshall defended a strong national union, Jefferson was eager to limit the powers of Congress in the name of states' rights. In fact, Jefferson and Marshall shared much in common, and their differences were temperamental as well as philosophical. By outmaneuvering Jefferson in case after case, Marshall helped to transform the Court from an embattled backwater to the leader of a strong and independent branch of the federal government.

The story continues after the Civil War with Justices John Marshall Harlan and Oliver Wendell Holmes, Jr., who clashed over the limits of majority rule. Harlan, who was named after the great chief justice and served on the Court from 1877 to 1911, combined a passionate commitment to protecting the rights of African-Americans with an equally firm devotion to defending the power of the federal government to protect the economically weak and disadvantaged. Holmes, by contrast, emerged from his service in the Union army as a nihilist and was so skeptical of judicial power that he voted to uphold some of the darkest laws in American history. Holmes belittled Harlan's lack of intellectual subtlety. But Harlan's vision of racial and economic egalitarianism—closely tied to his upbringing in a slaveholding family—has been dramatically vindicated by history. Holmes's radical devotion to judicial abstinence, for better or worse, has little constituency today.

The next clash of temperament focuses on Hugo Black and William O. Douglas, who were appointed by Franklin D. Roosevelt in the 1930s and served until the early 1970s. Although they began as close friends and allies, the liberal icons Black and Douglas drifted apart during their long service together, due partly to the dramatic differences in their temperaments. Black was a fiercely competitive former senator who believed that judges had to restrain themselves to protect democracy; Douglas was a brilliant and self-indulgent maverick who was more concerned with imposing his unique vision of justice than with the finer points of legal doctrine. Although Black considered Douglas a genius, he disapproved of Douglas's constant drinking and womanizing, and his disrespect for the Court as an institution. By the end of their tenures, Black had transformed the law in his own image while Douglas found himself increasingly marginalized as a judicial lounge act.

The final pairing, from our own era, examines the conservatives William H. Rehnquist and Antonin Scalia. Although early observers predicted that the brilliant and witty Scalia would be a formidable leader on the Court while Rehnquist would be less flexible, the opposite dynamic materialized. Scalia, an intellectual pit bull who is more concerned with ideological purity than building coalitions, found few acolytes on the Court for his doctrinaire judicial philosophy. By contrast, the pragmatic and politically savvy Rehnquist won the respect and affection of his colleagues, and under his leadership the Court remained generally in the political mainstream, moving modestly to the right on cases involving crime and states' rights as the country became more libertarian, while preserving generally moderate positions in cases involving the culture wars—from abortion to gay rights. Because he exercised power selectively and strategically, Rehnquist, like his most effective predecessors, including Marshall and Warren, brought the Court to new heights of self-confidence and generally maintained its public legitimacy.

The conclusion of the book reflects broadly on the relationship between judicial temperament and judicial success. Each of the four chapters contrasts a judicial pragmatist with a less accommodating temperament: Marshall versus Jefferson; Harlan versus Holmes; Black versus Douglas; Rehnquist versus Scalia. In all of these pairings, the more influential and effective justice was the one more willing to moderate the application of his principles in the name of the broader good of the Court and the country. The conclusion explores the views of the new chief justice, John Roberts, about the role of judicial temperament throughout history and offers some observations about Roberts's efforts to promote unanimity and consensus.

Many histories of the Supreme Court focus on judicial philosophy, ideology, and politics. This book examines the ways that the success of individual justices, and of the Court as a whole, reflects the interaction between judicial philosophy and judicial temperament. As we will see, the connections between the most successful justices—from Marshall to Harlan to Black to Rehnquist to Roberts—transcend ideology and reflect shared strengths of character and temperament. These judicial temperaments have shaped the country we live in today.

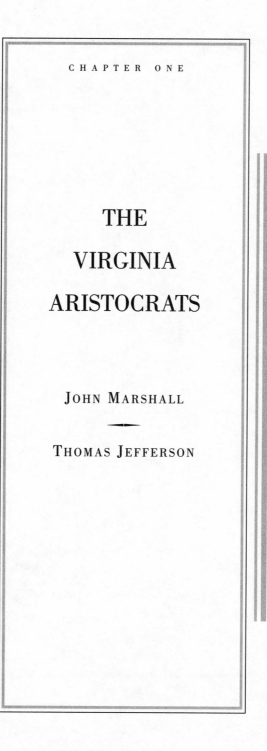

CHAPTER ONE

THE
VIRGINIA
ARISTOCRATS

JOHN MARSHALL

THOMAS JEFFERSON

O n Monday, March 2, 1801, President-elect Thomas Jefferson
wrote to Chief Justice John Marshall, asking him to administer the oath of office two days later at noon in the Senate
chamber, adding that he expected to be on time. "I shall with much pleasure attend to administer the oath of office on the 4th," Marshall replied
with appropriate formality, "& shall make a point of being punctual."[1]

This strained effort at cordiality persisted throughout the inaugural ceremonies, the first time in American history that the White
House and Congress had passed from one party to the other. With the
showy informality for which he was famous, Jefferson walked the brief
distance from his boardinghouse to the Capitol, followed by a re-
spectable parade of dignitaries. Unlike his predecessor, John Adams,
who was criticized for his kingly pretensions, Jefferson wore plain
clothes and carried no sword. The two political rivals behaved civilly
to each other, although at one point during the ceremony, Marshall
inadvertently turned his back on the new president.

President-elect Thomas Jefferson's letter of March 2, 1801, in which he asked Chief Justice John Marshall to administer the oath of office, despite their personal and political antagonism.

On the morning of the inauguration, Marshall had written a letter to a friend making clear where his political allegiances rested now that the judiciary was the only branch of government that his party, the Federalists, controlled. "Of the importance of the judiciary at all times but more especially the present, I am very fully impressed and I shall endeavor in the new office to which I am called not to disappoint my friends," he wrote pointedly. Perhaps to put himself into a less partisan frame of mind, he conceded that Jefferson was not as extreme as some of his supporters. "The democrats are divided into speculative theorists and absolute terrorists," he observed. "With the latter I am not disposed to class Mr. Jefferson." The letter then broke off so Marshall could administer the oath of office, but he returned after the ceremony to add some wan praise for the inaugural address he had just witnessed, in which Jefferson declared, "We are all republicans, we are all federalists," referring to the political principles of majority rule and national union. "It is in the general well judged and conciliatory," Marshall wrote. "It is in direct terms giving the lie to the violent party declamation which has elected him, but it is strongly characteristic of the general cast of his political theory."[2]

Marshall's guardedness about Jefferson was entirely reciprocated. They were distant cousins who had circled each other warily during the tumultuous years leading up to Jefferson's election. As early as 1795, when Marshall was reelected to the Virginia state legislature as a Federalist, Jefferson, who had recently left the government, complained to James Madison that Marshall's "lax lounging manners" and ability to win over Republicans by posing as a moderate had guaranteed his popularity.[3] Five years later, in the heat of the presidential campaign, Jefferson complained to James Monroe that Richmond had become a hotbed of "federation and Marshallism, and this latter spirit, I thought nothing should be spared to eradicate." But the election of 1800 was a clash of political principles more than a clash of personalities. The Federalists, led by Adams, supported a strong federal government to preserve the union, feared unchecked majority rule, and hoped that independent federal courts would check democratic excesses—which the Federalists interpreted to include criticisms of Adams himself. The Republicans, led by Jefferson, were suspicious of national power and the federal courts, believed strongly in states' rights and the rule of local majorities, and insisted that most constitutional disputes should be decided by elected legislatures rather than by unelected judges.

In November 1800, the election was thrown into the House of Representatives after Jefferson and his running mate, Aaron Burr, finished in a tie with seventy-three electoral votes each. (In those days, electors could only vote for president and the runner-up became vice president; the Founders had not anticipated the rise of political parties and presidential tickets.) Rumors spread of a Federalist plot to deprive Jefferson of the presidency and to install Marshall, who was then serving as Adams's secretary of state. Adams, having lost his bid for reelection and recognizing that the judiciary would be the last stronghold of his party, unexpectedly appointed Marshall chief justice of the United States on January 27, 1801, and the lame-duck Federalist Senate confirmed him a few days later. When Marshall took his oath as chief justice on a rainy day in February, wearing his plain black robe, Congress still had not chosen a president, and the Court was so weak and enfeebled that few newspapers took notice of the event. Still, the lame-duck president and Congress worked frantically to consolidate the power of Federalists in the judiciary before it was too late. Congress created a series of new judicial offices, to give Adams the chance to make midnight appointments, and also reduced the size of the Supreme Court to deny Jefferson the chance to make appointments of his own. On February 17, the House elected Jefferson as president on the thirty-sixth ballot; on March 1, three

President John Adams stayed up late into the night in the waning days of his administration signing "midnight appointments" of judges and other federal officials. These appointments gave rise to the controversy of *Marbury v. Madison* and the establishment of judicial review.

days before Jefferson's inauguration, Adams stayed up late signing the new judicial commissions, which were notarized by John Marshall, still performing double duty as a lame-duck secretary of state. In the confusion of the moment, however, not all of the commissions were delivered to their intended recipients—including one appointing William Marbury to be a justice of the peace for the District of Columbia.

It was hardly a surprise that Jefferson was offended by Adams's court packing: three years later, he wrote to Abigail Adams that her husband's midnight appointment of Jefferson's political enemies was "personally unkind" and "the one act of Mr. Adams's life, and one only

[that] ever gave me a moment's personal displeasure."[4] Nevertheless, after taking the oath of office, Jefferson behaved with relative moderation. He did not attempt a complete purge of Federalist officeholders but only those guilty of misconduct or those appointed after Adams knew he had been defeated.[5] And in a bipartisan gesture, he invited Marshall to administer the oath of office.

After Jefferson's inauguration on March 4, the newly elected Republican Congress repealed the Judiciary Act that had created the new judgeships and changed the size of the Supreme Court. Jefferson also ordered his new secretary of state, James Madison, not to deliver the commissions that Adams's appointees had never received. William Marbury sued, asking the Supreme Court to order Madison to deliver his commission. In December 1801, when Marshall asked Madison to appear in Court to defend his refusal to deliver the commissions, Jefferson reacted angrily. The Federalists "have retired into the judiciary as a stronghold," he wrote, and "from that battery all the works of republicanism are to be beaten down and erased."[6] Madison and Jefferson ignored Marshall's request, and Madison refused to appear.

The legal question in *Marbury v. Madison* was technical and narrow: did Marbury have a right to his commission, and, if so, did the Supreme Court have the power to order Madison to deliver it to him? The case put Marshall in what appeared to be a no-win situation, even setting aside his own role in creating the mess that made it possible. If he ruled for his party and ordered the White House to deliver Marbury's commission, Jefferson and Madison would simply ignore him, revealing the Court to be weak and ineffective. If he ruled that Marbury had no right to the commission, he would seem to be bowing to political pressure and his Federalist supporters would be furious. Marshall extricated himself from this exquisite dilemma with an act of judicial jujitsu that, two centuries later, still inspires awe for its craftiness. In February 1803, Marshall handed down the opinion for a unanimous Court. He ruled that Marbury did indeed have a right to his commission, but the Supreme Court could not order Madison to deliver it because the federal statute that authorized the Court to issue orders of that kind was itself unconstitutional. Imagine the confusion among the Republicans! They could hardly object to the outcome, since Marshall had given them what they wanted in the short term: no commission for Marbury or any of the other "midnight judges." By boldly and unequivocally asserting the power of judicial review—the power of federal courts to strike down laws that clashed with the Constitution—Marshall strengthened judicial authority over the long term, in ways that his opponents at the time could hardly imagine.

Although judicial review had become increasingly accepted in the fifteen years since the ratification of the Constitution, its status before *Marbury* was still uncertain and the unanimous decision was hardly a foregone conclusion. Today, judicial review is the foundation of the Supreme Court's power. And yet despite the broad implications of Marshall's opinion in *Marbury,* Republicans and Federalists in Congress declined to criticize it because neither party objected to the immediate result. Years later Jefferson recognized the degree to which he had been outmaneuvered. He complained to Justice William Johnson, his favorite Supreme Court appointee, that Marshall's practice of "traveling out of his case to prescribe what the law would be in a moot case not before the court, is very irregular and very censurable."[7] At the time, however, he accepted the result in *Marbury* with relative equanimity, turning his attention to other matters, such as the impeachment of Federalist judges that some Republicans hoped would eventually unseat Marshall.

How did the thin-skinned Jefferson and the famously genial Marshall come, within a few years, to detest each other? Although Jefferson never served on the Supreme Court, his conflict with Marshall came to shape the constitutional battles of the early Republic far more than Marshall's clashes with his colleagues—largely because Marshall had few clashes with his colleagues, and because none of his judicial opponents was remotely as large a figure as the Sage of Monticello, whom Marshall derided as "the great Lama of the Mountain." One of the many paradoxes of Jefferson's legacy is that he was on the wrong side of most of his battles with Marshall—involving national power, judicial independence, checks on majority rule, and states' rights—yet has been appropriately celebrated in history as America's most enduring and influential prophet of democracy and equality. Jefferson was consistently outfoxed by Marshall because his romantic and visionary temperament, which insisted on carrying most disputes back to first principles, tended to stake out radical and extreme positions in the name of ideological purity. By contrast, Marshall, whose temperament was defined by modesty, conviviality, moderation, and incrementalism, had a unique talent for getting along with those who disagreed with him and for leading by gentle persuasion. In his thirty-four years on the bench, he established the power of an independent Supreme Court to strike down federal and state laws that violated the Constitution and insisted on the obligation of the states to obey federal laws with which they disagreed—both principles that Jefferson vainly denied.

"I am in love with his character, positively in love," Justice Joseph Story gushed about his friend Chief Justice Marshall.[8] And Story was not in the habit of gushing. Marshall was indeed lovable: even his political opponents liked him, with the unique exception of Jefferson, whose hatred he reciprocated. The more one learns about Marshall's temperament, the harder it is not to admire him for being crafty and appealing at the same time. Marshall's modesty was at the heart of his character and his jurisprudence, and it is obvious from the endearing first line of the brief "Autobiographical Sketch" that he wrote at Story's request in 1827: "The events of my life are too unimportant, and have too little interest for any person not of my immediate family, to render them worth communicating or preserving."[9] His modesty was obvious in his appearance: he was loose-jointed and good-humored, with disheveled clothing and an unpretentious gait. "Marshall is of a tall, slender figure, not graceful or imposing, but erect and steady," Story wrote in a famous description of the chief justice. "His hair is black, his eyes small and twinkling. . . . His dress is very simple . . . his language chaste but hardly elegant. In conversation he is quite familiar. . . . He possesses great subtilty of mind, but it is only occasionally exhibited. I love his laugh—it is too hearty for an intriguer—and his good temper and unwearied patience are equally agreeable on the bench and in the study."[10]

Anecdotes about Marshall's modesty and conviviality are abundant. His fellow soldiers in Washington's army at Valley Forge recalled him as the best-tempered man they knew, uncomplaining in the face of adversity, and always ready to entertain them with a stream of amusing anecdotes. During his years on the Supreme Court, he did his own grocery shopping at the market near his home in Richmond, Virginia; once, when a newcomer to town saw the shabbily dressed chief justice carrying a turkey, he mistook him for a servant and tossed him a coin, which Marshall cheerfully accepted, to carry his own bird home. He was proud of his skill in pitching quoits—a game involving a kind of round horseshoe—and could be observed at the Quoits Club in Richmond toward the end of his life downing Madeira and rum punch, getting down on his hands and knees earnestly measuring the distance between his quoit and those of his opponents, and then shouting in unaffected happiness when he won.[11] It is hard to imagine the withdrawn and aristocratic Jefferson in a similar posture.

Marshall's appealing personality had obvious political benefits. During more than two decades in politics, he never lost an election, even when running from a Virginia district where most of the

Republican voters rejected his Federalist politics but voted for him because they liked him.[12] He had a knack for remaining friends with his political opponents: because of their mutual affection Patrick Henry crossed party lines to support him during his race for Congress. Geniality was also key to Marshall's influence on the Court. He made arrangements for his fellow justices to room together at Brown's boardinghouse, where they lived and worked until 1830. Over glasses of Marshall's prized Madeira, they discussed cases and socialized together on intimate terms. (After the justices resolved, in an unfortunate burst of temperance, to drink only on days when it rained, Marshall pointed out that on sunny days "our jurisdiction extends over so large a territory that the doctrine of chances makes it certain that it must be raining somewhere.")[13] And because of Marshall's pleasant temperament, he remained on good terms with justices whose politics were less moderate than his, from the conservative Federalist Samuel Chase to the Jeffersonian Republican William Johnson.

Modesty, conviviality, moderation, good humor—to some of his biographers, Marshall's constellation of appealing qualities makes him seem almost too good to be true. But there are, of course, countervailing character traits to fill out the picture. One of the most cool-eyed assessments of Marshall came early in his career from Theodore Sedgwick, the Federalist Speaker of the House of Representatives, who found Marshall's moderate Federalism a little pale for his taste. Sedgwick observed in the young congressman an eagerness to be liked that caused Marshall, for good and ill, to calibrate his conclusions throughout his career in response to what public opinion would tolerate. "He is a man of very affectionate disposition, of great simplicity of manners and honest and honorable in all his conduct," Sedgwick wrote to the Federalist leader Rufus King. "He is attached to pleasure, with convivial habits strongly fixed. He is indolent, therefore; and indisposed to take part in the common business of the House. He has a strong attachment to popularity but [is] indisposed to sacrifice to it his integrity; hence it is that he is disposed on all popular subjects to feel the public pulse and hence results indecision and *an expression* of doubt. . . . He is disposed to . . . express great respect from the sovereign people, and to quote their opinions as evidence of truth."[14]

Although Sedgwick lamented Marshall's hunger for popular approval, it served him well during his career on the Court. The combination of Federalist principles and a democratic manner was, in the end, the key to Marshall's strength, and helped him to succeed on a scale that eluded more doctrinaire Federalists and Republicans.

The charge that Marshall was too fond of popularity was not the harshest of those levied against him. Those came from Jefferson, who as early as 1796 accused Marshall of legal acrobatics. "When conversing with Marshall, I never admit anything," Jefferson is said to have declared. "So great is his sophistry you must never give him an affirmative answer or you will be forced to grant his conclusion. Why, if he were to ask me if it were daylight or not, I'd reply, 'Sir, I don't know, I can't tell.' "[15] Jefferson's charge that Marshall was too cunning by half became a kind of Republican dogma. By 1810, Jefferson was urging President Madison to appoint justices with enough backbone to stand up to Marshall on the bench. "The state has suffered long enough from the want of any counterpart to the rancorous hatred which Marshall bears to his country and from the cunning and sophistry within which he is able to surround himself," he complained.[16] Marshall, for his part, viewed Jefferson as an ambitious demagogue. "His great power is over the mass of the people and this power is chiefly acquired by professions of democracy," Marshall wrote of Jefferson's radical defense of states' rights. "Every check on the wild impulse of the moment is a check on his own power, and he is unfriendly to the source from which it flows. He looks, of course, with ill will at an independent judiciary."[17]

Jefferson and Marshall's mutual dislike generally unbalanced their judgment. But in charging Marshall with legal gymnastics, Jefferson was on to something. Marshall's judicial opinions and political positions were indeed "twistifications," as Jefferson put it in a nice phrase. Marshall had a knack for appearing to give his political opponents an immediate victory and then resorting to exquisite legalisms to deprive the victory of long-term effect, as he did in *Marbury v. Madison.* In a series of logical arabesques, he would walk up to the edge of endorsing the Republican position and then, at the last moment, announce that he had no choice but to reach the opposite conclusion, advancing the Federalist goals of extending judicial independence and federal power. In his less admirable moments, Marshall's pragmatic willingness to compromise, his sensitivity to what popular opinion would bear, and his strategic sensibility led him to trim his principles in the face of opposition. But Marshall himself always justified his caution in picking only those fights he could win with the practicality of a seasoned politician. "I am not fond," he wrote to Story, "of butting against a wall in sport."[18]

If Marshall's character can be sketched in primary colors, Jefferson's emerges from more elusive shades. Henry Adams, who said that Marshall's only weakness was that he "detested Thomas Jefferson," found Jefferson nearly impossible to capture. Nevertheless, Adams described the aestheticized delicacy of the aristocratic populist in the following sketch: "He built for himself at Monticello a chateau above contact with man. The rawness of political life was an incessant torture to him, and personal attacks made him keenly unhappy. . . . He shrank from whatever was rough or coarse, and his yearning for sympathy was almost feminine."[19]

The conflicts between John Marshall (left) and Thomas Jefferson came to define the constitutional battles of the early Republic. Although distant
cousins, the famously genial Marshall and the thin-skinned Jefferson came
to detest one another.

Jefferson was introverted, sensitive, thin-skinned, and averse to
conflict—all of which distinguished his character from Marshall's.
Above all, he preferred romantic abstractions to messy realities, tend-
ing to idealize all aspects of life. He invented a mythic past of lost liberties in England that he traced back to self-governing Saxon boroughs
and shires that predated the Magna Carta. In a section of the Declaration of Independence that the Continental Congress mercifully
deleted from his draft, he denounced King George III for having sub-
verted these ancient Saxon liberties and called for their resurrection.
Jefferson throughout his life lamented the loss of a pristine and imag-
inary past in the mists of history, in the same way that he invested the

yeoman farmer with utopian qualities of virtue and self-reliance. (His own farming efforts, by contrast, rarely made ends meet, and the only profit he ever made at Monticello came from a distinctly nonagrarian nail factory.) Jefferson's tendency to idealize went hand in hand with a tendency to demonize—he called his opponents "heretics" and his supporters acolytes of the "true faith."

In comparing Jefferson to his distant cousin, historians have tended to resort to dramatic antitheses. Marshall advanced aristocratic principles with democratic manners, while Jefferson did the opposite, defending the principle of unchecked majority rule from the ornamented isolation of his Monticello retreat. Marshall was a lawyer who preferred incremental change, Jefferson a philosopher who advocated radical reform. Marshall was sociable and willing to confront his opponents openly, Jefferson a loner, preferring political intrigue conducted by proxies rather than hand-to-hand combat. Marshall loved to laugh; Jefferson had no discernible sense of humor.[20] Marshall remained on good terms with his political opponents; Jefferson demonized them. Marshall was practical, Jefferson bookish. Marshall was indolent and liked to relax with with a drink and some horseshoes, Jefferson was obsessively self-disciplined and preferred the refined pleasures of the violin. And so on.

Jefferson's preference for philosophical abstractions over practical political realities—his opponents called him a "philosopher, visionary, speculator"—did indeed lead him to an intellectual radicalism that contrasted with Marshall's moderation, to Jefferson's detriment.[21] Unlike Marshall, Jefferson was often willing to carry his principles to their logical conclusions, at least in theory. This insistence on returning to first principles led to jarring lapses of judgment. He applauded the excesses of Shays's Rebellion, the 1786 populist uprising in Massachusetts against new taxes, with chilling glibness: "The tree of liberty must be refreshed from time to time with the blood of patriots and tyrants," he wrote. "It is its natural manure."[22] And as the French Revolution grew increasingly bloody in the 1790s, Jefferson never wavered in his belief that the principle of popular sovereignty had to triumph, no matter how many laws, institutions, and human beings were destroyed in its wake. In a letter to James Madison at the height of the French terror, he gave his radicalism free rein. "The earth belongs in usufruct to the living," he declared, adding that one generation may not bind another.[23] The contrast with Marshall, a conservative incrementalist who was horrified by the carnage in France, could not have been more stark; Marshall believed the whole point of a constitution was for past generations to prevent future ones from violating basic rights and liberties. Whether or not Jefferson deserves to be judged a "terrifying idealist, tinged with fanaticism," as one purported admirer put it, his belief that the past had no binding power over the present made him a prophet of constitutional transformation who had less to contribute to the process of constitutional preservation.[24]

It has become a cliché to say that Jefferson is defined by contradictions, but the cliché is unconvincing. There is nothing especially unusual in the fact that Jefferson was a defender of majority rule who shrank from contact with ordinary people, any more than Marshall was unusual in defending checks on majority rule with a common touch. Many of us embrace political principles in spite of—or perhaps because of—the tension with deep strains in our personality and character. The more pertinent question is: where and how did Marshall's and Jefferson's characters and political principles emerge?

Marshall and Jefferson had remarkably similar backgrounds. Both were related through their mothers to the Randolphs, one of the first families of Virginia. Both were the sons of largely self-educated fathers who came from Welsh farming stock, inherited small farms from their own fathers, and became successful land surveyors who made their fortunes in the West.[25] Although Marshall and Jefferson were born twelve years apart under similar circumstances in nearby Virginia counties, Marshall, the younger of the two, seems to have had a happier childhood. He idealized his father, with whom he served under Washington in the Revolutionary War, and would often spontaneously praise him as an adult. In his autobiography, Marshall recalled his father as "my only intelligent companion . . . both a watchfull parent and an affectionate instructive friend."[26] Marshall was also close to his mother, the well-educated daughter of a Scottish teacher, who inspired a respect for the intellectual abilities of women that he displayed throughout his life. And as the first of fifteen children, he learned to lead with a light hand, accepting responsibility for taming an unruly brood, but always exerting his authority by persuasion and example, winning his siblings' affection rather than disciplining them with heavy-handed shows of force. These early lessons in leadership proved invaluable when Marshall found himself at the helm of a similarly unruly group on the Court.[27]

Marshall's education, supervised by his father, was thorough but unsystematic: years later, he remembered with pleasure reading history and poetry at the age of twelve, and transcribing Alexander Pope's *Essay on Man*. Two years of private tutoring with local clergymen followed. After serving in the Revolutionary War, he enrolled at the College of William and Mary, where he spent several weeks attending lectures by George Wythe, Jefferson's own mentor, although Marshall had far less time under the great man's tutelage. The comprehensive lecture notes he compiled into a commonplace book show his skill in assimilating and organizing legal doctrine, but they also suggest that he was not entirely consumed by his studies: the margins of the manuscript are full of doodling references to "Polly Ambler," "Miss M. Ambler-J. Marshall," and—twice—simply "Polly." Marshall had fallen in love with the second daughter of Jacquelin and Rebecca

Ambler, whom he met during a party at their house in 1780 when he was twenty-five and she was not yet fourteen. They were married three years later and eventually had ten children, six of whom survived into adulthood. Marshall extravagantly idolized Polly, writing her letters during their long separations that recalled their courtship and paid her tender compliments. But Polly seems to have been less happy in the marriage: after losing four children within four years, she developed what we would now call depression—Jefferson unkindly called it a kind of "insanity"—which enfeebled her and often confined her to bed until she died in 1831, four years before Marshall. (Polly's depression may have been exacerbated by an unsigned letter she received from Marshall during his diplomatic mission to France, where he praised his landlady, a beautiful and eligible young widow, with whom some historians believe he had an affair.) Whether or not Marshall strayed in Paris, he doted on Polly extravagantly during the rest of their marriage, writing anxious letters to a neighbor begging him to quiet a barking dog at night, for example, in order to protect her fragile nerves. His grief at Polly's death was profound and unmistakable.

Marshall's worldview was shaped on the battlefield. With the coming of the Revolution, he enlisted in the Culpepper minutemen, where his father was a major, and was commissioned as a lieutenant in 1775, at the age of nineteen. His men admired him for his optimism, good humor, and ability to outrun and outjump them all, reportedly leaping in the air over six feet. (He was called "Silver Heels" because he wore stockings with silver heels that had been darned by his mother.) Marching through the countryside with bucktail hats, tomahawks, and hunting shirts emblazoned with the motto "Liberty or Death," the minutemen defeated the British at Norfolk during the Battle of the Great Bridge, where Marshall fought beside his father. After the unit was demobilized in 1776, Marshall enlisted in a Virginia regiment formed in response to General Washington's pleas for rein-forcements in the Continental army.

Both Marshall and his father then joined Washington's staff—Marshall as a deputy judge advocate and his father as one of the general's most valued advisers. Both men revered and idealized Washington, especially for his courage during the winter deprivations of Valley Forge in December 1777. There, the shortage of clothing, food, shoes, and blankets led to widespread starvation and disease—more than 3,000 troops were said to have died—and Marshall never forgot the images of the suffering that resulted from the failure of the state legislatures to respond to Washington's requests for supplies. For the rest of his life, he remained alert to the dangers of overzealous at-tachment to states' rights and the need for a vigorous national govern-ment to coordinate local activities during national emergencies.[28] In his autobiography, Marshall emphasized that his experiences in the Revolutionary army had made him a nationalist: "I had grown up at a time when a love of union and resistance to the claims of Great Britain were inseparable inmates of the same bosom," he wrote. In the army, he said, "I was confirmed in the habit of considering America as my country, and congress as my government." This vision of a strong fed-eral government serving the purposes of national unity would come to define Marshall's jurisprudence: he construed the U.S. Constitution to ensure that the depredations of Valley Forge would never be repeated.

After returning from the war, Marshall's burgeoning nationalism was reinforced by his experiences in the Virginia legislature. He was especially disturbed by Virginia's effort to repudiate the war debts owed to American merchants and to British creditors before the Rev-olution. Marshall was also alarmed by Shays's Rebellion, the antitax uprising in Massachusetts that Jefferson had glorified, which struck Marshall as an another example of the dangers of unchecked local mobs. All of these excesses of localism, Marshall confessed, helped him appreciate the parts of the newly proposed U.S. Constitution that made federal law supreme over state law, and persuaded him to participate as an elected delegate to Virginia's constitutional ratifying convention. As a delegate to the convention, he warned about the dangers of unchecked democracy and argued in favor of judicial review. By the end of the convention, Marshall had defended the constitutional doctrines that would define his tenure on the Supreme Court: the advantages of national power, the dangers of localism, the importance of judicial independence, the sanctity of property and contracts, and the centrality of fair judicial procedures.

Jefferson's upbringing and early experiences, while similar to Marshall's in some respects, produced a dramatically different temperament and character. From the start he seems to have been less doted on by his parents. Peter Jefferson, a successful farmer, surveyor, and local dignitary, gave his son habits of industry and startling self-discipline, but was frequently away from home on Western surveying excursions and did not appear to play the role of affectionate and "intelligent companion" that led Marshall to idolize his own father. In any event, Peter Jefferson died in 1757 when his son was fourteen, leaving sixty slaves, two sons, six daughters, and his widow. Although the evidence is sparse, Jefferson's relationship with his mother, Jane Randolph Jefferson, seems to have been distant if not openly tense, and after his father died, Jefferson threw himself into his studies away from home rather than submitting to his mother's care.

Like Marshall, Jefferson was placed at an early age under the classical tutelage of local Scottish parsons, but he soon developed an intense and hungry intellectuality, losing himself in the imaginative world of books. At the age of nine, he was reading the Latin and Greek authors in the original—an experience he later recalled as a "sublime luxury."[29] Jefferson's formative influences, however, were his teachers at the College of William and Mary, where he enrolled in

1760 at the age of seventeen. His favorite teacher was Dr. William Small, who taught him philosophy, history, logic and rhetoric, and who polished his manners as well. Other formative influences included Governor Francis Fauquier, who encouraged Jefferson to play the violin in his salon and improved his conversation at sparkling dinners, and above all, George Wythe, whose lectures Marshall would also attend. By the end of his time in Williamsburg, Jefferson was an exceptionally and impressively cultivated young man. In the famous observation of James Parton, he "could calculate an eclipse, survey an estate, tie an artery, plan an edifice, try a cause, break a horse, dance a minuet, and play a violin."[30]

Jefferson's teachers may have fired his imagination and polished his manners, but his character was shaped above all by the discipline of self-study. After two years of college, he undertook a rigorous five-year apprenticeship in law—far more extensive than Marshall's weeks of lectures—and set for himself a reading schedule that even today inspires awe for its consuming intensity. Here is the sixteen-hour daily reading schedule that Jefferson prescribed to a young lawyer who later wrote him for advice: from dawn until eight A.M., physical sciences, ethics and religion; eight to noon, law; noon to one, politics; one until dinner, history; dinner until ten P.M., literature, Shakespeare, criticism, and oratory; and then to bed.[31] It's hard to imagine Marshall, who was known for indolence, submitting to similar rigors.

In addition to becoming exceptionally well-read, Jefferson took from these long hours of communion with the classics a tendency to romanticize history, politics, and the law, to compare present realities to an imagined and largely invented utopian past always shimmering just beyond reach. Where Marshall had focused on the works of Blackstone, the great conservative defender of the supremacy of parliament, Jefferson was most inspired by Coke, the Whig defender of the common-law rights of Englishmen in their struggles against the monarchy. Coke put Jefferson in the habit of tracing principles back to their roots, with his emphasis on the ancient Saxon and Germanic foundations of English liberty that preceded the Norman Conquest and Magna Carta. Unlike Coke, however, Jefferson came to believe that these ancient liberties had been corrupted in a kind of fall from grace. Not for the first time, Jefferson constructed a prelapsarian secular fantasy about a pastoral utopia where men lived in simplicity, freedom, and harmony, only to have their idyll destroyed by corruption and tyranny. He clung tenaciously to this made-up history throughout his life. As many of his biographers have observed, there was something childlike—almost childish—in Jefferson's willingness, throughout his life, to construct fairy-tale visions of virtuous yeoman living in natural harmony, uncorrupted by government or laws.[32]

Jefferson also had a knack for ignoring inconvenient realities in his personal and political life that clashed with his romantic fantasies. His bungled marriage proposal at the age of twenty to Rebecca Burwell, the woman who would later marry Jacquelin Ambler and become John Marshall's mother-in-law, suggests a young man who lived in his own head, who idealized and abstracted a woman he barely knew, and who retreated in wounded self-pity when disappointed. This pattern of abstraction persisted throughout his personal life. His marriage to Martha Wayles by all accounts was happy; they had six children over the course of a decade, although all but three died in infancy. When Martha died in 1782, after the birth of their last child, Jefferson's torment, according to his daughter Patsy, was indescribable.[33] He continued for the rest of his life to profess no fonder wish than to retire to Monticello to be surrounded by his daughters and grandchildren, but the retirement was continually postponed. With his children, moreover, he assumed a fond but distant and slightly hectoring tone—like the one he used in setting out that exhausting schedule of self-improvement for the aspiring law student.

Jefferson's self-absorption and his weakness for abstraction complicated his personal life when he was in Paris as American ambassador in 1787. He sent for his daughter Polly, accompanied by his young slave, Sally Hemings. Although they were met by Abigail Adams on their arrival in London, Jefferson insisted that he was too busy to join them and had them make their way across the English Channel on their own.[34] Jefferson was at the moment engaged in what was at the very least an intense flirtation with Maria Cosway, the beautiful wife of a London society painter. After months of ardent perambulations with Maria—he broke his wrist at one point coltishly trying to jump a fence—Jefferson's feelings cooled when Maria failed to fulfill his impossible ideals, and he eventually withdrew from her, as he did from all other intimates, leaving her flummoxed and uncertain. By the same token, Jefferson's sexual relationship with Hemings—which seems to have been established by recent DNA tests beyond reasonable doubt—is another example of his powers of cognitive dissonance: after his death, he freed her children, apparently keeping a long-standing promise, but he neglected to free his longtime mistress.[35] More generally, Jefferson's ability to reconcile his abstract opposition to slavery with a suspicion that slavery could not be ended because "the blacks . . . are inferior to the whites in the endowments both of body and mind" further illustrates his knack for suppressing inconvenient personal conclusions that clashed with his stated ideals.[36] Of course, a simultaneous belief in the political equality and social inferiority of African-Americans was not unusual for Jefferson's time.

This preference for overlooking unpleasant realities while keeping his gaze fixed on idealized abstractions came to define Jefferson's constitutional vision as well. Although best remembered for his invocation of self-evident truths and inalienable rights in the Declaration of Independence, Jefferson's mature constitutional philosophy came

to center not on natural rights but on majority rule. "It is my principle that the will of the majority should always prevail," he wrote to
Madison from Paris when the Constitution was being debated in
1787. Jefferson's early constitutional views were most apparent in the
draft of the Constitution for Virginia, which he proposed in June
1776—not in the Declaration of Independence that would follow in
the next month. His main concern was democracy. He would have
guaranteed broad voting rights—something like universal white male
suffrage—and equal representation of voters in the House, with districts more or less based on population. (Marshall was less concerned
about extending the vote as broadly as possible.) Even more important, in Jefferson's view, was the provision for popular constitutional
amendments: Jefferson proposed that the Constitution could be
amended at any time by a vote cast on the same day by the people of
two-thirds of the counties in Virginia. He remained a lifelong critic
of the Constitution that Virginia actually adopted, which left "the
majority of the men in the state . . . unrepresented in the legislature" because of property-based qualifications for voting that Marshall was more willing to approve.[37] And although Jefferson included
an influential section on "rights private and public"—which guaranteed religious liberty, freedom of the press, and a prohibition on
the importation of new slaves—he did not include many of the
rights Virginia ultimately protected in its Bill of Rights, including
freedom from unreasonable searches and seizures, freedom from
self-incrimination, and the right to challenge unconstitutional convictions through habeas corpus. These were the rights of fair judicial
procedure that Jefferson's opponents would accuse him of violating
as president.

His thoughts on judicial independence, initially ambivalent and
uncertain, became increasingly radicalized, as Jefferson—driven by
a combination of partisan anger and ideological purity—endorsed

unchecked majority rule. In the 1780s, Jefferson was more circumspect, suggesting that the judiciary could play a role as a "legal check" against legislative excesses—by participating, with executive branch officials, in a special council that could veto unconstitutional laws before they went into effect. As John Adams's vice president from 1797 to 1801, he declared the right of state legislatures—rather than judges—to "nullify" any laws they believed were unconstitutional. Once he became president, he threatened Federalist judges with impeachment and argued convincingly that the president, Congress, and the courts all have the "concurrent" authority to interpret the Constitution.[38] After leaving the White House, however, Jefferson's views became truly extreme, as he was driven to distraction by his dislike of the Marshall Court. Writing to Madison in 1821, when both were out of office, Jefferson seemed to deny the power of the Supreme Court to strike down unconstitutional laws, suggesting that constitutional change could come only through formal amendments. This provoked Madison to demur that the framers of the Constitution had clearly intended to make the Court the final judge of conflicts between the state and federal governments.[39] Jefferson ended his life, therefore, as something close to a pure majoritarian, convinced that state legislatures, rather than independent judges, should be the ultimate arbiter of constitutional questions.

Jefferson's and Marshall's political disputes shaped both men's views about judicial independence, as well as defining the constitutional agenda for the Supreme Court during Marshall's tenure as chief justice. The difference between their views first emerged in 1798, before Marshall was even on the Court, over the Alien and Sedition Acts. These emerged from the furor that followed a secret diplomatic mission by Marshall to France, where he was sent to make peace with Charles-Maurice de Talleyrand, the French foreign minister in whose wily cunning Marshall met his match. Talleyrand demanded a bribe

before agreeing to negotiate, and forced Marshall and his fellow diplo-
mats to deal with three deputies, whom Marshall referred to in coded
dispatches as X, Y, and Z. After the "XYZ affair" was publicized in
America with 10,000 pamphlets printed with Marshall's encouragement (and at Congress's expense), Jefferson referred sneeringly to the
publicity as "the XYZ dish cooked up by Marshall."[40] Anti-French indignation led to war fever, which the Federalist Congress exploited in
1798 to pass the Alien and Sedition Acts. The Alien Act allowed the
president to deport aliens without a hearing, and the Sedition Act made
it a crime to publish "false, scandalous, and malicious writing" against
the president or Congress. Since the law expired on March 3, 1801, the
last day of President Adams's term, and did not cover criticism against
Jefferson, the Republican vice president, it was a transparent effort to
protect the Federalists against Republican criticism. During the two
and a half years the Sedition Act remained on the books—which Jefferson called "the reign of witches"—the Federalists tried and convicted ten Republicans under the noxious law.[41]

Marshall's and Jefferson's very different responses to the Alien
and Sedition Acts cast light on the differences in their philosophies
and temperament, and culminated in their war over the proper role of
the judiciary. Marshall returned from France to a hero's welcome in
Philadelphia, and Jefferson twice stopped by his boardinghouse. (The
vice president left a note lamenting that he was so "lucky as to find
Marshall out," but then inserted the prefix *un* before *lucky;* Marshall
later is said to have declared that the note was one of the few times
Jefferson had told the truth.)[42] After having coyly declined a series of
proffered appointments, Marshall agreed to run for Congress at George
Washington's request, and his success in getting elected as a Federalist from a largely Republican district in Virginia was a tribute to his
ability to win over his opponents through folksy charm and bonhomie.
During the campaign, Marshall was in a tough spot: if he supported

the Alien and Sedition Acts, he would lose support in his Republican district; if he opposed them too strongly, he would alienate the leaders of his own party. He navigated this shoal with typical élan, staking out a moderate position that neither satisfied nor infuriated extremists in either party. "I am not an advocate for the Alien and Sedition Bills," Marshall bravely wrote to a Virginia paper at the height of the campaign. "Had I been in Congress when they passed, I should, unless my judgment could have been changed, certainly have opposed them." But Marshall made a nod toward true believers in his own party by adding a lawyerly proviso: "I do not think them fraught with all those mischiefs which many gentlemen ascribed to them." Although he expected they would expire before he was called to vote on them, Marshall promised that if forced to choose: "I shall indisputably oppose their revival."[43]

Marshall's deft response earned him the suspicion of the conservative true believers who were known as High Federalists, but it may also have won him the election, since it persuaded Patrick Henry, Virginia's leading Republican, to endorse his ideological antagonist. "Tell Marshall I love him, because he felt and acted as a Republican, as an American," Henry announced.[44] In Congress, Marshall kept his promise. After his election, Republicans demanded the repeal of the sedition laws, and Marshall crossed party lines to cast the tie-breaking vote in favor of the repeal, which passed 50–48. If Marshall had voted with his own party, the Federalist speaker would have broken the tie by voting against repeal. Both during the campaign and after it, Marshall showed political courage and an attachment to constitutional principle, but always with a pragmatic sense of what was politically feasible.

Jefferson's response to the Alien and Sedition Acts was far more ideological. While serving as vice president, Jefferson was understandably upset by the tendency of Federalist judges and grand juries

to indict Republicans for their opinions under the Sedition Act—
including the representative of Jefferson's own congressional district.
He also feared that he himself might be prosecuted under the act. But
because he had no faith in federal courts controlled by Federalists, he
thought the right of free expression should be protected entirely by
state legislatures accountable to the people. As a result, he hit on a
cure for the Sedition Acts that was nearly as bad as the disease. With
James Madison, he secretly drafted the Virginia and Kentucky Reso-
lutions, which were based on the idea that state legislatures should be
free to interpret the Constitution and make clear their opposition to
the tyrannical acts of the national government. This proposition was
uncontroversial enough—Alexander Hamilton had recognized the
rights of states to protect civil liberties in the Federalist Papers. But
in the Kentucky Resolution, Jefferson went further. He declared that
the Union was a compact among independent and sovereign states;
that the framers had set up no ultimate interpreter of the Constitution;
and that each state legislature, therefore, had "an equal right to judge
for itself" infractions and the mode of redress. In cases where Congress had unconstitutionally assumed power, Jefferson declared, the
appropriate remedy was "nullification"—by which he meant that
each state could refuse to follow federal laws with which it disagreed.
This form of defiance is implicitly rejected by the Constitution, which
makes federal laws supreme over state laws. But then Jefferson went
further still: in a letter to Madison, he proposed not only that states
had the power of nullification but that, if the federal government persisted in trying to enforce unconstitutional laws, the states had the
right to secede from the Union.[45] Madison talked Jefferson out of this
despairing and radical conclusion, but he resurrected it at the end of
his life, when his views encouraged Southern secessionists in the de-
structive path that would ultimately lead to the Civil War.

The Alien and Sedition Acts expired at the end of Adams's term, and Jefferson succeeded him in 1801. After Jefferson's first confrontation with Marshall as chief justice, in *Marbury v. Madison,* the president accepted his Pyrrhic victory—perhaps because the Republican assault on the Federalist judiciary had bigger targets than an obscure justice of the peace. The Republicans decided to impeach Federalist judges who seemed unusually partisan on the bench, starting with an insane and alcoholic New Hampshire district judge, John Pickering, who was convicted in the Senate on a party line vote. The Republicans next turned their sights on the Supreme Court itself, starting with Justice Samuel Chase, a High Federalist whose fears of unchecked democracy and harangues against Jefferson from the bench made John Marshall look like the moderate he was. When Jefferson heard of a particularly vitriolic attack on him by Chase, he tacitly encouraged the justice's impeachment with his usual feline indirection. "Ought this seditious and official attack on the principles of our Constitution . . . go unpunished?" he wrote to one of the leaders of the House of Representatives. "And to whom so pointed as yourself will the public look for the necessary measures?" Jefferson then added with silken disingenuousness, "I ask these questions for your consideration, for myself, it is better that I should not interfere."[46] The House took Jefferson's less than subtle hint and impeached Chase in 1805 for his "highly arbitrary, oppressive, and unjust" conduct on the bench. Chase's trial in the Senate was presided over by Vice President Aaron Burr, who had killed Alexander Hamilton in a duel the previous summer, prompting jokes about how the judge was being tried by a murderer, rather than the other way around. Chase was ably defended by Luther Martin, an anti-Federalist who became one of the greatest appellate advocates of his day, despite his habit of appearing intoxicated before the bench. Refreshed with his usual stimulants, Martin made a powerful case that impeachments should be limited to crimes and should not be used as a weapon against political differences.

In a dramatic moment, Chief Justice Marshall was called to testify on behalf of his voluble colleague. But the testimony did not show Marshall at his best. On the contrary, instead of wholeheartedly defending Chase, Marshall fell over himself to accommodate his accusers. "The Chief Justice really discovered too much caution—too much fear—too much cunning," a witness recorded of Marshall's testimony, adding that Marshall should have been more "frank and explicit."[47] In the face of political resistance, Marshall went so far as to suggest that instead of resorting to impeachments, Congress should be able to reverse legal opinions that it viewed as unsound. The performance put Marshall's strategic pragmatism in its least sympathetic light, revealing his fears that if the Chase impeachment had succeeded, he himself would be next on the block. Nevertheless, Marshall's willingness to compromise may have impressed Republican moderates, who unexpectedly fell out with Chase's chief Republican prosecutor, John Randolph, over an unrelated dispute. As a result, Chase was acquitted and the most serious threat to judicial independence in a generation repudiated. When Randolph, after Chase's acquittal, proposed constitutional amendments allowing for the removal of any federal judge by the president if a majority of both houses of Congress agreed, the amendment was rejected. Many in both parties ultimately recognized that if Chase were impeached for his political unpopularity, any judge could meet the same fate. The acquittal of Chase established a precedent of judicial independence that allowed judges of both parties to disappoint the presidents who appointed them. And to Jefferson's intense distress, that tradition soon established itself on the Marshall Court.

During his eight years in office, Jefferson made three appointments to the Supreme Court, which he viewed as opportunities to destroy all traces of its hostile Federalist majority. "The revolution is incomplete so long as that fortress is in the possession of the enemy," the radical Republican Richard Giles wrote to Jefferson in 1801.[48] But when it came time to name Supreme Court justices, Jefferson chose moderate Republicans and distinguished state judges who cared about the Court as an institution and ended up supporting Marshall in his efforts to extend national power.[49] Jefferson's three appointees were William Johnson, Brockholst Livingston, and Thomas Todd. The former chief justice of the Kentucky Supreme Court, Todd was an expert in property law who would disappoint Jefferson by siding with Marshall and filing only one dissent in his nineteen years on the bench. Livingston, a former judge on the New York State Supreme Court, was an expert in commercial law who filed only eight dissents during sixteen years and was noted for his good humor. (He even published an epic poem under the pseudonym of Aqualine Nimble-Chops.)

Jefferson's closest acolyte was his first appointee, William Johnson. Although an ardent Republican during his time as Speaker of the New Jersey House of Representatives, Johnson infuriated Republican partisans in 1807 by citing Marshall's opinion in *Marbury v. Madison* when objecting to the Supreme Court's decision to order the testimony of two accomplices of Aaron Burr in his trial for treason.[50] And the following year Johnson clashed with Jefferson over the president's controversial decision to declare an embargo on all foreign trade in order to avoid taking sides in the war between France and Britain. The embargo was a failure, both economically and constitutionally. Exports plummeted in a year by nearly $100 million and thousands of American sailors were put out of work. Henry Adams later observed that Jefferson's decision to call out the army and navy to enforce the embargo made a mockery out of his purported principles of strict construction and resulted in the abridgement of more civil liberties than anything perpetrated by Great Britain during the Revolutionary War. Justice Johnson put a wrench into Jefferson's plans when he held that the discretion to detain ships suspected of violating the embargo belonged to the port inspectors, not the president; Jefferson ordered his inspectors to ignore the ruling and relied on an expansive decision by a Federalist district judge in Massachusetts upholding the constitutionality of the embargo under Marshall's broad vision of Congress's power to regulate interstate commerce.[51] For many Federalists, Jefferson's hypocrisy was complete.

During Marshall's first four years on the bench, the Court handed down forty-six decisions, and all of them were unanimous.[52] Marshall wrote the opinion for the Court in all forty-two of these cases in which he participated. As early as 1801, in *Talbot v. Seeman*, he introduced the practice of issuing a single opinion, styled the Opinion of the Court, rather than allowing each justice to express his own view separately, which was the English custom. In vigorously promoting unanimous opinions, Marshall hoped to shore up the Court's authority as being above politics. Jefferson wrote to Justice Johnson denouncing Marshall's practice of having the Court deliver a single opinion, which he said prevented the public from knowing whether the decisions really were unanimous and protected "the lazy, the modest & the incompetent."[53] Johnson replied that soon after his appointment, he delivered a dissenting opinion, and for the rest of the term, was continually lectured by Marshall about "the indecency of judges cutting at each other, & the loss of reputation which the Virginia appellate court had sustained by pursuing such a course etc. . . . I therefore bent to the current."[54]

The dissenting opinion to which Johnson referred came in an 1810 case called *Fletcher v. Peck*. The case involved one of the most corrupt land deals in history, involving 35 million acres in the Yazoo territory, which now comprises most of Mississippi and Alabama. The Georgia legislature had sold the land to New England land investors at very low rates in exchange for massive bribes. Attacking the deal as flamboyantly corrupt, a subsequent group of Georgia legislators passed a law rescinding the deal. Federalists called on the federal courts to

A rare group portrait of some of the members of the Marshall Court in the old House of Representatives, painted by Samuel F. B. Morse in 1821. From left to right: Congressman Hugh Nelson, Justice Bushrod Washington, Justice Brockholst Livingston, and Chief Justice John Marshall. Under Marshall's leadership, the justices not only heard cases together but also lived together in the same boardinghouse and shared Marshall's excellent Madeira. (In the Collection of the Corcoran Gallery of Art)

protect commercial interests, including those of the original land investors; Republicans supported the power of elected state courts to protect farmers and more recent settlers on the land. In *Fletcher*, Marshall wrote an opinion for the Court siding with the original purchasers, holding that the new Georgia law violated the constitutional provision which says, "No State shall . . . pass any . . . Law impairing the Obligation of Contracts." The decision, the first time the Supreme Court had struck down a state law as a violation of the Constitution, was tremendously important. Emphasizing that private property and contracts could not be lightly interfered with by local majorities, Marshall helped to create a stable regulatory environment for the growth of the national economy. In a passage that must have made Jefferson apoplectic, Marshall warned about the dangers of populist excesses: "Whatever respect might have been felt for the state sovereignties, it is not to be disguised that the framers of the constitution viewed, with some apprehension, the violent acts which might grow out of the feelings of the moment," he wrote, "and that the people of the United States, in adopting that instrument, have manifested a determination to shield themselves and their property from the effects of those sudden and strong passions to which men are exposed." In his dissenting opinion, Justice Johnson agreed that the Georgia law was invalid, but insisted that it violated principles of natural justice rather than the contracts clause of the Constitution. He noted that "the states and the United States are continually legislating on the subject of contracts," and predicted that Marshall's interpretation would "operate to restrict the states in the exercise of that right which every community must exercise, of possessing itself of the property of the individual, when necessary for public uses." But neither of the other two Jefferson appointees joined Johnson in his lonely dissent.

Disappointed by his own nominees, Jefferson turned his attention to urging sounder ones on his protégé and successor, James Madison. In 1810, when Jefferson was sued for damages in connection with disputed land in New Orleans arising out of the Louisiana Purchase, the case ended up in Marshall's circuit in Richmond, Virginia. Jefferson urged Madison to replace the local district judge with someone of more reliably Republican leanings: "The state has suffered long enough from the want of any counterpart to the rancorous hatred which Marshall bears to his country and from the cunning and sophistry within which he is able to surround himself," Jefferson wrote. "His twistifications of the law in the case of Marbury, in that of Burr, and the late Yazoo case show how dexterously he can reconcile law to his personal biases."[55] When it came time to appoint a new justice in 1811, and to create the first Republican majority on the Court, Jefferson bombarded Madison with advice about candidates. Jefferson recommended his former attorney general, Lincoln Levi, who had tangled with Marshall in *Marbury v. Madison,* but Levi turned down the appointment. After two other candidates declined the job, Madison, who needed a New Englander for geographic balance, settled on Joseph Story, one of the most prominent Republicans in Massachusetts. Jefferson mistrusted the future Harvard Law School professor as a "pseudo-Republican" because during his brief service as a congressman he had voted to repeal Jefferson's embargo, and because he had gone on to serve as counsel for the land speculators in *Fletcher v. Peck,* along with John Quincy Adams, the son of the former president.

As it turned out, Jefferson was right to worry. Story would prove to be Marshall's closest friend and ally on the bench, forging a long relationship of genuine affection and intellectual collaboration in the service of nationalism and property rights. "It is certainly true, that the Judges here live with perfect harmony, and as agreeably as absence from friends and from families could make our residence," Story wrote happily to his wife a year after his appointment. "Our intercourse is perfectly familiar and unconstrained, and our social hours when undisturbed with the labors of law, are passed in gay and frank conversation."[56] As Story's account suggests, part of Marshall's strength as a leader was his insistence that justices of different political persuasions live and work together in the same boardinghouse. By contrast, Jefferson was so averse to political conflict that his White

House dinners were segregated along political lines: only Federalists or Republicans were invited on a given evening, and Jefferson went to great lengths to avoid any political conversation, mesmerizing the guests instead with his encyclopedic knowledge of topics from natural history to French travel. The result was dazzling, but it was hardly conducive to bipartisan negotiation or political compromise. As a result, Jefferson lacked the influence over moderate Federalists that Marshall maintained over moderate Republicans.

Jefferson's Federalist critics called him a hypocrite, betraying principles in practice that he defended only in his idealizing imagination. But it was Jefferson's pragmatic willingness, as president, not to take his strict constructionist principles to their logical conclusion that saved his presidency. In addition to his support for sedition prosecutions of his critics, he presided over the Louisiana Purchase, the largest expansion in America's landmass in history, even though according to his own constitutional principles, Congress and the president almost certainly lacked the power to authorize the purchase from France. Although Jefferson himself initially suggested that the purchase would make "blank paper of the Constitution," and could only be justified by a constitutional amendment, he abandoned his constitutional scruples for fear of upsetting the deal. In justifying his accommodation, Jefferson found the resources to praise the virtues of pragmatism over ideological purity—surely one of the greatest of his many exercises in cognitive dissonance. "What is practicable must often control what is pure theory; and the habits of the governed determine in a great decree what is practicable," he declared improbably.[57] But the belated embrace of pragmatism was his greatest political achievement: faced with a conflict between his romantic ideal of a youthful America ever expanding westward and legalistic objections about strict constructionism, he preferred to embrace the more vivid ideal and to throw over the lesser one. For him, pragmatism was just one more tool in the greater service of his democratic vision.

Marshall's pragmatism was more consistent, however, and therefore more effective. With judicial power on increasingly firm footing, Marshall proceeded to use his Supreme Court opinions to advance his twin goals of allowing Congress to unify the national economy and preventing state politicians from interfering with contracts and property rights. In some cases, Marshall's rulings coincided not only with his political beliefs but also with his economic interests. As an enthusiastic land speculator in Kentucky, Marshall fought a lifelong battle to protect his investment against efforts by the Virginia legislature to seize disputed parts of the title. When a case involving his own land came before the Supreme Court in 1813, Marshall recused himself, but his loyal deputy, Justice Story, defended the sanctity of private contracts, holding in *Fairfax's Devisee v. Hunter's Lessee* that federal treaties with Britain trumped Virginia's efforts to confiscate the land of British loyalists, which Marshall and his brother had subsequently acquired. Jefferson's deputy, Justice Johnson, wrote a vigorous dissent arguing that Virginia had the power to confiscate the lands. With Jefferson's support, the Virginia Supreme Court responded to the decision defiantly, announcing that the federal law that gave the Supreme Court the power to review civil decisions by state courts was itself unconstitutional. The U.S. Supreme Court, again speaking through Justice Story, promptly reversed the Virginia court, asserting its power to review state court civil decisions in *Martin v. Hunter's Lessee* (1816). This time, Justice Johnson concurred. He was tempted to applaud the Virginia court for its spirit of resistance, but couldn't tolerate the radical challenge to the Union. Johnson reiterated the Jeffersonian idea that the Union was a compact among sovereign states, and that the Supreme Court could not destroy state sovereignty; it could only guarantee national uniformity when it came to the interpretation of federal laws. When "angry vindictive persons of men . . . made their way into state judicial tribunals," Johnson agreed with the majority, "there ought to be a power where to refrain or punish, or the union must be dissolved."

The culmination of Marshall's nationalist vision came in *McCulloch v. Maryland* (1819). For a unanimous Court, now composed of five Republicans and two Federalists, Marshall upheld Congress's authority to charter the Bank of the United States, the centerpiece of Alexander Hamilton's plan to expand the money supply, create a national currency, and retire the Revolutionary War debt. During the Washington administration, Hamilton had fought with Jefferson and Madison about whether Congress had the constitutional power to charter a national bank. He won the battle when Washington signed the bill chartering the bank in 1791. The bank was generally considered a rousing success, and by 1816 even President Madison had abandoned his former constitutional objections and signed the charter for a second bank into law. Jefferson, however, was more radical than his protégé on constitutional questions and continued to insist that the bank was unconstitutional. This view became more widespread after the bank was blamed for the financial downturn following the panic of 1818, and several states, including Maryland, passed taxes on it. These taxes were challenged in court, and in 1819 the Marshall Court seized the opportunity to side with Congress and the bank over the recalcitrant states.

There was nothing especially novel about Marshall's opinion in the *McCulloch* case: he resurrected the same arguments that Hamilton had used to persuade Washington to endorse the Bank of the United States a generation earlier, over Jefferson's objection. Marshall noted that the Constitution gives Congress the authority to pass all laws "necessary and proper" for executing its constitutional powers and insisted that these words should be construed broadly, in a practical spirit. (The fact that the Jeffersonian opponents of the bank, who claimed to hate judicial power, were calling for breathtaking judicial activism in asking judges to second-guess Congress was one of the many ironies of the case.) Marshall, however, chose the path of judicial restraint. "Let the end be legitimate, let it be within the scope of the constitution, and all means which are appropriate, which are plainly adapted to that end, which are not prohibited but consist with the letter and spirit of the constitution, are constitutional," he wrote. Although Marshall's reasoning wasn't original, his opinion was arguably more important than *Marbury v. Madison,* and it was one of the nineteenth century's most significant contributions to the growth of federal power. If Marshall had endorsed Jefferson's strict construction of the scope of congressional power, federal courts would have been asked to second-guess the necessity of nearly every law that Congress passed.

In addition to recognizing Congress's power to charter the bank, Marshall also emphasized that the states had no power to tax it—a more controversial conclusion. In the process, he rejected the exotic vision of states' rights that Jefferson had advanced before he became president. Jefferson and other opponents of the bank insisted that the Union was a compact of sovereign states, any one of which could substitute its own views on constitutional questions for those of Congress. Marshall countered that national sovereignty is vested in the people of the United States as a whole, not the people of each individual state, and because the bank, chartered by Congress, represented the sovereign people as a whole, it should be "supreme within its sphere of action" and could not be thwarted by dissenting states.

Jefferson's reaction to the *McCulloch* case suggests a peevish extremism that had become more pronounced with age. He and his supporters had been outmaneuvered once again by Marshall, forced as they were into an awkward position—they found themselves arguing that the Court should be trusted to strike down an act of Congress, but not trusted to restrict the powers of the states.[58] When he read the attacks on the decision published by the states' rights partisan Spencer Roane, Jefferson said he endorsed "every tittle" of the essays, but went even further than Roane in denying the Court's exclusive power to interpret the Constitution. "When the legislative or executive functionaries act unconstitutionally, they are responsible to the people in their elective capacity," he wrote. The only "safe depository of the ultimate powers of the society" was "the people themselves."[59] Jefferson said it was "dangerous" to exempt judges from this popular check, suggesting that state legislatures that disagreed with Supreme Court decisions should be free to defy them. Jefferson's embrace of nullification as a response to overreaching judicial authority became more explicit after he read another attack on *McCulloch* by John Taylor, an ardent states' rights defender from Virginia. The Supreme Court had no power to review the constitutionality of state laws or to enjoin the decisions of state courts, Taylor insisted, because "the spheres of action of the federal and state courts are as separate and distinct as those of the courts of two neighboring states."[60] Once again, Jefferson applauded this attack on national supremacy in Manichean terms, describing Taylor's polemic as "the true political faith to which every catholic republican should steadfastly hold."[61]

Marshall understood that Jefferson's vision would thwart the effort by the framers of the Constitution to create a system of national laws that all citizens were obliged to follow, whether they agreed with them or not. He wrote a series of pseudonymous pamphlets in response to Roane, explaining to his Federalist colleague Justice Bushrod Washington that "I find myself more stimulated on this subject than on any other because I believe the design to be to injure the Judges and impair the Constitution."[62] In a case called *Cohens v. Virginia*, Marshall unequivocally rejected Jefferson's nullification vision. The case involved the Cohen brothers, who had been convicted of violating a Virginia law regulating the sale of lottery tickets. They claimed their operation had been authorized by a federal law setting up the lottery in Washington, D.C. When the Supreme Court agreed to hear the case, Jeffersonians in Virginia once again tried to defy the justices: the Virginia legislature, willfully ignoring the Court's earlier decision in *Martin v. Hunter's Lessee,* passed a resolution denying the Court's power to review the decision of the Virginia state court, which had insisted that a Virginia law banning lotteries was valid despite the federal law to the contrary. With typical craftiness, Marshall gave a nominal victory to Virginia—holding that Congress had not intended to authorize the sale of lottery tickets outside of the District of Columbia, and therefore there was no conflict between state and federal law. The Cohens were out of luck. But he reserved the more important victory for friends of national power, emphasizing that Congress did have the power to authorize a Virginia lottery if it chose to do so, despite state laws to the contrary. The *Cohens* case also established the important principle that the Supreme Court could review criminal as well as civil cases arising out of state courts, to assure national uniformity. "In war, we are one people," he wrote. "In making peace, we are one people. In all commercial regulations, we are one and the same people."

Marshall's parry seemed to drive Jefferson to new heights of extremism. He warned that the Federalist judiciary was pushing what he saw as a confederation of independent states toward consolidation, and he insisted that judges should ultimately be accountable to the will of the people. In response to the *Cohens* case, Jefferson wrote a furious letter to Justice William Johnson insisting that federal courts, including the Supreme Court, should not be able to review controversies between states and their own citizens, even when federal rights were involved. He denied Marshall's suggestion that the Supreme

Court should be the ultimate arbiter of disputes between the states and the nation, insisting that "the ultimate arbiter is the people of the Union," exercising their power of constitutional amendment.[63] In statements like this, Jefferson seemed to deny entirely the Supreme Court's power to hand down binding interpretations of the Constitution, making it impossible to enforce the supremacy of the national government.

As the end of his life approached, Jefferson was succumbing to despair about imagined conspiracies of national consolidation. In 1825, he wrote a letter to the radical Republican William Giles that seemed openly to endorse the possibility of secession. Denouncing President John Quincy Adams's attempts to consolidate national power over the states, Jefferson called for states' rights advocates to protest each encroachment "as a temporary yielding to a lesser evil, until their accumulation shall outweigh that of separation."[64] Opponents said Jefferson had gone mad or senile, but whenever he was out of government, he was never able to resist carrying a philosophical principle to its logical conclusion, no matter how extreme the consequences. Madison as usual kept his head better than his patron, writing to Jefferson that he had no doubt that the framers of the Constitution intended the federal courts to be a "final resort" to decide conflicts between federal and state law, and that this intention was clearly expressed by the provisions declaring that the federal constitution and laws shall be the "supreme law of the land," and that the jurisdiction of federal courts shall extend to all controversies arising under those supreme laws.[65] Jefferson never forgave his protégé for being a constitutionalist rather than a true believer in majority rule. On his deathbed, just before he breathed his last, Jefferson lamented that Madison had always been too accommodating. "But ah!" he exclaimed, "he could never in his life stand up against strenuous opposition."[66] The equation of any pragmatism with heresy was characteristic, and it provides one reason why, in his battles with Marshall, Jefferson was consistently outmaneuvered.

Jefferson died on July 4, 1826. As for Marshall, he served on the Court for nine more years, until his own death on July 6, 1835. The final decade was not entirely happy. There were the usual indignities of age, including a painful operation for kidney stones, performed without anesthetic by the aptly named Dr. Physick. The death of Polly Marshall in 1831 filled him with grief. And his beloved Court became a little more fractious: the justices stopped living together in the same boardinghouse and dissents became more frequent. But even the justices appointed by Marshall's political antagonists, from Jefferson to Andrew Jackson, continued to embrace Marshall's vision of national unity, largely because those presidents defied the demands of their party extremists and appointed moderates instead. Marshall was initially distressed by the election of Andrew Jackson in 1828 ("Should Jackson be elected, I should look upon the government as virtually dissolved," he wrote in a widely published letter), and perhaps because of his discontent he became uncharacteristically aggressive in confronting the Jackson administration in a battle he knew in advance he could not win.

The Cherokee Indians case, *Worcester v. Georgia,* was Marshall's last hurrah on behalf of national supremacy in the face of state usurpation. After gold was found on land belonging to the Cherokee Indians, the state of Georgia passed a series of laws seizing the Cherokee territory and nullifying all Cherokee laws and customs. A Vermont minister, Samuel Worcester, was convicted of violating one of the Georgia laws, which required non-Cherokees to get a license from the state before living in the territory, and he sued, arguing that the Georgia law violated federal treaties guaranteeing the Cherokees their land. In one of his most passionate opinions, Marshall agreed, striking down Georgia's entire system of laws regarding the Cherokees as "repugnant to the Constitution, laws, and treaties of the United States."[67] President Jackson is famous for having supposedly reacted to the decision by saying, "John Marshall has made his decision, now let him enforce it." The comment was probably apocryphal, but the state of Georgia simply ignored the decision, and Jackson made no effort to enforce it.

Because of their dissatisfaction with the centralizing decisions of the Marshall Court, southern states like Georgia and South Carolina in the 1820s and 1830s grew increasingly radical in their denunciations of judicial authority. Marshall worried that the talk of states' rights would lead to secession and the dismemberment of the Union. The intellectual leader of this effort, Senator John C. Calhoun, invoked Jefferson as an authority and resurrected an early draft of the resolution Jefferson had drafted in opposition to the Alien and Sedition Acts, in which he announced that "every state has a natural right . . . to nullify of their own authority all assumptions of power by others within their limits."[68] Things came to a head when South Carolina passed a declaration of nullification in 1832, refusing to comply with a federal tariff that it claimed was unconstitutional.

But unexpectedly, and to Marshall's great relief, President Jackson issued a proclamation to the people of South Carolina insisting that they could not choose which federal laws to follow, affirming that the Supreme Court had the ultimate power to decide the constitutionality of laws, and stressing that its decisions had to be obeyed. Marshall, surprised and pleased, became one of Jackson's most improbable fans, and took special pleasure swearing him in at his second inauguration the following March. When Marshall died three years later, Jackson returned the compliment, praising the chief justice's opinions for their "energy and clearness which were peculiar to his strong mind, and gave him a rank amongst the greatest men of his age."[69]

Marshall's success in winning over his last political opponent

Marshall administering the oath of office to President Andrew Jackson. The two political rivals were initially wary but came to respect each other.

was an appropriate capstone to a brilliant career. Displaying all the qualities of temperament that Jefferson lacked—incrementalism, accommodation, practicality, philosophical moderation, and a great deal of political savvy—he had transformed the Supreme Court from a weak and largely ignored body to a national institution whose rulings commanded bipartisan respect. But the key to Marshall's success was his unique combination of confidence and restraint. He boldly asserted the Supreme Court's power to strike down laws in theory, but only exercised this power in practice when he knew that public opinion would support his position. In this sense, he shared Jefferson's concern about the will of the people, but was willing to check transient passions on behalf of fundamental and widely accepted principles. Marshall was also generally more adept than his rival at reading the popular mood.

In the years leading up to the Civil War, Abraham Lincoln and his Republican supporters claimed that they were the true Jeffersonians, in attacking judicial activism and championing unalienable human rights, and they insisted that the Southern Democrats had perverted Jefferson's legacy. "All honor to Jefferson," Lincoln announced in 1859, who had the courage to recognize the "abstract truth"—that all men are created equal—and to "embalm it" in the Declaration of Independence as "a rebuke and a stumbling block to the very harbingers of re-appearing tyranny and oppression."[70] The Democrats countered by decrying Lincoln's lionizing of Jefferson as "barefaced humbuggery," insisting instead that the party of states' rights was the true heir to the legacy of the Sage of Monticello. The fact that Jefferson could plausibly be invoked by both parties during the run-up to the Civil War is a reminder of the protean quality of his thought. Wrong on all of the great constitutional issues of his age, he was profoundly right about the abstract truths of equality and democracy, and his vision was abstract enough to be earnestly invoked on both sides in most of the constitutional battles in the nineteenth and twentieth centuries.

The more we learn about Jefferson, the harder he is to admire as a constitutionalist. Instead, his greatness comes in the force of his personal example—as a polymath, a philosopher, an aesthete, and a genius. Temperamentally, he provides an antitype for the qualities that make for a judicious temperament—in his remoteness, radicalism, impracticality, intense intellectuality, and devotion to abstract ideals over concrete principles. That he was willing to compromise these ideals as a practical politician made him a far more effective president than he would otherwise have been. And as the leading philosopher of the American experiment, Jefferson also shows that there may be more important qualities than judicial temperament when it comes to achieving greatness—such as recognizing and defending abstract truths that inspire future generations, regardless of the practical consequences.

By contrast, Marshall was vindicated by history on all the constitutional issues where Jefferson was wrong—on the scope of national power, the importance of checks on government power enforced by independent courts, and the sovereignty of the people of the United States as a whole, rather than of individual states. He outfoxed Jefferson repeatedly, not only because of his ideas but because of his temperament—the moderation, modesty, gregariousness, strategic cunning, reluctance to fight losing battles, and willingness to conserve judicial power for those skirmishes in which judges could count on the support of the nation. Marshall recognized, in the end, that Jefferson was correct that democratic majorities were the ultimate source of political authority in America, although he was wrong that temporary local majorities always had to have their way. By insisting on enforcing fundamental constitutional limitations on government power, but only those that the people were willing to accept, Marshall, rather than Jefferson, remade the Constitution in his own image.

CHAPTER TWO

THE
LEGACY
OF THE
CIVIL WAR

JOHN MARSHALL HARLAN

OLIVER WENDELL HOLMES, JR.

J ustices John Marshall Harlan and Oliver Wendell Holmes, Jr., were both tall and self-confident Civil War veterans: Harlan was barrel-chested, strapping, and bald, while Holmes was razor-thin and leonine, with a luxuriant military moustache. Temperamentally, however, they were opposites: where Holmes was elegant, bloodless, aristocratic, and aloof, Harlan was emotional, gregarious, and prone to delivering extemporaneous stump speeches in open court with such passionate indignation that the veins on his neck stood out. Whenever Harlan began to hector his colleagues at the justices' private conferences, Holmes, always urbane, addressed him condescendingly as "my lion-hearted friend" and declared, "That won't wash." (The accommodating chief justice, Melvin Fuller, tried to make peace between the two antagonists by mimicking a washboard and declaring in soothing tones: "Still I keep scrubbing and scrubbing.")[1] Harlan and Holmes respected each other's military background during the nine years they served together, from Holmes's arrival in 1902 until Harlan's death in

73

1911, and on Holmes's seventieth birthday, Harlan charmed his unsentimental colleague by leaving a bunch of violets at his place on the bench. Nevertheless, Holmes referred to Harlan in private as "the last of the great tobacco-spittin' judges" and announced that Harlan's mind was "like a great vise, the two jaws of which cannot be closed closer than two inches of each other."[2] Harlan, for his part, grumbled that Holmes's constitutional views were "unsound" and his opinions clouded by "obscure phrases."[3]

One of their fiercest clashes came in 1903, in a case involving voting rights. As federal support for Reconstruction collapsed in the 1890s, southern states adopted new state constitutions that used a variety of ruses to prevent nearly all African-American voters from casting ballots, in open defiance of the Fifteenth Amendment to the Constitution, which prohibits racial discrimination in voting rights. One of the most notorious of these state constitutions, adopted by Alabama, imposed a series of strenuous qualifications for new voters, unless they had already been registered. For example, anyone descended from a veteran of earlier American wars—in which blacks had been ineligible to serve—could register automatically; everyone else had to pass complicated tests of literacy and character. The purpose and effect of the scheme was to disenfranchise all the black voters without disenfranchising a single white voter.

This transparent discrimination was challenged by five thousand black citizens of Montgomery County, Alabama, led by Jackson Giles, a janitor at the local federal courthouse and president of an organization devoted to fighting for black voting rights. When the case, *Giles v. Harris,* finally reached the Supreme Court in 1903, Giles's lawyer accurately declared that "a more high-handed and flagrant case of the nullification of the Fourteenth and Fifteenth Amendments to the Constitution of the United States . . . can never be presented to the courts of the country." He added, "The honor of this nation is

bound to suffer in the estimation of the world if its solemn constitutional guarantees made to the negro shortly after the late civil war . . .
are allowed to go unenforced."[4]

The Supreme Court—in an opinion by Justice Holmes—
laconically rejected the black voters' arguments. Holmes cared intensely about honor and the Civil War: he viewed his own service in
the Union army as the most important event of his life and drank a
glass of wine each year on the anniversary of the battle of Antietam,
where he was wounded in the neck and was expected to die. But
Holmes was entirely unmoved by the plight of black voters, whose arguments he dismissed with perverse satisfaction. Acknowledging that
the Alabama voter registration scheme perpetrated the equivalent of a
fraud on the Constitution, he nevertheless declared that the Supreme
Court could not correct the injustice by ordering the registration of
black voters because it would become an accomplice to the fraud. Unless court officers were prepared to supervise the voting in Alabama,
Holmes objected, any judicial orders would be ignored. Therefore, he
concluded sardonically, African-American voters should seek relief
not from the courts but from the very state legislators who had barred
them from voting.

Holmes's torturous legalisms were too much for Justice Harlan,
who wrote a characteristically vigorous dissenting opinion on behalf
of African-American civil rights. Harlan, a former slaveholder, one of
only two southerners on the Court, had seen the reality of Ku Klux
Klan violence on the ground. When he ran for governor of Kentucky
in 1871, he was appalled by the lynching and terrorism that thwarted
the constitutional rights of the freedmen. This firsthand experience
with southern racism had converted Harlan from a passionate opponent of the Reconstruction amendments into their most ardent supporter on the Supreme Court. Having run for office as a Republican in
Kentucky, Harlan knew the importance of getting black votes, and as

John Marshall Harlan (left) and Oliver Wendell Holmes, Jr., respected each other's service in the Union Army, but were otherwise at odds. Holmes condescended to Harlan, and Harlan considered Holmes's constitutional views unsound.

early as 1888, wrote to President Benjamin Harrison, noting with approval that black voters in Kentucky represented about a fourth of the Republican total. But after 1900, as the Southern Democrats' efforts to disenfranchise blacks began to succeed, Harlan complained to President William Howard Taft that "we are approaching a real crisis in the South. In the former Confederate states, or in most of them, there is a fixed purpose to destroy the right of the negro to vote despite the provisions of the Constitution."[5] It's hardly surprising, therefore, that Harlan made clear in his dissenting opinion that he believed the Alabama voter scheme violated the Constitution. Jackson Giles was entitled "to relief in respect of his right to be registered as a voter,"

Harlan declared, because the courts were competent "to give relief in such cases as this."

The exchange between Holmes and Harlan in the *Giles* case was characteristic of their wary interactions. Holmes today is revered as a liberal hero because he wrote a famous dissenting opinion defending the constitutionality of New York's maximum working hour laws for bakers in 1905. ("The Fourteenth Amendment does not enact Mr. Herbert Spencer's Social Statics," Holmes wrote in a memorable aphorism, even though he himself was the only true Social Darwinist on the Court.) But although Holmes voted to uphold progressive laws, he also voted to uphold illiberal and even fascistic laws. During his long tenure on the Court from 1902 to 1932, he voted to uphold virtually all laws, because his restrained view of judicial authority stemmed from his view of politics as war and of life as a Darwinian struggle for power. Holmes believed so little in fundamental truth that he was willing to ignore even relatively clear constitutional restraints on legislative power, such as the Fourteenth Amendment's prohibitions on racial discrimination.

For much of American history, Harlan was dismissed as a moralizing eccentric while Holmes was lionized as a democratic visionary. But today, Harlan's dissenting opinions about civil rights, civil liberties, and national power have been embraced by the Court and vindicated by history, while the radical majoritarianism and judicial abstinence represented by Holmes has hardly any academic or popular constituency. By contrast, John Marshall Harlan, who served on the Court from 1877 to 1911, combined a passionate commitment to protecting the rights of African-Americans with an equally firm devotion to defending the power of the federal government to protect the economically weak and disadvantaged. Harlan's most famous opinion was his dissent in *Plessy v. Ferguson,* in which he, alone among the justices, insisted that the compulsory segregation of blacks and whites on railway cars violated the Constitution. "Our constitution is color-blind and neither knows nor tolerates classes among citizens," Harlan wrote. Harlan has the unique distinction of having prefigured the civil rights and civil liberties revolution, while Holmes is remembered primarily for the First Amendment dissents at the end of his life, when he abandoned his lifelong devotion to judicial abstinence and finally refused to carry his own philosophy to its logical extreme.

During Harlan's and Holmes's long tenures, which spanned from the Reconstruction to the New Deal eras, the central constitutional battles involved the scope of the Thirteenth, Fourteenth, and Fifteenth Amendments, ratified after the Civil War to protect civil rights and economic rights for African-Americans and all citizens. In the decades leading up to the Civil War, the national parties embraced several different visions of national power. The most extreme states' rights Democrats, led by Senator John C. Calhoun of South Carolina, insisted that each state had the power to secede from the Union if Congress abridged the natural rights of citizens, including the right to own slaves. Moderate Republicans, such as Abraham Lincoln, countered that Congress had the power, if it chose, to ban slavery in the federal territories. Because there was no clear national majority for any position on slavery, the Democrats increasingly called on the Supreme Court to resolve the constitutional controversy. In the infamous 1857 decision, *Dred Scott v. Sandford,* the Court, under the leadership of Chief Justice Roger Taney, foolishly accepted the invitation. Unequivocally endorsing the position of the most radical states' rights Democrats, the *Dred Scott* majority declared that Congress had a constitutional obligation to protect slavery in the territories and no power to ban it. Taney's decision to constitutionalize the radical political views of Calhoun proved a strategic error, because those views were rejected by a majority of moderate Republicans and Democrats. Although the *Dred Scott* decision did not actually precipitate the Civil War, it allowed the new Republican Party of Lincoln to cast the Supreme Court as a reviled symbol of judicial tyranny, and made a mockery out of the claim by the Democratic Party of Jefferson and Buchanan that it was devoted to a limited role for judges in American politics.

After the Civil War, *Dred Scott* was reversed in several stages. The Thirteenth Amendment (1865) abolished slavery and involuntary servitude. Nevertheless, southern states proceeded to adopt a series of infamous "Black Codes" that imposed harsher punishments on blacks than whites and denied the freedmen the right to own property or to make contracts. In 1866, Congress passed a Civil Rights Act that repudiated the Black Codes by guaranteeing all citizens "of every race and color" the same rights to make and enforce contracts, own property, and sue and be sued. Because of continuing doubts about Congress's constitutional authority to pass the Civil Rights Act, Congress proposed and the states ratified the Fourteenth Amendment to the Constitution (1868), which provides that states cannot deny or abridge the fundamental rights of citizens, including equal protection of the law and the right not to be deprived of life, liberty, and property without due process of law. The Fourteenth Amendment transformed the relationship between the federal government and the states by empowering the national government to force the states to respect equal rights. But how dramatically it accomplished the transformation was hotly disputed. The most enthusiastic Republicans, such as Congressman John Bingham of Ohio, the author and chief sponsor of the Fourteenth Amendment, believed that it gave the federal courts as well as Congress the power to force the states to respect many of the rights enumerated in the original Bill of Rights, including free speech, freedom of religion, and fair criminal procedure. More moderate Republicans believed that Congress, rather than the courts, should take the lead in enforcing fundamental rights, and also believed that Congress could act only when the states passed discriminatory laws, and had no power to legislate against private acts of discrimination. On the Supreme Court, Harlan consistently championed the broad vision of congressional and judicial power outlined by Chief Justice John Marshall and extended by John Bingham and the other Radical Republicans, while Holmes preferred a Jeffersonian deference to the will of the majority so extreme that it verged on judicial self-abnegation.

How was it possible that Harlan, the southern slaveholder and Kentucky Whig-turned-Republican became a prophet of racial and economic equality, while Holmes, the son of a Massachusetts abolitionist, became a radical skeptic of abolitionism and of all constitutional ideals? The answer, for both Harlan and Holmes (as for Marshall and Jefferson), seems to have originated in their attitude toward the Union, shaped by their service in the Union army during the Civil War. The only consistent touchstone in Harlan's political universe was constitutional nationalism and the sanctity of the Union. Like his father, who served as a U.S. congressman from Kentucky, Harlan's heroes were John Marshall, for whom he was named, and Henry Clay, a fellow Kentuckian and one of the founders of the Whig Party. "My father was an ardent admirer of John Marshall," Harlan recalled. "He was equally ardent in his opposition to the views of constitutional law . . . entertained by Thomas Jefferson. . . . He regarded 'Jeffersonianism' as an evil that needed to be watched and overcome."[6]

Like his father, Harlan "gloried in being a Whig," until the party collapsed under its own contradictions. The Whig Party, formed in the early 1830s, opposed the exaltation of states' rights and embraced Marshall's vision of broad federal power as an engine for economic expansion. The Whigs elected two presidents—William Henry Harrison in 1840 and Zachary Taylor in 1848—and tried to carve out a middle position in the slavery debate, supporting gradual emanci-

Harlan and his wife, Malvina, on their wedding day in December 1856. Malvina Harlan later wrote a memoir about their devoted life together.

pation while rejecting, as threats to the social order, the immediate abolition or extension of slavery. Harlan and his father were steeped in this tradition—both owned slaves and scorned abolitionists while insisting that their own slaves and others should be gradually emancipated. As a youth, Harlan remembered seeing a slave driver angrily whipping a slave in the street; his father angrily called the man a "damned scoundrel," impressing the family with his moral indignation. In a more Jeffersonian spirit, Harlan's father sired an out-of-wedlock son with a slave owned by his wife's family, whom he tried to enroll in school, treated decently, and eventually freed in exchange for $500 from the son himself. Throughout his life, Harlan maintained cordial relations with his accomplished half-brother, who made his fortune in California. Harlan also inherited twelve slaves from his father, and he prided himself on treating them well. His wife wrote about the family slaves with the paternalistic affection that passed, at that time and place, for racial enlightenment.

Harlan's Whig nationalism was further reinforced during his law studies at Transylvania University, where his teachers denounced nullification and secession and defended the constitutional vision of Hamilton, Clay, and John Marshall. The Whig straddle made sense in the Kentucky of Harlan's youth, which, swayed by Clay's leadership, abandoned Jeffersonianism in the 1820s and became enthusiastically pro-Union while supporting the status quo on slavery. But as the political constituency for the pro-Union and pro-slavery position evaporated in the 1850s, so did the Whigs, giving way to a series of splinter parties. Harlan opportunistically joined several of them in a frantic and unsuccessful attempt to chase the disappearing political center.

He started with the nativist Know-Nothing Party in 1854, best known for its anti-Catholicism and opposition to immigration. ("Put None but Americans on Guard" was the party motto.) The Know-Nothings supported the Union, opposed secession, but also insisted that Congress had no power to interfere with the slave policies of the individual states. Harlan ran unsuccessfully for Congress in 1859 as a Know-Nothing, and during the campaign, he praised the *Dred Scott* decision for holding that Congress had the duty to protect slavery and no power to exclude it from the federal territories. Democratic newspapers attacked him for inconsistency—just three years earlier, he had insisted that each territory should decide the slavery question on its own—and ridiculed him as a "hybrid opportunist [who] has accomplished as many somersaults in his brief career as any man in the country."[7]

Despite his political gymnastics, Harlan's devotion to the Union remained unswerving. He used the soapbox of the editorial page of the *Louisville Courier* to lobby against secession. In 1861, at the age of twenty-eight, he raised his own regiment—the Tenth Kentucky Infantry—and became a colonel in the Union army. His regiment had a knack for showing up at the battlefield after the fighting was over, too late for bloodshed but just in time to bask in the reflected glory associated with the cleanup. Harlan managed to earn a reputation for heroism by getting the better of Confederate forces at Rolling Fork Bridge, where he was praised for protecting the Union railway lines. Despite—or perhaps because of—this relatively light duty, Harlan seems to have been a gregarious figure who won the affection of his men with reciprocated loyalty, athletic bonhomie, and sympathetic understanding of their interests. His association with Catholics and German immigrants helped him to overcome some of his opportunistic nativism. Recollections of Harlan by his soldiers call to mind similarly enthusiastic recollections of those who served under John Marshall: "When the soldiers came from the war they had diverse tales to tell of their beloved colonel," recalled Champ Clark, who would later serve as Speaker of the U.S. House of Representatives. "Among other things they said he could outrun, outjump, and outwrestle any man in the regiment. . . . After their first engagement— the battle of Mill Springs—the colonel told them frankly that if any of them felt like running he did not blame them, for all that prevented him from fleeing was his shoulder-straps."[8]

As a Kentuckian, Harlan also displayed a sense of compassion for the enemy: recognizing a friend who had joined the Confederate army but returned to central Kentucky to see his wife, Harlan prevented his men from arresting the friend and sending him to his death by placing his foot under the brake of the handcar they were driving, an act of generosity the friend never forgot. Harlan distinguished himself sufficiently in office for Lincoln to recommend his promotion to brigadier general in 1863, but because his father had died, he resigned from the army instead. On learning of his resignation, his men passed a resolution declaring that Harlan had "won the love and esteem of his whole command, by his amiable manners, unflinching integrity, and his indefatigable attention, to all his duties."[9]

Holmes's war was far less amiable than Harlan's, and ultimately more transformative. Throughout his life, Holmes insisted that his three years as a lieutenant in the Civil War had influenced his judicial philosophy even more than his thirty years on the Supreme Court. As a Harvard student, he had been fired by his mother's antislavery ideals, scorning the glib frivolity of his father, a Harvard medical school professor and celebrity journalist who wrote comic sketches for *The Atlantic Monthly*. Soon after the war began, in the spring of 1861, Holmes dropped out of college and enlisted in the Massachusetts militia, two months before receiving his degree. When he signed up, he expected a brief and glamorous war, in which he would be cosseted with other aristocratic Boston Brahmins, a term that his father coined to describe the well-bred, scholarly caste to which the Holmes family belonged. As the other enlisted men camped out in New York City on the way to the battlefield, Holmes and his Harvard classmates had a lavish champagne dinner at Delmonico's. Servants accompanied them to the front.

On the battlefield, Holmes experienced horrors that would define his temperament and outlook for the rest of his life. Six months after enlisting, at the Battle of Ball's Bluff in October 1861, he was shot in the chest. A fellow soldier removed the ball, and the wound was filled with lint. Although expected to die, Holmes was back in battle by the spring, writing home to his parents of the "indifference one gets to look on the dead bodies in gray clothes wh[ich] lie all around . . . the swollen bodies already fly blown and decaying, of men shot in the head, back or bowels."[10]

Holmes viewed his service in the Union Army as the most important event of his life; until his death in 1935 (two days before his ninety-fourth birthday), he kept his Civil War uniform in his bedroom closet with a note declaring that it was stained with his own blood.

Holmes's second wound occurred at the Battle of Antietam, on September 17, 1862, the bloodiest in American history. (At the end of the battle, 6,000 men were dead and 17,000 wounded—more than twice as many dead as in any other war in the nineteenth century.) Obeying an order to retreat, Holmes was conscious of how it would play in the newspapers, recalling that *Harper's* magazine had praised him for having been shot at Ball's Bluff "in the breast, not in the back." During these reflections on the battlefield, he was shot in the back of his neck, the bullet "passing straight through the central seam of coat & waistcoat collar coming out toward the front on the left hand side."[11]

Although eager for respite after recovering once more, Holmes realized that the code of honor required his return to the battlefield. He imagined the glory that would come to him in later life if he were "thrice wounded." He achieved his ambition. His third wound occurred in an encounter with a Confederate rear guard as he approached Fredericksburg in the spring of 1863. Attacked by cannon fire as he stopped at a canal, he was shot in the heel. This minor wound took the longest to heal—almost seven months—and Holmes wished his foot had been amputated so he might have been spared further fighting.

Holmes kept the relics of his ordeal until the end of his life. After his death in 1935 (two days before his ninety-fourth birthday), his executors found in a safe-deposit box a tiny parcel with two musket balls and the inscription: "These were taken from my body in the Civil War." In his bedroom closet, his Civil War uniforms were found with another note declaring that the stains were his own blood.[12] His hunger for recognition as a war hero expressed itself in military metaphors, which suffused his speeches and judicial opinions. And his worldview was transformed.

Holmes began the war as a committed abolitionist, but he emerged from it with contempt for abolitionism and for all forms of moral certainty. As his doubts about the purpose of the carnage became increasingly strong, Holmes came to lionize a friend and college classmate, Henry Abbott. Little Abbott, as he was known, openly scorned abolitionism, Lincoln, and the Emancipation Proclamation. He was noted, nevertheless, for his extraordinary courage under fire, and for his cavalier willingness to expose himself to danger that ultimately proved fatal on behalf of a cause in which he did not believe. Abbott's example persuaded Holmes that war itself was a brutal waste, and the only thing that could redeem its senseless carnage was the professionalism and effectiveness of individual soldiers—honor could be achieved, in other words, not by intensity of belief but by the iron self-discipline that led to ultimate success in a Darwinian struggle whose ends were immaterial.[13]

Holmes expressed this dark vision in the most famous speech he ever gave, "The Soldier's Faith," delivered at Harvard on Memorial Day, 1895: "I do not know what is true," he declared. "I do not know the meaning of the universe. But in the midst of doubt, in the collapse of creeds, there is one thing I do not doubt . . . and that is that the faith is true and adorable which leads a soldier to throw away his life in obedience to a blindly accepted duty, in a cause which he little understands, in a plan of campaign of which he has no notion, under tactics of which he does not see the use."[14] The speech so impressed Theodore Roosevelt ("By Jove, that speech of Holmes's was fine") that it led the future president to appoint Holmes seven years later to the Supreme Court.

The war gave Holmes a nihilistic suspicion of certitudes of all kind, but he had special scorn for the certitudes of abolitionists that had initially motivated him to enlist. "The abolitionists had a stock phrase that a man was either a knave or a fool who did not act as they (the abolitionists) *knew* to be right," he wrote in 1929. "When you know what you know persecution comes easy. It is as well that some of us don't know that we know anything."[15] Holmes's suspicion of abolitionist ideals proved to be especially unfortunate during his tenure on the Supreme Court, since some of the most important cases of his tenure required him to construe the meaning of the Reconstruction Amendments, in which the abolitionists had attempted to inscribe their ideals of equality into the Constitution. With no patience for these ideals despite their constitutional endorsement, Holmes upheld laws—such as the racial discrimination at issue in the *Giles* case— that violated clearly enumerated constitutional protections. In effect, Holmes's personal disillusionment with abolitionism led him to ignore the meaning of the Fourteenth Amendment and to subvert the abolitionists' constitutional achievement. In most cases involving race, one scholar observes, Holmes believed that "if the white South as the 'de facto dominant power in the community' wanted to subordinate its black citizens under the thinnest cover of formal-legal equal treatment, there was nothing the federal courts could or should do about it."[16]

But Holmes's "lasting disgust for come outers" who were morally "cocksure" was not limited to abolitionists.[17] The lesson that Holmes took from the war—that moral certitude culminates in violence— led him to a radical skepticism about any claims of absolute truth, whether or not they were embodied in the Constitution.[18] Holmes believed that the only test of truth for individuals was what they could not help believing, and the only test of truth collectively was what the majority wanted. He saw democratic debates in violent, military terms—as an opportunity for the strong to impose their will on the weak—and applauded this outcome because of his belief that when the will of majorities was thwarted, actual violence might result. This led him to a radically restrained view of judicial power: he believed that judges should uphold virtually all laws, in the interest of clearing the way for majorities to do whatever they liked.

"If the people want to go to Hell, I will help them," Holmes wrote to his friend Harold Laski. "It's my job."[19] For Holmes, the chips in a democracy should fall wherever the people wish. "I am so skeptical as to our knowledge about the goodness or badness of laws that I have no practical criticism except what the crowd wants," he wrote, even as he confessed that he "loathe[d] the thick-fingered clowns we call the people."[20]

After returning from the war, Holmes became obsessed with the idea that he had to make his name before the age of forty, and devoted his thirties to intense bursts of work on legal scholarship, which he carried around in a green bag that he never allowed to leave his side, for fear it would be destroyed by fire. To the degree that Holmes believed anything intensely after the war, he seems to have been devoted to Social Darwinism—that is, the belief that only the fittest races, ideas, individuals, and groups would survive in the brutal competition of life. In an article on the gas stokers' strike in London in 1872, he applauded the law under which the strikers were sentenced to a year in jail, believing as he did that all war led to brutal casualties: "In the last resort a man rightly prefers his own interest to that of his neighbors," he wrote. "The more powerful interests must be more or less reflected in legislation; which, like every other device of man or beast, must tend in the long run to aid the survival of the fittest."[21]

Holmes developed his radical majoritarianism in his major work of scholarship, *The Common Law,* published in 1881, which began with a memorable manifesto against the rigidity of legal formalism. "The life of the law," he announced, "has not been logic: it has been experience. The felt necessities of the time, the prevalent moral and political theories, intuitions of public policy, avowed or unconscious, even the prejudices which judges share with their fellow-men, have had a good deal more to do than the syllogism in determining the rules by which men should be governed."[22] Holmes took from the battlefield a Darwinian affinity for natural selection, and insisted that the common law—that is, law made by judges, rather than legislatures—reflected, like all law, the will of forces that were dominant at any point in history. Law, therefore, was both a cause and an effect of natural selection. Holmes insisted that power and class prejudice, not abstract principles of natural justice or previous legal precedents, determined legal development, and "the prophecies of what courts will do in fact, and nothing more pretentious, are what I mean by law."[23] Holmes developed this bracingly realistic credo during twenty years of service on the Massachusetts Supreme Judicial Court, where he wrote more than a thousand opinions and consistently deferred to the wishes of the legislature. He seemed to embrace the British view that the legislature was sovereign and that its power was virtually unbounded, giving short shrift to the understanding of the American Founders that the people were sovereign, and imposed limitations on the legislature by adopting written constitutions. On the Massachusetts court, he earned a mistaken (and to him amusing) reputation of being a friend to labor after he wrote a dissenting opinion defending the rights of unions to organize peaceful strikes, picket, and boycott on behalf of better working conditions. But his opinion showed no fear of the effects of industrial combinations: on the contrary, it defended the idea that workingmen should be entitled to combine forces in the hope of matching, or perhaps destroying, the power of their employers in a fair, although brutal, competition. "Free competition means combination, and . . . the organization of the world, now going on so fast, means an ever increasing might and scope of combination," he wrote in *Vegelahn v. Guntner* (1896). "It seems to me futile to set our faces against this tendency. Whether beneficial on the whole, as I think it, or detrimental, it is inevitable."[24]

When Justice Horace Gray of Massachusetts died in 1902, President Theodore Roosevelt needed another New Englander. (At the time, tradition held that the Court should represent all regions of the country.) Roosevelt was favorably disposed to Holmes because he misinterpreted his 1895 Memorial Day speech as bellicose; this thin reed was enough to convince the president that Holmes would uphold the government's power to expand the American empire without granting full constitutional protections to the territories. For these reasons, Roosevelt appointed Holmes, at the age of sixty-one, to the Supreme Court.

If Holmes was an antislavery idealist whom the war converted into a radical skeptic, Harlan was a political opportunist whom the war converted into an antislavery idealist. The war may have taught Harlan lessons about leading with a light touch, but it had no immediate influence on his politics: on returning to civilian life, Harlan continued his awkward political straddle, trying to combine pro-Union nationalism with antiabolitionism. He was elected attorney general of Kentucky on the conservative Union Party ticket, and supported General George McClellan, Lincoln's Democratic opponent, in the presidential election of 1864. He initially opposed all of the Reconstruction legislation protecting the rights of African-Americans that he would later defend as a Supreme Court justice. He denounced the Thirteenth Amendment, which abolished slavery, as "a flagrant invasion of the right of self-government" and insisted that the war had been fought to preserve the Union, not to give "freedom to the Negro." He denounced the abolitionists for proposing constitutional amendments that "would work a complete revolution in our Republican system of government."[25] And, according to a political enemy, he declared in 1866 that "he had no more conscientious scruples in buying and selling a Negro than he had in buying and selling a horse."[26] Despite his attacks on the Radical Republicans, Harlan was overwhelmingly defeated twice in 1867: when he ran for U.S. senator and then ran for reelection as Kentucky attorney general, both times on the Constitutional Union ticket.

Finally recognizing the futility of trying to straddle the race question, Harlan was forced to pick sides. Unable to stomach the states' rights Democrats because of his intense nationalism, he switched to the Republican Party in 1868 and embraced its egalitarian vision with a convert's zeal. In an effort to win votes from newly enfranchised African-Americans, he embraced racial equality and anticorporate populism with equal vigor. Running for governor in 1871, and again in 1875, he supported the Thirteenth and Fourteenth Amendments with the same enthusiasm he had previously devoted to denouncing them, confessing his flip-flop with cheerful candor: "It is true that I was at one time in my life opposed to conferring these privileges" upon African-Americans, he conceded during the 1871 campaign, but "I have lived long enough to feel and declare . . . that the most perfect despotism that ever existed on this earth was the institution of African slavery." He concluded rousingly: "Let it be said that I am right rather than consistent."[27] In the same campaign, Harlan witnessed the carnage of Ku Klux Klan terrorism and lynching. The refusal of state Democrats to stem the violence persuaded him of the importance of federal intervention to enforce civil rights. In addition to supporting civil rights legislation during Reconstruction, Harlan also campaigned against railroad monopolies and on behalf of a graduated income tax, suggesting that corporate power posed as much of a threat to liberty as slave power.[28]

Harlan lost both of his races for governor because the Republicans still could not command majorities in Kentucky, but they could win presidential elections. His energetic campaigning on behalf of Rutherford B. Hayes in 1876 ultimately won him a seat on the Supreme Court. Hayes needed a reform-minded Republican southerner to assuage Southern Democrats and satisfy Southern Republicans, and Harlan fit the bill. "Confidentially and on the whole is not Harlan the man?" the president asked a political intimate. "Of the right age—able—of whole character—industrious—fine manner, temper and appearance."[29] To general acclaim (with the exception of Northern Republicans, who suspected his commitment to civil rights), Harlan was appointed to the Court in 1877, at the age of forty-four.

If Holmes took from the war the lesson that moral certainty leads to violence, Harlan absorbed the opposite lesson: namely, that moral waffling leads to political defeat. He may have fought for the Union rather than for emancipation; but once he finally embraced the goals of Reconstruction, he brandished them with messianic enthusiasm, as if trying to atone for his former ambivalence by the purity of his faith. To justify his conversion to himself, he had to repudiate his former views about slavery entirely and unequivocally. Having made scores of campaign speeches from 1868 until his appointment to the Court in 1877 apologizing for his racial errors, and having loudly proclaimed his Republican faith after his nomination to mollify a skeptical Senate, Harlan had little choice but to became an egalitarian crusader to vindicate his reputation; the fact that he had a lifelong suspicion of Democrats made the transformation easier.[30] When all this was combined with a personality with a fondness for viewing every issue in moral absolutes (even as he scrambled for political advantage), it is less surprising that the former slaveholder became the most passionate defender of civil rights of his time

Harlan displayed this commitment throughout his long tenure on the Court, where there was little variation between his politics and his jurisprudence. He read the principles of the moderate Republicans into the Constitution with the same fervor that John Marshall read the principles of the moderate Federalists into the Constitution. But Harlan's jurisprudence, like Marshall's, appears to be something more than result-oriented, because in both cases, the principles they embraced as their own had also been ratified by the nation as fundamental law. Both Marshall and Harlan understood that the great constitutional question of their respective eras concerned the scope of Congress's power, which both of them construed broadly, deferring to Congress rather than trying to construe its powers strictly in order to protect the autonomy of states.

The Court that Harlan joined was still recovering from the self-inflicted wound suffered in the *Dred Scott* case. Hardly at the apogee of its power, the Court had recently moved from its cramped home in the Capitol basement, used since 1810, to the more elegant appointments of the old Senate chamber.[31] Although the new accommodations included a robing room, so the justices no longer had to get dressed in front of the audience, there were often empty seats in the courtroom, a reflection of the Court's still unsettled role in American life.

Harlan's new colleagues were far less keen than he was to preserve the legacy of Reconstruction. By 1873, President Grant had abandoned vigorous federal enforcement of civil rights in the South and had issued pardons to convicted members of the Klan. The same year, he appointed as chief justice Morrison Waite, a competent but obscure Ohio lawyer who was so surprised to receive a telegram informing him of his nomination that he thought it was a joke. The intellectual leaders of the Waite Court before Harlan's appointment were three justices with no passion for civil rights: Stephen Field, Samuel Miller, and Joseph Bradley. Although appointed by Lincoln, Field was a Unionist Democrat from California who had little sympathy for Reconstruction: his consuming interest was private property, and he became a passionate advocate of the laissez-faire view that the Fourteenth Amendment protected inalienable rights of private property and economic liberty from state and federal regulation. Samuel Miller, another Lincoln appointee, was a moderate Republican who, like Harlan, had grown up in Kentucky and attended Transylvania University. He was a nationalist who voted with the Court to invalidate the most egregious forms of state-sponsored discrimination against African-Americans—as in the *Strauder* decision, in 1880, which struck down, over Field's dissent, a state law that said only whites could serve on juries. But Miller was skeptical of broad national power to enforce civil rights, and his majority opinion in the

Slaughterhouse Cases (1873) eviscerated the promise of the Four-teenth Amendment by insisting that the states had no obligation to respect the fundamental economic and civil rights that the original Constitution prohibited only the federal government from abridging. Finally, there was Joseph Bradley, a Grant appointee and former rail-road lawyer from New Jersey who generally supported Hayes's policy of withdrawing federal troops from the South in exchange for Southern Democrats' support of his disputed election and had no enthusiasm for Reconstruction; instead, his passion was for protecting business from unreasonable state regulations.

Harlan's first and most important opportunity to construe the scope of national power to protect civil rights came in 1883, six years after he joined the Court. By an 8–1 vote, with Harlan alone dissent-ing, the Court struck down the federal Civil Rights Act of 1875, the high-water mark of liberal Reconstruction. The Civil Rights Act, which forbade racial discrimination in places of public accommoda-tion, including railways, inns, and theaters, had become a campaign issue during Harlan's second run for governor of Kentucky in 1875. As a candidate, Harlan took the position that the act guaranteed equal rights to African-Americans in public conveyances such as railroads, not special rights, as the Democrats charged. The constitu-tional challenge that the Supreme Court decided involved five consol-idated test cases, collectively known as the *Civil Rights Cases,* which were brought by a series of African-American plaintiffs who had been denied access to various public accommodations. George Tyler, for example, had been barred from McGuire's Theater in San Francisco; Sallie J. Robinson, a young biracial woman, had boarded a train in Tennessee and was refused entrance to the separate "ladies" car set aside for white women. State law in all five cases did not require the discrimination; instead, the railroads and theaters had decided to dis-criminate on their own. The majority opinion in the *Civil Rights Cases* by Justice Bradley seemed almost impatient that African-Americans had not managed to achieve civil equality without federal aid. "When a man has emerged from slavery, and by the aid of beneficent legislation has shaken off the inseparable concomitants of that state, there must be some stage in the progress of his elevation when he takes the rank of a mere citizen, and ceases to be the special favorite of the laws," Bradley declared. Because the Civil Rights Act regulated acts of private discrimination, rather than state-sponsored discrimination, he concluded, Congress had no power to pass it.

The *Civil Rights Cases* provoked one of Harlan's greatest dissents, uniting his now fervent concern for black civil rights with his determination to protect a broad vision of national power. After Bradley announced his opinion, Harlan delivered an extemporaneous oral dissent from the bench in such vigorous language that mass meetings of African-Americans convened around the country to send Harlan expressions of gratitude. Harlan had trouble reducing his oral dissent to writing and found himself paralyzed by an uncharacteristic case of writer's block. His wife solved the problem by locating the inkwell with which Chief Justice Roger Taney had written his infamous *Dred Scott* decision and placing it quietly on Harlan's desk. When Harlan found the memento, according to his wife, the memory of the role the inkwell had played in oppressing blacks acted "like magic" in clarifying his thoughts, and "his pen fairly flew."[32]

The written dissent that emerged accused the majority of resorting to "narrow and artificial" logic to reduce the promise of the Reconstruction Amendments to "splendid baubles." Harlan's strongest argument was that Congress's power to regulate interstate commerce gave it the authority to regulate discrimination by railroads in the course of interstate travel. He also argued convincingly that innkeepers and railroad corporations had traditionally been obligated to serve the public without discriminating, because they exercised "quasi-

public functions" rather than being considered purely private enti-
ties. He also insisted plausibly that the framers of the Fourteenth
Amendment had intended Congress, rather than the courts, to decide
what kind of laws were necessary to enforce the constitutional guarantees of equality, and accused the majority of usurping the powers of
Congress. The Court had ignored Chief Justice John Marshall's broad
vision of national power, he insisted, and in the process threatened "a
radical change in our system of government." Harlan's dissent was
criticized as sentimental and legally eccentric by many newspapers at
the time, including the *New York Times*. But it also provoked a moving
tribute from the black leader Frederick Douglass, who wrote, "The
marvel is that, born in a slave State, as he was, and accustomed to see
the colored man degraded, oppressed and enslaved, and the white
man exalted . . . he should find himself possessed of the courage to
resist the temptation to go with the multitude."[33]

When Holmes joined the Court in 1902, his record involving the
equal rights of African-Americans was abysmal: while Harlan viewed
race cases in terms of the effect on individual lives and the principles
of Reconstruction, Holmes was more concerned about deferring to the
will of local majorities, even when they were southern legislatures
trying to oppress racial minorities. In many important race cases during the period when Holmes and Harlan sat together, from 1902 to
1911, Holmes joined the majority in denying the claim of an African-
American plaintiff, and Harlan filed a dissent that would have granted
it. Holmes's refusal to enforce civil rights might be excused as part of
his general reluctance to second-guess the choices of political majorities to impose their will on minorities. But even in cases where the
constitutional violations were relatively clear, Holmes often went out
of his way to overlook them.

Consider the cases involving peonage—a southern scheme, tantamount to slavery, that consigned black workers to compulsory

service after they built up debts they were unable to repay. (Under peonage schemes, the indebted peon had to continue to work for his master until his debt was paid off.) Harlan never had any doubt that being forced to work to pay off debt violated both the Thirteenth Amendment's ban on involuntary servitude and federal statutes that prohibited peonage: he dissented in four out of the five peonage cases that came before the Court between 1905 and 1911. But Holmes was far more grudging in these cases, resorting to legal technicalities to deny relief to black workers whenever possible. In 1908, for example, Holmes, writing for a majority of the Court, refused to strike down an Alabama peonage law that made refusal to perform a labor contract evidence of an employee's intent to defraud his employer, to be punished by ruinous fines as well as imprisonment. Harlan vigorously dissented. Three years later, in *Bailey v. Alabama,* Harlan joined a majority of the Court in striking down the same Alabama law as a violation of the Thirteenth Amendment. The Court noted the sad facts of the case, in which Alonzo Bailey, an African-American man, made a contract to work for one year for $12 a month, with a $15 advance payment, but quit after working for just one month. Bailey was fined $30 and sentenced to hard labor. A majority of the Court noted that the law was clearly intended to circumvent the federal ban on peonage: it would be illegal for the state to seize Bailey and force him to work until he paid off his debt; and therefore the state could not achieve the same result indirectly, by imprisoning Bailey for intent to defraud his employer. In a particularly brutal dissent, Holmes expressed indifference to the fact that Alabama was resorting to technicalities to circumvent the federal and constitutional bans on peonage: "Breach of a legal contract without excuse is wrong conduct, even if the contract is for labor," Holmes wrote, and if the state "intensifies the legal motive for doing right" with criminal fines as well as civil liability, "it does not make the laborer a slave."

The most important conflicts over race that arose between Harlan and his colleagues concerned the constitutionality of segregation—on railroads, in residential housing, and in schools. In his most famous opinion, Harlan dissented in *Plessy v. Ferguson* (1896), the case in which all the other justices voted to uphold a Louisiana law requiring the separation of white and black passengers on railway cars. The only inequality, Justice Henry B. Brown wrote for the majority, was the false "assumption that the enforced separation of the two races stamps the colored race with a badge of inferiority. If this be so, it is not by reason of anything found in the act, but solely because the colored race chooses to put that construction on it." In his memorable dissent, Harlan, by then the only southerner and former slaveholder on the Court, drew on his firsthand experience in Kentucky to note what was obvious to anyone who had grown up in that region: "Every one knows that the statute in question had its origin in the purpose, not so much to exclude white persons from railroad cars occupied by blacks, as to exclude colored people from coaches occupied by or assigned to white persons," he wrote. "The thin disguise of 'equal' accommodations for passengers in railroad coaches will not mislead any one, nor atone for the wrong this day done," Harlan concluded, emphasizing that the law was "conceived in hostility to, and enacted for the purpose of humiliating citizens of the United States of a particular race."

By modern standards, Harlan was hardly a racial egalitarian: "In respect of civil rights, all citizens are equal before the law," he insisted, but in the same opinion said he had no doubt that the "white race" would remain the "dominant race in this country . . . in prestige, in achievements, in education, in wealth and in power," as long as it held "fast to the principles of constitutional liberty." The unsettling paean to civil equality combined with economic and intellectual inequality was characteristic of Republicans of Harlan's era, including

Lincoln. But the dissent is nevertheless a masterpiece, because it res-
urrects the original understanding of the Reconstruction amendments
and predicts accurately that the Court's decision to uphold separate
but equal railway cars would one day be as reviled as the *Dred Scott*
decision.

Holmes was not on the Court that decided *Plessy,* but he made
his own views on segregation clear in other cases. He had little interest in the way that Jim Crow operated in practice, or in the actual
purpose of segregation—namely, to humiliate and degrade. Unlike
Harlan, the practical politician, Holmes was too enamored of his own
philosophy to dirty his hands with facts ("I hate facts," he responded,
when Justice Louis Brandeis urged him to study them for a change)
and his opinions in segregation cases made this antipathy clear.[34]
Holmes and Harlan clashed in 1908 in a case involving Berea College, a private college founded by religious abolitionists in Kentucky
in the 1850s. The college was fined $1,000 for violating a 1904 Ken-
tucky law that banned any corporation or person from operating a
school with white and black pupils. A majority of the Court, with
Holmes concurring, upheld the conviction on the ground that Kentucky
law gave the state legislature the power to amend corporate charters.
Harlan wrote a vigorous dissent calling the law "an arbitrary invasion of
the rights of liberty and property guaranteed by the Fourteenth Amendment against hostile state action." He said that if the state could
prevent white and black students from voluntarily mixing in public
schools, it could just as well prohibit white and black citizens from sitting together in church or shopping at the same markets. "Have we
become so inoculated with prejudice of race that an American government, professedly based on the principles of freedom, and charged with
the protection of all citizens alike, can make distinctions between such
citizens in the matter of their voluntary meeting for innocent purposes
simply because of their respective races?" Harlan asked.

Holmes's answer appeared to be yes—he went beyond his racially indifferent colleagues in straining to uphold segregation of all kinds. In a railway segregation case decided in 1914 after Harlan's death, the Court upheld an Oklahoma law requiring separate but equal accommodations for whites and blacks but took issue with a provision of the law allowing railroads to provide sleeping and dining cars for whites but not, in cases of insufficient demand, for blacks. Holmes wrote a private memorandum suggesting that he considered this provision to be entirely reasonable.[35] Three years later, in one of the few victories for racial equality in the Progressive Era, the Court in *Buchanan v. Warley* (1917) struck down a residential segregation law that prohibited black people in Louisville, Kentucky, from buying property in white neighborhoods. Had the Court upheld the law, it would have ushered in official, rather than informal, American apartheid. But in an unpublished dissent he decided at the last minute not to issue, Holmes argued that the case should have been dismissed. Charles Buchanan, a white real estate agent, had bought property in a white neighborhood on behalf of William Warley, the black head of the NAACP, and when Warley defaulted on the contract, Buchanan sued him for the purpose of creating a test case that would challenge the law in court. In his unpublished dissent, Holmes attacked Buchanan for challenging "a wrong to someone else."[36] According to Holmes's cramped logic, finding someone with standing to challenge the law might be impossible, and therefore the wrong might persist without a legal remedy.

Holmes did not vote against civil rights claims in every case. He joined the Court's decision to strike down state voting laws containing grandfather clauses that automatically registered white citizens whose ancestors had registered when blacks could not vote. In 1927, he wrote an important opinion for the Court in *Nixon v. Herndon*, striking down a Texas law that barred blacks from participating in the Texas Democratic primaries, which were tantamount to general elections in a virtually one-party state. Still, this was hardly an act of judicial courage—the Texas law was the only one of its kind in the country—and Holmes's legally imprecise opinion relied on the Fourteenth Amendment rather than the Fifteenth Amendment—further suggesting his indifference to the legal legacy of Reconstruction. Although Holmes generally deferred to dominant public opinion, his sorry performance in race cases suggests that his disillusionment with abolitionist principles was so strong after the Civil War that he went out of his way to thwart or belittle even those principles that were explicitly enumerated in the Constitution.

Once Harlan and Holmes became colleagues, the contrast in their personalities and temperaments became more pronounced. Harlan was self-righteous, voluble, moralistic, and deeply religious; he viewed the Constitution and its amendments as a fulfillment of America's divine purpose to spread liberty and equality throughout the globe. A memorable description of Harlan's constitutional faith came from Justice David Brewer, who said Harlan "goes to bed every night with one hand on the Constitution and the other on the Bible, and so sleeps the sweet sleep of justice and righteousness."[37] Harlan was a constitutional formalist who believed that the written text expressed immutable and unchanging principles of liberty and equality that should be preserved by impartial judges. (Holmes, by contrast, was a legal realist who insisted that law reflected shifting moral and political realities—the law, he insisted, was nothing more than what judges said it was.) Harlan was a fundamentalist in religion as well as constitutional interpretation: he exhorted his children not to take religion lightly and faithfully attended Presbyterian Sunday services with his beloved wife, Malvina, to whom he was devoted, and who reciprocated his regard by writing a charming diary about their happy marriage that was published a century later.

By his own account, Harlan's happiest professional experience was the twenty years he spent as a lecturer on constitutional law for evening students at the Columbian University in Washington, D.C., now the George Washington University Law School. Arriving at 7 P.M., often dressed in a tuxedo, mopping his brow with a bandanna, and enthusiastically chewing tobacco, Harlan would address the "young gentlemen of the law class" with the zeal of an evangelist and the timing of a circus barker, speaking in a resonant voice with a slight southern drawl. He entertained the crowd by describing his own dissenting opinions and then adding, after a deadpan pause, "But of course I was wrong."[38]

Drawing on techniques of biblical typology, which interpreted the Old Testament as a prefiguration of the New, Harlan insisted that the Revolutionary War, which attacked monarchy and aristocracy, had foreshadowed the Civil War, which eradicated the racial caste system.[39] The Reconstruction amendments, he believed, constitutionalized the egalitarian spirit and natural rights of the Declaration of Independence. But in other respects, Harlan was no Jeffersonian: he preferred George Mason's draft of the Virginia Bill of Rights to the work of Jefferson, the Whig Party's bogeyman, and taught his students to revere the nationalism of John Marshall and Joseph Story. He maintained that the people of the United States (rather than the people of the individual states) were sovereign, and liked to close his lectures by reading aloud from the Supremacy Clause of the Constitution, which makes the Constitution and federal laws supreme over state laws and obliges state judges to follow their commands. ("Is there any country on the earth that has in its statutes or laws a provision like that?" he would marvel. "Not one.")[40] Reconceiving the Civil War as a divinely ordained penance for the scourge of slavery, he insisted that America, as God's chosen people, would serve as an example of equality throughout the world, and presciently predicted that even England, inspired by America's example, would eventually replace its House of Lords with an elected Senate.[41]

Holmes, by contrast, was neither religious nor moralistic; when shot on the battlefield, he realized he did not need religious faith but instead could take consolation in his philosophy of skeptical unbelief. Later, his wife declared that they would both be Unitarians because "in Boston one has to be something and Unitarian is the least you can be."[42] Perhaps because Holmes, unlike Harlan, could not justify his life by taking consolation in faith, he was intensely self-regarding and obsessively focused, from his earliest years, on burning his mark upon the world. As a youth, he began a program of disciplined reading and self-improvement that was matched only by Jefferson in its Stakhanovite intensity, and he stuck to it until the end of his long life, laboriously recording each of the works of philosophy, literature, and history he read each year and leavening the relentless self-improvement with murder mysteries. His ambition was so palpable and thoughtless of others that he alienated his colleagues at Harvard Law School by hastily resigning from a professorship that had been created especially for him in order to take a judgeship that opened unexpectedly. Professor James B. Thayer groused of Holmes that he was "selfish, vain, thoughtless of others."[43] And his friend from youth, William James, described Holmes as "a powerful battery, formed like a planing machine to gauge a deep, self-beneficial groove through life."[44]

Throughout his life, Holmes fretted that he was not as celebrated and fawned over as he thought he should be. His childless marriage was happy but peculiar. By his own accounts, he devoted most of his energy to his work, with little emotional energy left over for his wife, Fannie, with whom he enjoyed a teasing and playful but highly unequal rapport: he called her Dickie, she called him Holmes; in the evenings, she read to him as he played solitaire. Fannie wor-

The Supreme Court circa 1904, with Harlan seated second from the left and Holmes standing at the far left. When Holmes said of Harlan's arguments, "That just won't wash," the accommodating chief justice, Melville Fuller (seated at center), tried to make peace by mimicking a washboard and declaring: "Still I keep scrubbing and scrubbing."

shiped him, as did all of the flattering young acolytes he liked to surround himself with in his old age to reassure him that he deserved more worldly adulation than he was already receiving. Holmes returned Fannie's regard by flirting flamboyantly with other women at public functions and carrying on an affair of emotional infidelity, at the least, with Lady Castletown, an Irish aristocrat he sought out on his solo trips to England. As with Jefferson, Holmes's compulsive flirtations seemed to be a form of emotional distancing rather than engagement and seemed to have more to do with gratifying his own ego than with actual sexual or romantic conquest. But they were hurtful to Fannie, who had to listen to President Theodore Roosevelt marvel at Holmes's ability to flirt even with an elderly dinner partner, because "the sex instinct is so strong in him."[45]

The differences in the temperaments and perspectives of Harlan and Holmes were obvious in many areas of the Court's jurisprudence, where Harlan emphasized the importance of protecting constitutional liberty and Holmes the importance of deferring to democratic majorities. As soon as Holmes joined the Court, his Social Darwinism clashed with Harlan's messianic egalitarianism in a series of cases involving the growing American empire. In the opening years of the twentieth century, following the Spanish-American War and President William McKinley's resounding reelection victory in 1900, the Court issued a series of rulings that the Constitution did not follow the flag, to use the popular slogan, and that sugar and tobacco imported from the newly conquered territories in the Caribbean and the Pacific could be subject to protectionist tariffs. (These rulings prompted the cartoon character Mr. Dooley's famous remark: "No matther whether th' constitution follows th' flag or not, th' supreme coort follows th' iliction returns.")[46] Harlan vigorously dissented in these cases, insisting that the Constitution does follow the flag and its guarantees applied to the new territories from the moment they were acquired. Theodore Roosevelt appointed Holmes to the Court in 1902 in part because his bellicose speeches reassured the new president that Holmes would side with the imperialists in the so-called insular cases, which raised the question of whether newly acquired territories in Puerto Rico and the Philippines would have to respect all the rights guaranteed by the U.S. Constitution, such as the right to jury trial. Holmes did not disappoint his patron. To Roosevelt's delight, he joined the pro-imperialist majority on the Court, holding in *Hawaii v. Mankichi* in 1903 that only the most basic guarantees of constitutional due process applied to colonies like Hawaii—and the right to a jury trial was not among them. Harlan, in dissent, wrote a characteristically apocalyptic jeremiad, insisting that the Constitution had to be supreme over all people subject to the authority of the United States and lamenting the fact that, "under the influence and guidance of commercialism and the supposed necessities of trade, this country had left the old ways of the fathers, as defined by a written Constitution." The reference to the corrupting influence of commerce was telling. Harlan believed devoutly in the idea of American exceptionalism, and feared that only greed could divert the United States from its divine mission.[47]

In addition to questions about race and empire, the greatest drama that consumed the Court from the Reconstruction era to the New Deal was the constitutionality of progressive economic regulation. Congress and the states passed a series of laws to protect health, safety, and economic equity, and the conservative Court struck several down. Harlan and Holmes tended to dissent in these cases, both favoring deference to legislatures, although their personal views about economic regulation were diametrically opposed. Harlan, whose populist economic views were a vestige of the Whig Party of an earlier era, embraced John Marshall's broad vision of the Commerce Clause, which held that the federal government should have broad authority over economic policy to encourage growth and entrepreneurship. At the same time, he was suspicious of big money and corporate interests and feared that "aggregations of capital" would impose "another kind of slavery" on the American people: in his view, the Court's decisions favoring corporate wealth were just as bad as those upholding Jim Crow.[48] His sympathy for economic underdogs seems to have been fanned by class anxiety and financial instability. Constantly in debt in his efforts to support his three sons, often on the verge of bankruptcy, he viewed the rich as unpatriotic and coddled. "I never knew a *very* rich man who was not astute in attempting to evade the payment of his share of taxes," he wrote to a friend.

This made Harlan an enthusiastic supporter of the federal income tax enacted in 1894 by a Democratic Congress and a Democratic president, Grover Cleveland. When the Court struck down the income tax a year later, Harlan became apoplectic on the bench. One newspaper reported that, in delivering his extemporaneous dissent, he "pounded the desk [and] shook his finger" at Chief Justice Fuller, expressing himself "in a tone and language more appropriate to a stump speech at a Populist barbecue than to an opinion on a question of law before the Supreme Court of the United States."[49] Harlan was so incensed that historians believe he leaked the result of the case, including intimate details about what had occurred in the justices' conference, to the *Chicago Tribune*, which accurately forecast the voting in advance. While the majority opinion charged that the "present assault on capital was a prelude to socialism," Harlan responded that precedents from the Marshall era and the Civil War had established Congress's power to tax incomes, and he accused the Court of exalting the rich over innocent citizens "who ought not to be subjected to the dominion of aggregated wealth any more than the people of the country should be at the mercy of the lawless." Predicting that the decision would "sow the seeds of [class] hate and mistrust," he called for a constitutional amendment explicitly to authorize an income tax. In 1913, two years after Harlan's death, the American people obliged by ratifying the Sixteenth Amendment.

Although Holmes, too, generally voted to uphold progressive economic laws, he, unlike Harlan, had contempt for the laws he was upholding. "It has given me great pleasure to sustain the Constitutionality of laws that I believe to be as bad as possible because I thereby helped to mark the difference between what I would forbid and what the Constitution permits," he declared. Holmes had no interest in or concern for the poor, weak, and economically disadvantaged: he viewed Socialism and pacifism as the foolish doctrines of weak-minded do-gooders and sentimentalists. ("Doesn't this squashy sentimentality of a big minority of our people about human life make you puke?" he wrote a friend. "Oh bring in a basin.")[50] His own sympathies were entirely with capitalists, who openly acknowledged the brutality of human competition, and he believed that competition meant that the strong would inevitably combine forces to destroy the weak.

In the fifteen years after Holmes joined the Court, the justices became increasingly activist in cases involving economic liberties, striking down ten federal laws. (By contrast, during the sixty years between the founding and the Civil War, only two federal laws were invalidated, in *Marbury v. Madison* and *Dred Scott.*) Holmes dissented in four of these cases, and declared that he would have been perfectly happy if the Court lost its power to invalidate acts of Congress, as long as it retained the ability to strike down unconstitutional acts by the states. During the same period, however, the Court provoked even more criticism for its willingness to strike down economic regulations passed by progressive state legislatures, such as minimum wage and maximum hour laws. Both Harlan and Holmes dissented from this trend: both generally supported the ability of state legislatures, when exercising their "police powers," to pass regulations in the interest of protecting health, safety, and morals. On a list of his favorite decisions, Harlan included no fewer than eighteen cases where he supported the exercise of a state's police power, allowing the states to ban the sale of liquor, lottery tickets, and margarine, to regulate garbage collection and Sunday trains, and to compel vaccinations.[51] But while Harlan generally applauded these regulations, Holmes characteristically found them puritanical and paternalistic. It is one of the jokes of history that Holmes, the aristocratic amoral Social Darwinist, has

Joseph Lochner, the owner of this bakery in Utica, was arrested in 1902 for employing a worker for more than sixty hours a week. The Supreme Court's decision three years later to strike down New York State's maximum hour law became a symbol of conservative judicial activism.

been recast as a tender-hearted progressive, while Harlan, the economic populist and moralist, has received less attention for his championing of economic judicial restraint. This odd verdict results largely from their respective performances in one of the most famous regulatory cases in the history of the Court, *Lochner v. New York*.

Soon after it was decided in 1905, *Lochner* became an epithet for the excesses of conservative judicial activism on behalf of economic liberties, although the majority opinion today has been resurrected by libertarians who suggest it may have gotten a bum rap. The case involved the constitutionality of a New York law prohibiting bakers from working more than sixty hours a week or ten hours a day. By a 5–4 vote, the Court struck down the law. (The vote in conference had originally gone the other way, and Harlan, who dissented, had originally been assigned to write the majority opinion.) In his opinion for the Court, Justice Rufus Peckham asked whether the law could be justified as a reasonable regulation of health or safety—in which case it could be upheld as legislation in the public interest—or whether it was a special interest "labor law," designed to favor one class of unionized workers at the expense of employers, with no broader benefits to the public. Baking was not an unusually dangerous or unhealthy profession, Peckham declared, and because bakers required no special protection, they could fend for themselves in an unregulated labor market. Therefore, Peckham announced, the law must have been passed not for the legitimate purpose of protecting health and safety, but for the illicit purpose of helping a special interest group. For this reason, it violated the freedom of contract protected by the Fourteenth Amendment of the Constitution and had to fall.

Both Holmes and Harlan dissented. Although Harlan's dissent has been largely forgotten by history, it is more legally convincing than Holmes's showier and better-known alternative. Harlan accepted the legal framework that the majority was trying to apply, which American courts had embraced since the Jacksonian era. According to this familiar libertarian framework, courts had a responsibility to distinguish legitimate health and safety regulations from illicit attempts to favor one group of economic competitors over another. Harlan took for granted that the Fourteenth Amendment to the Constitution was originally intended to protect freedom of contract, and assumed, with the framers of the Fourteenth Amendment, that employers and employees should generally be able to bargain on equal terms in an unregulated labor market. Harlan also agreed with the Court that the appropriate way of distinguishing permissible health and safety regulations from

111

impermissible "class legislation," or special preferences for labor over capital, was to focus on the character of the industry being regulated. The only question on which Harlan and the majority disagreed was whether baking was an unusually dangerous profession, like mining, and whether bakers therefore were a vulnerable class of workers entitled to special protection by the state.

Rather than second-guessing the New York legislature's conclusions on this point, Harlan's dissent focused on the virtues of judicial restraint. Courts, he said, should not strike down laws unless they were "plainly, palpably" unreasonable, and in the face of uncertainty, should defer to the judgments of elected legislators. Focusing, once again, on the facts and political reality on the ground, Harlan said it was perfectly reasonable for the New York legislature to conclude that baking was a dangerous profession in need of regulation. He quoted a treatise on "Diseases of the Worker," noting "the labor of the bakers is among the hardest and most laborious imaginable" because it has to be performed at night in overheated workshops. Anticipating the fact-intensive opinions of Justice Louis Brandeis, he quoted statistics about the average working day in several European countries. He was especially moved by the fact that Congress and many state legislatures were passing maximum hour laws, and most had chosen eight hours as a reasonable maximum. He concluded by quoting Chief Justice Marshall's view that states should have broad discretion to protect health and predicted "a decision that the New York statute is void under the Fourteenth Amendment will, in my opinion, involve consequences of a far-reaching and mischievous character; for such a decision would seriously cripple the inherent power of the States to care for the lives, health and well-being of their citizens." Thus Harlan nicely struck a blow for federalism in the course of quoting the great nationalist. Harlan's dissent is workmanlike but entirely persuasive. Rather than denouncing his colleagues, he convincingly challenged them on their own terms.

Holmes's far more elegant dissent, by contrast, entirely ignored his colleagues and refused to engage in their debate about how to apply existing legal tests for distinguishing health and safety laws from special interest legislation. With extraordinary confidence and colloquial ease, Holmes made clear that he had no interest in legal precedents or in the intentions of the framers of the Fourteenth Amendment; for him these were petty technicalities to be swept away by the power of his rhetoric. "This case is decided upon an economic theory which a large part of the country does not entertain," he began confidently. "If it were a question whether I agreed with that theory I should desire to study it further and long before making up my mind. But I do not conceive that to be my duty, because I strongly believe that my agreement or disagreement has nothing to do with the right of a majority to embody their opinions in law. . . . The Fourteenth Amendment does not enact Mr. Herbert Spencer's Social Statics."

Although memorable as aphorisms, all of Holmes's legal claims were open to question. The economic theory on which the case was decided—that legislatures should be able to protect health and safety but not favor some workers over others—was one that the country and the framers of the Fourteenth Amendment largely accepted. There was room for disagreement about the application of that theory, but not, in 1905, about the constitutional status of the theory itself. The invocation of Herbert Spencer's *Social Statics* was an inspired rhetorical effect: by naming an exotic-sounding libertarian treatise—a memorable concrete example rather than an easily forgotten abstraction— Holmes succeeded in making the majority opinion look esoteric and out of touch. Holmes was being coy, however, when he said he didn't know whether he agreed with Spencer; Holmes was in fact an

113

enthusiastic Spencerian. As he had done in civil rights cases, Holmes was less interested in respecting conventional legal materials than in repeating his glib view of law as a Darwinian struggle for power in which majorities should triumph over minorities. He declared, "I think that the word liberty in the Fourteenth Amendment is perverted when it is held to prevent the natural outcome of a dominant opinion, unless it can be said that a rational and fair man necessarily would admit that the statute proposed would infringe fundamental principles as they have been understood by the traditions of our people and our law." Of course, the question of whether the law infringed fundamental principles was ultimately one involving factual judgments, not philosophical abstractions, but Holmes, unlike Harlan, was an armchair empiricist who had no interest in facts when they interfered with his aphorisms.

The different perspectives of Holmes and Harlan about the dangers of economic aggregation also emerged in cases involving the Sherman Antitrust Act, which Congress passed in 1890 to rein in monopolies and trusts that were increasingly perceived as greedy and rapacious. Holmes thought the act a foolish and ineffective law that was constitutionally questionable when applied to smaller companies; Harlan enthusiastically praised it as a way of countering "the greatest injury to the integrity of our social organizations [which] comes from the enormous power of corporations."[52] In 1895, the Court refused to apply the Sherman Act to the American Sugar Refining Company, which had acquired almost complete control of the manufacture of refined sugar in the United States, on the grounds that Congress had the power to regulate commerce but not manufacturing. Justice Harlan wrote the only dissent, largely following Chief Justice Marshall's broad vision of congressional authority under the Commerce Clause. He insisted that commerce, according to the Constitution, includes not only the interstate movement of goods but "interstate trade in any of its stages." Harlan also could not resist editorializing against "overshadowing combinations . . . governed entirely by the law of greed and selfishness." His vision was finally vindicated in 1948, when the Court overturned the sugar trust case, holding that manufacturing and commerce are so closely related that Congress could regulate both.

The year after his appointment, Holmes had an opportunity to express his own qualms about the Sherman Act in the *Northern Securities* case, which involved a railway combination formed by two competing railroad magnates, James Hill of Northern Pacific and E. H. Harriman of Great Northern. In a 5–4 decision written by Justice Harlan, the Court held that the combination violated the Sherman Act, which prohibited "every contract, combination . . . or conspiracy, in restraint of trade or commerce." Holmes wrote a separate dissent, which began by protesting his general inclination to bow to the will of the majority. "I think it useless and undesirable, as a rule, to express dissent," he began. He insisted that the act was intended to suppress combination, not competition, and therefore it would be undesirable to extend it to small local mergers as well as large trusts. To hold otherwise, he said, "would make eternal the *bellum omnium contra omnes*"—the war of each against all—"and disintegrate society so far as it could into individual atoms. . . . It would be an attempt to reconstruct society." Holmes believed, in other words, that the strongest groups were entitled to the spoils of fair competition, as an alternative to incessant violence. His apostasy infuriated President Roosevelt, the trustbuster-in-chief, who said of his recent appointee: "I could carve out of a banana a judge with more backbone than that."[53]

Holmes and Harlan clashed again over the meaning of the Sherman Act in the *Standard Oil* case of 1911, a civil suit aimed at breaking up John D. Rockefeller's giant trust. The Court, with Holmes's support, construed the act to forbid only "undue restraints" of trade or commerce, and therefore modified the order to break up Standard Oil, allowing subsidiary corporations of the cartel to create new combinations, as long as they avoided duplicating the existing ones. Harlan dissented, accusing the majority of ignoring the plain language of the Sherman Act, and creating, by judicial fiat, a looser restriction on "unreasonable" combinations, rather than any and all combinations. Holmes, the majoritarian legal realist, trusted courts to decide what kind of economic restraints were unreasonable, while Harlan, the formalist, thought judges had no power to make exceptions from the clear prohibitions that Congress adopted. In an angry analogy, Harlan compared the slavery prohibited by the Civil War amendments and "another kind of slavery sought to be fastened on the American people; namely the slavery that would result from aggregations of capital in the hands of a few individuals and corporations controlling, for their own profit and advantage exclusively, the entire business of the country, including the production and sale of the necessities of life."

Harlan's dissent in the *Standard Oil* case proved to be his last, and he delivered it with memorable aplomb. Having refreshed himself with whiskey, he denounced his colleagues from the bench in improvised language that is said to have made them blush, language that his new colleague, Justice Charles Evans Hughes, called "not a swan song but the roar of an angry lion."[54] After a rejuvenating summer break in Canada, Harlan returned to Washington for the opening of the new term in October 1911, but became ill on the bench and was taken home with severe bronchitis. Within a day, his fever turned into pneumonia and Harlan fell into a coma; he died on October 14, at the age of seventy-eight. "I'm sorry I kept you all waiting so long," he said to his wife and children before expiring.[55] A moving memorial service was held at the Metropolitan A.M.E. Church, a leading African-American church in Washington, D.C., where Harlan was praised for emphasizing "the duty of the favored to the ill-favored; of the strong to the weak."[56]

This was never a duty that moved Holmes during the twenty-one years he continued to serve on the Court after Harlan's death. During those two decades, Holmes continued to champion judicial abstinence, his Social Darwinism reaching its most unsettling expression in 1927, when he wrote for an 8–1 majority and upheld eugenic sterilization laws directed at the mentally disabled. "Three generations of imbeciles," Holmes wrote in his opinion, "are enough." Holmes didn't know or care that Carrie Buck, whose mandatory sterilization he upheld, was hardly mentally disabled: Buck's daughter made her school's honor roll before she died of measles in the second grade. In a subsequent letter to his friend Harold Laski, Holmes made clear that he agreed enthusiastically with the Virginia sterilization law. "Establishing the constitutionality of law permitting the sterilization of imbeciles," he wrote, "gave me pleasure."[57] Having read Malthus on overpopulation, as well as Charles Pearson's book *National Life and Character*, which predicted that American and English Anglo-Saxons would be swamped by the brown and yellow races, Holmes believed that only brutal methods for population control—including euthanasia of the unfit—could ensure the survival and improvement of the white race.[58] "If there is a thing I loathe," he wrote toward the end of his life, "it is the sentimental squashiness of a big minority of our time—Religious squeams about taking human life. . . . The Universe is predatory . . . all life except the very lowest is at the expense of other life. . . . I do despise the upward and onward."[59]

If Holmes were simply a radical majoritarian who believed that courts should almost never strike down laws, as he suggested in cases involving civil rights and economic regulation, his reputation as a visionary would not have survived the second half of the twentieth century. Today, however, he is largely remembered for his eloquent dissenting opinions in the 1920s defending the rights of free speech. Near the end of his life, Holmes came to see laws restricting free speech as a threat to the ability of clashing groups in American democracy to struggle for power. In the years following World War I, he wrote stirring defenses of the First Amendment in a series of dissenting opinions that also relied on metaphors of conflict and struggle. "The best test of truth is the power of the thought to get itself accepted in the competition of the market," he wrote in *Abrams v. United States* in 1919. But he was not sentimental about the ultimate outcome of the battle for ideas. "If in the long run the beliefs expressed in proletarian dictatorship are destined to be accepted by the dominant forces of the community, the only meaning of free speech is that they should be given their chance and have their way," he declared in *Gitlow v. New York* (1925). In the end, even his free speech activism reflected his broader belief that the strong would always dominate the weak, and it was the job of judges to help them do so.

Holmes's view of free speech was initially far narrower than Harlan's. In *Patterson v. Colorado* (1907), Holmes wrote a remarkable majority opinion for the Court upholding the right of state court judges to hold a newspaper editor in contempt for publishing cartoons that ridiculed the judges themselves. The populist editor, Thomas Patterson, had supported an amendment to the state constitution that would have provided home rule for the city of Denver, and he was furious when Republican members of the state supreme court struck down the home rule amendment. After he published editorials and cartoons mocking the court for being in the pocket of utility corporations, the court convicted him of criminal contempt and fined him $1,000. In a glib and terse majority opinion, Holmes upheld the conviction, adopting a cramped view of the First Amendment as preventing all "previous restraints upon publications" but allowing "the subsequent punishment of such as may be deemed contrary to the public welfare." Endorsing the narrow British view of free expression that had been rejected by the framers of the Civil War amendments, Holmes held further that the truth of the publication was irrelevant; publications that "tend to obstruct the administration of justice" could be punished whether or not their criticisms were true.[60] Harlan's powerful dissenting opinion insisted that free speech was one of the privileges and immunities of national citizenship that the states as well as Congress should have to respect. Since the framers of the Fourteenth Amendment had been galvanized by the attempts of southern states to suppress the speech of abolitionists, Harlan's view was far more faithful than Holmes's to the original understanding of the amendment.

During his first years after Harlan left the Court, Holmes continued, at least at first, to support the suppression of free speech and political protest. After World War I, for example, a series of Socialists were convicted of having obstructed the armistice by circulating pamphlets criticizing the draft. One such pamphlet argued that the draft was unconstitutional and urged readers to join the Socialist Party and petition their congressmen for repeal of the draft laws. In *Schenck v. United States* (1919), Holmes wrote an opinion for a unanimous Court upholding the conviction of Charles Schenck for circulating the pamphlet. Holmes began cavalierly by asserting that the pamphlet must have been intended to influence people to obstruct the draft, even though it called for the repeal of the draft by peaceful means. In one of the most famous paeans to free speech in American history, he then offered the following observation: "The most stringent protection of free speech would not protect a man in falsely shouting fire in a theatre and causing a panic. . . . The question in every case is whether the words used are used in such circumstances and are of such a nature as to create a clear and present danger that they will bring about the substantive evils that Congress has a right to prevent." These ringing sentences have come, over the years, to stand for a broad libertarian protection for free speech. But Holmes offered them as a justification for suppressing free speech. In the next breath, he declared: "When a nation is at war many things that might be said in time of peace are such a hindrance to its effort that their utterance will not be endured so long as men fight and that no Court could regard them as protected by any constitutional right."

Once again, Holmes could not resist the military references. But Holmes's civil libertarian friends at *The New Republic* and Harvard Law School were appalled. Despite his claim that speech had to create a "clear and present danger" to be suppressed, Holmes presented no evidence that the call for peaceful protest against the draft actually threatened this level of harm. A week later, Holmes went on to write two more unanimous opinions for the Court upholding the conviction of Jacob Frohwerk, who published antiwar articles in a German newspaper, and Eugene V. Debs, the Socialist Party candidate for president in 1912, who defended three Socialists who had been imprisoned for espionage as "martyrs for freedom." Neither of these illiberal opinions made any reference to the idea of a "clear and present danger."[61]

How did Holmes transform himself from being a vigorous supporter of the government's power to suppress free speech into one of free speech's most vigorous defenders? The transformation seems to have been precipitated by his readings over the summer of 1919, as the prosecution of antiwar dissenters continued to grow. Holmes was especially struck by an article by Professor Zechariah Chaffee of Harvard Law School, *Freedom of Speech in War Time*, which he discussed with the author. Flattering Holmes in the way that Holmes required, Chaffee convinced the justice to refine his "clear and present danger" test so that it came to stand for the opposite of what Holmes had originally meant—namely, that speech could be banned only if it threatened to create imminent harm, rather than if it simply had a "bad tendency" that might eventually produce harm in the remote future. With the encouragement of Chafee and other acolytes, Holmes dissented in the next case involving the prosecution of antiwar dissenters, *Abrams v.*

United States (1919). The majority upheld the conviction of Russian immigrants who had circulated pamphlets urging a strike to protest the deployment of American troops to Russia after the Bolshevik revolution. Holmes objected that the connection between the pamphlets and the possibility of illegal activity was too remote: "It is only the present danger of immediate evil or an intent to bring it about that warrants Congress in setting a limit to the expression of opinion where private rights are not concerned." He added one of the most inspiring odes to the value of free speech ever written: "When men have realized that time has upset many fighting faiths, they may come to believe even more than they believe the very foundations of their own conduct that the ultimate good desired is better reached by free trade in ideas." The metaphor of free trade and market competition was consistent with Holmes's general view of life as a vigorous and sometimes violent struggle; and although hard to reconcile with a general tendency to defer to laws that interfered with economic competition, it is consistent with his Jeffersonian devotion to majority rule at all costs. Censorship of political speech, after all, chokes the free flow of information on which a properly functioning democracy depends, and therefore interferes with the formation of future majorities that Holmes believed were the only test of truth.

Although Holmes provided the poetic metaphors that envelop our modern conception of free speech, other justices provided the legal foundations. It was Justice Louis Brandeis, joined by Holmes in his concurring opinion in *Whitney v. California* (1927), who emphasized that speech could not be banned unless the danger it threatened was imminent, serious, and expressly advocated—a position that a majority of the Court finally embraced in the 1960s. And in the *Gitlow* decision in 1925, a majority of the Court finally agreed that the First Amendment restrained the states as well as Congress, vindicating the position that Harlan had first advocated two decades earlier. In *Gitlow*

Holmes, as always, was less interested in the technical details: he filed yet another beautiful and memorable dissenting opinion, making explicit the connection between his vision of free speech and his vision of life as a Darwinian struggle: "Every idea is an incitement. . . . Eloquence may set fire to reason." If anyone thought he had gone soft in his old age, he took care to dispel the error, later insisting that his dissent in *Gitlow* guaranteed nothing more than "the right of a donkey to talk drool about the proletarian dictatorship, etc."[62]

During his last years on the Court, Holmes was celebrated less for his free speech dissents than for his dissents in the cases involving economic liberties that led up to the New Deal. As early as 1918, he wrote a dissent for four justices, including Brandeis, objecting to the Court's decision to strike down the federal Child Labor Law, which prohibited the interstate shipment of any product manufactured with child labor. (As in the antitrust cases, the conservatives continued to insist that Congress's power to regulate commerce did not extend to the regulation of manufacturing.) "If there is any matter upon which civilized countries have agreed," Holmes wrote with characteristic panache, "it is the evil of premature and excessive child labor. . . . It is not for this Court to . . . say that [prohibition] is permissible as against strong drink but not as against the product of ruined lives."

In the twilight of his career, Holmes became, to progressives, a true national hero. On his ninetieth birthday, in 1931, a live national radio broadcast celebrated his achievements, and Holmes replied to the tributes, speaking into a microphone for the first time, and closing with the words of a Latin poet: "Death plucks my ear and says, Live—I am coming." The next year, after suffering what he called a "pull-down" that made writing difficult, he retired reluctantly from the Court. On March 8, 1933, Holmes's ninety-second birthday, President Franklin D. Roosevelt, who had been inaugurated just four days earlier, called at his Washington townhouse to pay his respects to the great judge and to ask his advice. Holmes replied, characteristically, with a martial metaphor. "Mr. President, you are in a war; I, too, was in a war. There is only one rule in a war. Form your battalions and fight."[63]

Roosevelt took Holmes's advice. As the Court attempted to strike down the New Deal recovery program on the same narrow conception of interstate commerce that Holmes had opposed, Roosevelt proposed a court-packing plan in 1937 that would have given him the right to appoint a new justice for every member of the Court who refused to retire after turning seventy. Although the court-packing plan was defeated in the Senate, the Court changed its mind later that year about the constitutionality of the New Deal and began to uphold economic legislation that it had previously struck down. (The swing justice, Owen J. Roberts, unexpectedly changed his position, an about-face called "the switch in time that saved nine.") The child labor case was reversed, the distinction between commerce and manufacturing was abandoned, and Holmes's dissenting opinions became the law of the land. Under the new legal regime, Congress could regulate any activity that affected interstate commerce, even if the activity itself did not involve commerce, such as growing wheat in the backyard for personal consumption. In the most prominent sign of the new legal order, the Court, in *West Coast Hotel v. Parrish* (1937), upheld a state minimum wage law for women and minors and overruled a *Lochner*-era decision (from which Holmes had dissented). "The Constitution does not speak of freedom of contract," Chief Justice Charles Evans Hughes declared for the Court, tacitly accepting Holmes's charge in *Lochner* that the Court had read its own idea about freedom of contract into the Constitution. Noting that the economic reality of the Depression had dislodged old assumptions about the ability of workers and employers to fend for themselves in a properly functioning labor market, the Court emphasized that the burden of caring for the unemployed would be imposed on the nation as a whole. Thus, Holmes, by good luck and good timing, had managed to predict the legal order of the future, and he was hailed at his death as a visionary who had imagined the constitutional transformation ahead of schedule.

Who was more influential, in the end, Holmes or Harlan? There is no question that Holmes was more brilliant than Harlan—just as Jefferson was more brilliant than Marshall. And Holmes's greatest achievements, like Jefferson's, were the dazzling and varied achievements of his life itself—as an intellectual, philosopher, talker, and cynic, he was unsurpassed. "Life is an art not a thing which one can work out successfully by abstract rules," he confessed to Lady Castletown. "It is like painting a picture."[64] It is impossible not to admire the cultivated panache and disciplined force with which Holmes created his own legend and imposed it on posterity. In addition to sharing Jefferson's genius as a polymath, Holmes, like Jefferson, was more European than American, and was as instinctively drawn to England as Jefferson was to France. Holmes was also Jeffersonian in his radical skepticism of judicial power and in his support for the virtually unchecked power of popular majorities to do whatever they pleased. Just as Jefferson would have given Congress the power to overturn Supreme Court decisions, so Holmes was perfectly happy to surrender the Court's ability to strike down acts of Congress, and he, like Jefferson, believed in radical judicial abstinence. As a Massachusetts nationalist, Holmes delivered the obligatory obeisance to Marshall: in a speech celebrating the centennial of Marshall's accession, he wrote generously, "If American law were to be represented by a single figure, skeptic and worshiper alike would agree without dispute that the figure could be one alone, and that one John Marshall." But Holmes's tribute to Marshall was otherwise tepid, and President Theodore Roosevelt thought the address "unworthy of the subject," indicating that Holmes had shown a "total incapacity to grasp what Marshall did." Indeed he had: Holmes rejected Marshall's vigorous vision of judicial power, and could never have praised Marshall as forcefully as did Henry Cabot Lodge, the man who persuaded Roosevelt to appoint Holmes, who declared on the same anniversary: "At one stroke . . . Marshall asserted the supremacy of the Constitution and the power of the court in relation to the other branches of the National Government."[65] The truth is, Holmes believed little in the supremacy of the Constitution and had sneered throughout his life at the idea of natural rights.[66] He may have been correct on the broad question of the importance of judicial deference to legislative majorities, but because he could not resist taking his principles to their logical conclusions in most cases, the purity of his vision has little constituency today.

It was Harlan, the natural heir to his judicial namesake, who embraced Marshall's vision of judicial power in the service of nationalism. Harlan was an emotionalist, a moralist, a Republican proselytizer, and something of a ham, but he understood and shared the vision of the framers of the Reconstruction amendments and sought to preserve that vision from the assaults of increasingly illiberal local legislative majorities. Harlan has tended to be dismissed over the years as a muddled judge who was simply lucky that his result-oriented political preferences were eventually vindicated by history. But that ungenerous verdict fails to do justice to the magnitude of his achievement. Alone among the justices of his era, he understood the three central goals of the Reconstruction amendments—to protect the equal civil rights of African-Americans, to extend the Bill of Rights to bind the states, and to empower Congress to protect economic liberties and civil rights as broadly as it believed necessary.

During the Warren Court era in the 1950s and 1960s, Harlan's prophetic dissenting opinions were dramatically vindicated. Harlan's dissent in *Plessy v. Ferguson* became a kind of bible to Thurgood Marshall: as a lawyer challenging segregation in the 1950s, he liked to read it aloud for inspiration as he prepared to argue *Brown v. Board of Education.* When the Court finally struck down school segregation in 1954, the *New York Times* hailed the landmark *Brown* decision as a belated endorsement of Harlan's views.[67] As early as 1955, one distinguished scholar listed the Harlan dissents that the Supreme Court, Congress, and constitutional amendments had already codified as law. They included not only his opinion in *Plessy* but also his broad reading of the antitrust laws, his defense of judicial deference in economic cases, and his defense of the federal income tax. During the 1960s, under Chief Justice Warren's leadership, even more of Harlan's dissents became law, including his insistence that the Fourteenth Amendment extended most of the guarantees of the Bill of Rights to the states and his insistence that Congress had broad power, under the Thirteenth and Fourteenth Amendments, to punish private acts of discrimination.[68] Harlan's dissent in the *Civil Rights Cases* was finally vindicated when Congress passed the Civil Rights Act of 1964 and the Supreme Court upheld it. It may have taken almost a hundred years, but as Holmes's devotion to unchecked majority rule went out of fashion, Harlan's devotion to national power and constitutional equality appeared increasingly prophetic.

CHAPTER THREE

LIBERTY AND LICENSE

Hugo Black

—

William O. Douglas

I n 1965, after nearly three decades as liberal allies on the Supreme Court, William O. Douglas and Hugo Black disagreed strenuously about the right to privacy. The dispute arose in *Griswold v. Connecticut,* a challenge to Connecticut's archaic law that forbade married couples from using contraceptives. At the justices' private conference, Black, a celebrated free speech absolutist, said he could not see how the law violated the First Amendment rights of free speech or assembly. "The right of husband and wife to assemble in bed," he declared, "is a new right of assembly to me." Douglas spoke next and took issue with Black's position. Freedom of assembly included all intimate and personal associations, he insisted, and there was nothing more personal than the marital relationship. After the justices voted 7–2 to strike down the Connecticut law, with Douglas in the majority and Black in dissent, Chief Justice Earl Warren asked Douglas to draft an opinion for the Court. Douglas wrote opinions more quickly than any justice since Holmes, and at this point in his career he often scribbled drafts, which his clerks called "plane-trip specials," in less than twenty minutes during his frequent week-end lecture tours. In no time at all, Douglas produced a slapdash effort. "The association of husband and wife is not mentioned in the Constitution nor in the Bill of Rights," Douglas declared. "But it is a form of association as vital in the life of a man or woman as any other, and perhaps more so. . . . It is a coming together for better or for worse, hopefully enduring, and intimate to the degree of being sacred."[1]

Douglas's draft was skeptically received by his colleagues, not only because it was hastily written, but also because they were dubious about Douglas's paean to the sanctity of marriage. The sixty-seven-year-old Douglas was on the verge of divorcing his third wife, whom he met when she was a twenty-three-year-old college student (she had written asking him for help on a senior thesis praising his judicial philosophy). After less than two years of marriage, he was abandoning her for his fourth wife, a twenty-year-old college student he had picked up in a restaurant while she was waiting on his table. The other justices were also unconvinced by Douglas's shoddy legal reasoning. At the urging of Justice William Brennan, Douglas wrote a new draft locating a right to privacy not only in the First Amendment but also in what he called, using an astronomical metaphor, "penumbras, formed by emanations" from various other amendments, including the Third, Fourth, and Fifth Amendments. "Various guarantees create zones of privacy," Douglas concluded lyrically, and the specter of police searches of "the sacred precincts of marital bedrooms" was "repulsive to the notions of privacy surrounding the marriage relationship."

Douglas's reference to "penumbras" and "emanations" provoked laughter among several law clerks and a sharp rebuke from his old ally, Hugo Black. Black had been hailed months earlier in a *Time* magazine cover story which noted that more of his dissents had become majority opinions than those of any other justice. The article suggested that "the 'Warren Court' [was] more accurately called the 'Black Court' after its chief philosopher."[2] Black considered his dissent in *Griswold* to be the most difficult he ever had to write, because he found the Connecticut law personally "abhorrent, just viciously evil, but not unconstitutional."[3] In his dissent, he criticized Douglas for substituting vague abstractions about "privacy" for the more precise protections against unreasonable searches and seizures, compelled self-incrimination, and restrictions on free speech guaranteed by the text of the Constitution. "I like my privacy as well as the next one, but I am nevertheless compelled to admit that government has a right to invade it unless prohibited by some specific constitutional provision," he wrote, later paraphrasing the rousing revival song "Give Me That Old Time Religion." Black criticized Douglas for resurrecting the freewheeling, natural law–based philosophy that the Court had used in the 1930s to strike down the New Deal and that both Black and Douglas had decisively repudiated in cases involving economic liberties ever since Franklin D. Roosevelt appointed them to the Court.

The conflict between Black and Douglas in the *Griswold* case epitomized the very different judicial philosophies and temperaments that had made both men close allies and liberal heroes in the 1940s and 1950s but caused them to drift apart, personally and professionally, in the 1960s, as they approached the end of their long careers. Black, the former senator from Alabama and former member of the Ku Klux Klan, became the most influential liberal strict constructionist in the history of the Court. A civil libertarian who believed in the text of the Constitution with a fundamentalist's fervor, Black defended free speech and fair criminal procedures on the Court for blacks and whites alike, but refused to enforce rights that did not appear explicitly

Hugo Black (left) and William O. Douglas were close allies and liberal heroes for more than three decades in the middle of the twentieth century, but they drifted apart, personally and professionally, at the end of their long careers.

in the Constitution. Black was a shrewd politician with a knack for convincing his colleagues through proselytizing and compromise, and *Time* magazine was right to suggest that his influence in many ways surpassed even that of Chief Justice Warren.

Although Douglas often voted with Black, his approach to his job was very different. It's hard to avoid the suspicion that Douglas often scribbled his opinions on the back of a cocktail napkin. Breezy, polemical, and unconcerned with the fine points of legal doctrine, they read more like today's blog entries than carefully reasoned constitutional arguments. Scorning the constraints of constitutional text and previous legal precedents as window dressing, Douglas was a re-alist who believed, like Holmes, that law was essentially politics. But while Holmes deferred to the decisions of democratic majorities, Douglas was flamboyantly unrestrained, viewing it as his personal mission to promote justice and to defend the individual against the tyranny of what he called "the Establishment" in case after case. Al-though viewed by Black and others as one of the brightest justices in the history of the Court—a borderline genius, in the rank of Holmes—Douglas was distracted for much of his tenure, devoting his energies instead to angling for the vice presidency and to compulsive bouts of drinking and adultery with college students, flight attendants, or any other women who crossed his path. And since Douglas, like Holmes, was a loner who insisted that "the only soul I had to save was my own," his lack of interest in persuading his colleagues ultimately marginalized him on the Court. Douglas's passionate individualism and egalitarianism continue to inspire many of his ideological sympa-thizers, but his lack of personal and professional discipline robbed him of the long-term influence that Black continues to enjoy among conservatives and liberals alike.

Both Black and Douglas were appointed by Franklin Roosevelt for a single purpose: to keep the Court out of the business of striking down economic legislation. After the Court, in 1937, abandoned its narrow interpretation of the Commerce Clause and began to uphold the New Deal, the Court had to decide whether cases involving hu-man rights—such as free speech, freedom of religion, and fair crimi-nal procedures—would be treated differently from cases involving the now controversial protections for property rights. In 1938, the Court announced that those human rights explicitly enumerated in the federal Bill of Rights were entitled to a higher degree of constitu-tional protection than economic and property rights. Roosevelt ap-plauded the so-called preferred position for human rights over property rights, improbably invoking Jefferson as the intellectual father of the New Deal. Indeed, everything about Roosevelt's program seemed to be based on the ideals of Jefferson's antagonists, Alexander Hamilton and John Marshall. Roosevelt centralized the federal administrative state, was indifferent to states' rights, and broadly rather than strictly construed the scope of congressional power. But Jefferson was the patron saint of the Democratic Party, and with his cheerful lack of concern for political contradictions, Roosevelt emphasized the parts of Jefferson's legacy that appeared to support the new economic order. Just as Jefferson had assailed the Supreme Court and called for judicial deference to majority will, so did Roosevelt; just as Jefferson had exalted human rights over property rights, Roosevelt did, too; and just as the aristocratic Jefferson had posed as a champion of the common man, the aristocratic Roosevelt followed in his footsteps.[4] Although the "long and splendid" day of Jeffersonian individualism had ended, Roosevelt declared in 1932, Jefferson would entirely approve of the New Deal's attempt to make the national government "a refuge and a help" rather than a threat to liberty.[5]

When it came time to choose Supreme Court justices, Roosevelt was drawn toward candidates who shared his Jeffersonian suspicion of judicial power in the field of economic regulation while embracing Marshall's view of strong national power, now institutionalized in the burgeoning administrative state. And he found his men in Black, appointed from the Senate in 1937, and Douglas, appointed when he was head of the Securities and Exchange Commission in 1939. Both Black and Douglas had supported Roosevelt's court-packing plan, which Black called a "wise" effort "to protect the people of this nation from judicial usurpation."[6] Black's political and intellectual hero was Jefferson, whom he admired from his early days as an Alabama trial lawyer for his opposition to economic privilege and his populist defense of local majorities against unelected judges. But on the Court,

Black placed himself more squarely in the nationalistic tradition of John Marshall Harlan, a distant relative whose portrait hung in his chambers. They shared an evangelical commitment to limiting judicial discretion while strictly enforcing constitutional limits on the power of the president, Congress, and the states. Douglas, too, styled himself a Jeffersonian, defending the rights of individual dissenters and nonconformists more single-mindedly than any other justice in the history of the Court. But while Black was a populist, Douglas was a progressive, and while Black resolved hard cases in favor of democracy, Douglas resolved them in favor of individual liberty.[7] Because of his character flaws as much as judicial philosophy, Douglas ended his career by embracing an especially freewheeling judicial activism that ultimately drew him apart from Black and marginalized his legacy. Black, on the other hand, became not only the intellectual leader of the Warren Court but also the leading critic of its excesses—in a way that foreshadowed the conservative counterrevolution of the Rehnquist and Roberts Courts on the distant horizon.

Hugo Lafayette Black was born in 1886 in Clay County, Alabama. He was delivered by Dr. John J. Harlan, his mother's cousin, whom Black claimed was distantly related to the great Supreme Court justice. Like John Marshall Harlan, Black absorbed the South's conflicted attitudes about race—both the conventional prejudices of his time as well as an evangelizing faith in equal treatment under law regardless of color. Black's father was a Democrat who had fought for the Confederacy in the Civil War and named his oldest son Robert Lee. Though Black recalled a log cabin childhood, his father was one of the most successful merchants in the area. Black's father drank heavily, and the memories of his bad behavior instilled in his moralistic son an enthusiasm for Prohibition and a lifelong suspicion of alcohol. Although Black was the youngest of eight children, he was his mother's favorite (she named him for a favorite novelist, Victor Hugo), and she gave him a passion for self-improvement through disciplined reading, which stayed with him throughout his life.

Black's formal education was not extensive: after being expelled from high school for breaking the switch of a teacher who was disciplining his teenage sister with it, he never graduated.[8] He went on to the fledgling University of Alabama Law School, composed of only two professors, who taught him that judges should interpret the law, not make it. Self-conscious about the gaps in his formal education, Black embarked on an impressive program of self-directed reading. In adulthood, Black continued to read a book a day—from Greek historians in translation to history and poetry—and the reading light over his bed wore a hole in the mattress. After graduating Phi Beta Kappa, he started out as a trial lawyer in Birmingham, and in one of his first cases, successfully represented an African-American convict who had been kept in prison for several weeks beyond his sentence.

In 1911, at the age of twenty-five, Black was appointed a local police court judge—a position he said taught him much about life—and his firsthand observation of how Birmingham police used the third degree to coerce African-American suspects to confess gave him a concern for fair procedures that he would take with him to the Supreme Court. After making his name as a fire-breathing reformer—"Hugo-to-Hell Black"—he was elected solicitor, or district attorney, in 1914.[9] He distinguished himself by lobbying to improve prison conditions for blacks and whites, and by publishing a report on coerced confessions. Then he became a personal injury lawyer, where his exhaustive preparation and instinctive affinity with jurors made him a rich man. But Black was not above resorting to race-baiting to win verdicts from sympathetic jurors. In his most unsettling performance, Black defended a Protestant minister who had murdered a Catholic priest after the priest performed the marriage of the minister's daughter to a Puerto Rican laborer. "You are a Catholic, aren't you?" Black asked several of the prosecution witnesses. He had a battery of floodlights installed in the courtroom, and he theatrically trained them on the swarthy Puerto Rican bridegroom at the climax of his testimony. "That will do. I just wanted the jury to see that man," said Black. And during his closing argument to the jury, most of whom were Klansmen, Black recited the official Ku Klux Klan prayer: "Our Father and our God. We, as klansmen, acknowledge our dependence upon Thee. . . ."[10] The jury, obligingly, ignored the evidence and voted to acquit the minister.

After deliberating for almost a year, Black decided to join the Klan in 1923. But his standard explanation in later years—"I went to a couple of meetings and spoke about liberty"—was false.[11] During his first race for the Senate, Black marched in parades and spoke at nearly 150 meetings, dressed in full Klan regalia. On the campaign trail, Black sounded many of the same populist themes that John Marshall Harlan had embraced before and after the Civil War, denouncing immigration, trusts, corporations, and "concentrated wealth."[12] (Black also shared Harlan's nativism and anti-Catholicism.) Awarded a Klan "grand passport" after winning the Democratic Senate primary in 1926, Black accepted it enthusiastically. "I know that without the support of the members of this organization," Black observed, "I would not have been called, even by my enemies, 'the junior Senator from Alabama.'"[13] The daughter of one of Black's first mentors recalled that when she ran into a closet as a little girl, a white Klan uniform embroidered with Black's name fell on her head. "Oh, that's Mr. Black's costume," said her mother. "He's going to wear it in a play Saturday night."[14] Years later, when a clerk asked him why he joined, Black replied simply: "Why, son, if you wanted to be elected to the Senate in Alabama in the 1920s, you'd join the Klan, too."[15]

In 1921, at the age of thirty-five, Black single-mindedly courted and married Josephine Foster, the daughter of a rich and distinguished political family from Tennessee. Although Black idealized Josephine until she died of unknown causes thirty years later, at the age of fifty-two, she was often depressed during their marriage. In particular, she seemed to resent his intense ambition and his expectation that she subordinate her life entirely to his. He was similarly controlling with his daughter and two sons, whom he frequently bombarded with suggested reading lists and other homilies about self-improvement. Hard-driving and intensely competitive, especially on the tennis court, Black had little patience for weakness in family members and colleagues.

In the Senate, he made his national reputation as an ardent New Dealer: when he proposed to create six million new jobs by requiring a thirty-hour national workweek, even Roosevelt privately questioned the constitutionality of the plan. He also denounced organized monopolies and earned a reputation as an economic radical. But he wasn't a radical on social issues; like his fellow southerners, he threatened to filibuster the antilynching bill that a majority of the Senate supported, claiming it threatened states' rights. He got Roosevelt's attention by chairing a Senate investigation in 1936 into fraudulent lobbying by public utilities opposed to federal regulation, and he used his subpoena power so aggressively that civil libertarians criticized him for violating constitutional rights of privacy. In a national broadcast that combined populism with moralism, Black denounced the utility lobby for "its size, its power, its capacity for evil." "You, the people of the United States, will not permit it to destroy you," he concluded melodramatically. "You will destroy it."[16]

During the court-packing battle, Black continued his program of self-education, staying up late in the Library of Congress to study the intellectual sources of American constitutional government, including the complete works of Jefferson, as well as Adam Smith's *The Wealth of Nations* and the records of the Constitutional Convention.[17]

Hugo Black's membership in the Ku Klux Klan during his early political career in Alabama came to light after his confirmation to the Supreme Court in 1937, causing him great embarrassment and giving political cartoonists an ample target.

He boasted of vanquishing one of his Senate opponents by quoting a passage of the *Fallacies of Anti-Reformers,* from volume 27 of the *Harvard Classics.* Guided by an article by Will Durant called *One Hundred Best Books,* he buried himself in the Greeks and Shakespeare; and he became such a partisan of Jefferson that the mere mention of Hamilton's name was enough to provoke fits of oratory. Later he would tell his clerks that Edith Hamilton's *The Greek Way* was "the best

preparation for the job I could think of." The experience of communing with original texts, along with his childhood reading of the
Bible, helped Black develop the rudiments of a strict constructionist
judicial philosophy. Judicial subjectivity, he believed, was the greatest evil, and subjectivity could be avoided by forcing judges to study
the text and original understanding of the Constitution, rather than
following their own "economic predilections.[18]

Roosevelt was in a bitter mood in 1937 after his court-packing
plan died in the Senate, and when it came time for him to fill his first
Supreme Court seat the same year, he relished the thought of nomi-
nating Black, one of the zealous supporters of court-packing. "To give
the rebels' part of the country so important an appointment, yet give it
to one of the two or three left-wingers in the Senate was a neat and
cruel irony to the rather vengeful President," wrote the columnists
Joseph Alsop and Turner Catledge.[19] Confirmed 63 to 16, Black
quickly took his judicial oath and then left for a vacation in Europe.
During his trip, the news of his Ku Klux Klan membership broke. To
quell the political firestorm that ensued—along with the widespread
jokes about how he could save money by dyeing his white robes
black—Black returned to deliver a live radio broadcast to one of the
largest audiences in history. Uncontrite and combative, he improbably denounced his opponents for fanning religious intolerance, admitted he had joined and then resigned from the Klan, and added for
good measure that some of his best friends were Catholic and Jewish.
The speech, somehow, seemed to do the trick: public opinion turned
in Black's favor, and the firestorm abated.

Three years later, Black mollified his critics by writing an opinion for the Court holding that the state of Florida violated the due process of law when it subjected four young African-American murder
suspects to dragnet arrests without a warrant, followed by five days of
abusive questioning without lawyers. Drawing on his own experience

observing the results of third-degree police tactics in Birmingham, Black wrote an eloquent paean to the importance of constitutional protection for the rights of all minorities. (In later years, he could never read the opinion without weeping.) The *New York Times* praised the opinion as "far and away the most direct, sweeping and brilliantly written application of the Fourteenth Amendment to human rights that has come from our highest Court."[20] It is also possible that the public scrutiny of Black's Klan membership provoked some useful introspection by the new justice about racial equality that would be reflected throughout his career on the Court.

If Black's upbringing gave him a populist's antipathy to special privileges and judicial subjectivity, Douglas's was focused on a narrower goal: the promotion of William Orville Douglas. Born in Minnesota in 1898, Douglas was the oldest son of a Presbyterian minister who died when he was five. He had an ambivalent relationship with his mother, Julia Fisk Douglas, who brought him up to believe that he could never be as good as his absent, idealized father, though he could try to be as smart. The mother had a peculiar ritual that haunted Douglas throughout his life: after reminding him that his father was a better man, she would recite a little speech she had composed to nominate her son to be president of the United States, complete with a quotation from Sir Walter Scott about the dangers of bearding a Douglas in his lair. This oedipal exercise instilled in Douglas an insatiable and lifelong desire for the presidency, which he wanted, according to a friend, "worse than Don Quixote wanted Dulcinea."[21] And it led him, throughout his life, to alter his political positions and invent the details of his biography in preparation for the presidential campaign that never materialized. As a child, for example, Douglas suffered bouts of the intestinal colic. Years later, he would convert this, in his first autobiography, *Of Men and Mountains,* into a case of polio that was never conclusively established: the more

Douglas, a westerner from Washington State, loved the outdoors, and his most lasting legacy includes his environmentalism.

Rooseveltian disease, he assumed, would play better on the campaign trail.

Unfortunately for Douglas, he was temperamentally unsuited for the presidency or for elective office of any kind. A maverick and a loner, he recoiled from the constant glad-handing and backslapping that any campaign requires. Whether or not Douglas was, as Black and many others believed, a "genius," he had a knack for hitting the intellectual jugular, aided by what he liked to boast was a photographic memory. This stood him in good stead at Whitman College, where he distinguished himself academically but failed to win a Rhodes Scholarship; the experience instilled in him an angry resentment toward "the Establishment" that he nursed until his dying day. He then made his way to New York, where he put himself through Columbia Law School with the help of his doting young first wife, Mildred, a schoolteacher. Because of his ability and prodigious capacity

for sustained work, Douglas was hired by Columbia soon after gradu-
ation to teach corporate law. He soon won a reputation as the "finest
law teacher in America," according to Robert Hutchins, the dynamic
young dean of Yale Law School, who lured Douglas to New Haven
with an impressive salary.

Douglas's reputation was based not on his classroom teaching,
which was shy and awkward, but on his headline-grabbing scholarship on corporate bankruptcy, which included extensive interviews
conducted by Douglas and his research assistants. Douglas's socio-
logical scholarship, pathbreaking for its day, convinced him of the
dangers of laissez-faire capitalism and the excesses of corporate consolidation. In 1934, he took these lessons with him to Washington,
where Joseph Kennedy, the head of the new Securities and Exchange
Commission, hired him to continue his investigations of corporate
wrongdoing. After succeeding Kennedy in 1937, Douglas earned a
reputation as "Mr. Trouble" with the corporate community, due to his
swaggering motto "Piss on 'Em."[22] Douglas was appropriately sensitive to the necessity of appeasing all of his political constituencies
and alternated between investigations into corporate fraud and more
moderate positions offered to appease Wall Street; in the end, he distinguished himself as one of the most successful SEC chairmen ever.
When Louis Brandeis retired from the Court in 1939, Roosevelt, who
wanted a westerner for the seat and thought Douglas played "an interesting game of poker," turned to the forty-year-old reformer. In many
ways, Douglas seemed an appropriate successor to the Jeffersonian
Brandeis, who celebrated local democracy and denounced capitalists
who profited from "other people's money."

As soon as he joined the Court, however, Douglas feared he had
made a terrible mistake. "At the start I did not particularly enjoy the
work of the Court," he confessed in his memoirs.[23] Chafing at the
monastic isolation of judicial work, Douglas began to plot ways of

getting back into the political arena and, eventually, the White House. He came closest in 1944, when Roosevelt expressed an oblique preference for Douglas over Harry Truman as his running mate, but later bowed to the Democratic bosses who doubted Douglas's popular appeal. In 1948, Truman offered Douglas the vice presidential nomination, but Douglas turned it down, apparently on the grounds that he didn't want to be a number two man to a number two man.[24] In 1951, angling for the Democratic presidential nomination the following year, Douglas embarrassed himself by declaring that the United States should recognize Communist China—a form of extrajudicial punditry that earned him a rebuke from President Truman. And in 1960, Douglas hoped to be picked as vice president by Lyndon Johnson. When Johnson was bested in the primaries by John F. Kennedy, Douglas drank himself into a stupor while on a camping trip, raving, "This always happens to me!"[25] Douglas never got over his failure to attain the electoral success that his mother had expected; when a law clerk asked at the end of the 1960s whether, if he had to do it over again, he would go on the Court, Douglas exploded, "Absolutely not! Because the Court as an institution is too peripheral, too much in the backwater on the Court. You're just too far out of the action here."[26]

The demise of Douglas's presidential ambitions around 1960 coincided with a marked change in his jurisprudence. In the 1940s and '50s, when Douglas still fancied himself a viable political candidate, his opinions were more sensitive to public opinion, and he infuriated his colleagues by changing his positions, apparently for political gain. But once he abandoned dreams of political success, Douglas became more romantically aggressive in his defense of the principle that individuals should not blindly follow convention, but should be free to assert themselves in the face of disapproval by the majority. Douglas summed up his creed in a 1963 speech called "The Bill of Rights

Is Not Enough." "Once speech, belief, and conscience are placed beyond the reach of government," he declared, "a nation acquires a spiritual strength that will make it a shining light to all who have never known the blessings of liberty, even to those behind the Iron and Bamboo Curtains."[27]

Black's textualist creed, by contrast, remained consistent. The Bill of Rights *is* enough, he believed, and he resisted efforts to expand or contract it. But his career, too, can be divided into two stages. During the 1940s and '50s, when the Court was more conservative under Chief Justices Harlan Fiske Stone and Fred M. Vinson, Black's passionate defense of the First Amendment made him, with Douglas, a liberal hero. In the 1960s, as the Court under Chief Justice Earl Warren became more expansively liberal and other justices joined Douglas in discovering new constitutional rights, Black's consistent concerns about judicial subjectivity led him to break with Douglas and made him appear more conservative. Although Douglas and other liberal justices complained that Black had changed at the end of his career, Black always insisted, with some plausibility, that it was the Court that had changed while his judicial philosophy remained the same.[28] But judicial temperament, as much as judicial philosophy, was responsible for the gradual estrangement between Black and Douglas; the moralistic Black disapproved of Douglas's drinking and womanizing, and Douglas's lack of concern for constitutional text, history, and precedent came to represent, for Black, the antithesis of what a principled judge should be. At the same time, Douglas came to see Black as a moralistic prude and lamented what he considered Black's jurisprudential rigidity and drift to the right. For many citizens today, the choice about who is more admirable—Black or Douglas—will depend on whose politics they find more congenial. But the fact that Black was more successful than Douglas in enacting his views into law is a reminder of the centrality of judicial temperament.

The differences between Black and Douglas were not immediately obvious when they joined the Court; they initially formed a united front in cases involving economic regulations. Both men had been appointed by Roosevelt to get the Court out of the business of striking down the New Deal, and with the aid of other Roosevelt appointees, they accomplished their mission in short order by broadly construing Congress's power to regulate interstate commerce. "Congress alone must determine how far [interstate commerce] . . . shall be free and untrammeled," Black wrote in a 1939 dissent. Two years later, the Court overturned the pre–New Deal cases from which Justice Holmes had dissented and ruled that Congress had broad discretion, under its authority to regulate interstate commerce, to pass laws concerning salaries, working hours, and factory conditions. Douglas believed that the Court was returning to the nationalistic vision of Marshall and Holmes. Although a textualist and an originalist, Black agreed that the federal government had to be allowed to change with the times: the government is not "powerless to meet new times, new circumstances and new conditions," he argued, and he was willing to stretch the Commerce Clause as far as it could be stretched.[29] (In other words, Black, unlike his conservative successors, was a textualist but not a strict constructionist.) Between 1941 and 1995, the Court would strike down no federal laws for violating the Commerce Clause, and Black never voted to do so during his tenure.

Black and Douglas also championed judicial restraint when confronted with economic regulations passed by the states: their constitutional villain was the 1903 *Lochner* case, and they were determined to end the practice of striking down state regulations as a violation of the constitutional guarantee of due process of the law. In 1955, Douglas wrote a unanimous opinion for the Court upholding an Oklahoma law that forbade opticians from making glasses without a prescription from a licensed ophthalmologist. The real purpose of the law was clear enough—a bit of anticompetitive protectionism from the ophthalmologists, who feared competition from the upstart predecessors of the LensCrafters chain. But Douglas held that courts should not strike down economic regulations unless they were completely irrational. As long as courts could invent some plausibly rational purpose for the law—such as the possibility that professional eye examinations might detect hidden diseases—then the law had to be upheld.

During their early years on the Court, Black and Douglas were drawn together by their common adversaries: Robert Jackson and Felix Frankfurter. Although all four justices had been appointed by Franklin Roosevelt, Jackson and Frankfurter viewed Black and Douglas as the leaders of a liberal "axis," while Black and Douglas dismissed Frankfurter and Jackson as judicial conservatives and traitors to the liberal cause. There were indeed philosophical differences between the two camps, especially in cases involving civil liberties: Black and Douglas, in the tradition of John Marshall Harlan, believed that judges should vigorously protect the liberties enumerated in the Bill of Rights, led by free speech, while deferring to legislatures in cases affecting economic liberties. By contrast, Frankfurter and, to a lesser degree, Jackson, in the tradition of Oliver Wendell Holmes, came to champion judicial restraint across the board. But the real animosities were fueled less by jurisprudence than by personality and temperament, producing clashes that were more angrily emotional than any others in the Court's history.

The most celebrated of these personality clashes occurred between Black and Jackson. A self-made country lawyer from Jamestown, New York, Jackson endeared himself to Roosevelt by his legal ability, sparkling prose, and considerable charm: he distinguished himself as solicitor general and attorney general before his appointment to the Court in 1941. FDR enjoyed his company so much that he included Jackson (along with Douglas) in his small group of

147

poker-playing intimates and invited Jackson to join him on long, informal fishing expeditions in the Florida Keys and the Bahamas. But for all his amiability and ability, Jackson had an Achilles' heel: a tendency to fly off the handle when he failed to get his way. This tendency nearly undid him in 1946, when Chief Justice Stone died unexpectedly. Jackson was on sabbatical from the Court, serving in Germany as the chief U.S. war crimes prosecutor at Nuremberg. Convinced that Roosevelt had promised to appoint him as Stone's successor, Jackson expected that Truman would honor the commitment as well. But the *Washington Post* reported that Black had threatened to resign from the Court if Jackson were promoted to chief, and Truman chose his own poker buddy, Fred Vinson, instead. Jackson considered Black to be ruthless and unethical, and had all but attacked him publicly for his failure to recuse himself from a case in which his former law partner had played a prominent part. Unhinged by Black's perfidy, Jackson cabled Truman an intemperate letter accusing Black of political extortion; for good measure, he cabled a similar letter to Congress. The outburst had the effect of embarrassing Jackson without ruffling the famously composed Black. And while Jackson had written pathbreaking opinions defending civil liberties before leaving for Germany, on his return he voted more frequently in favor of judicial restraint. This left the impression that he was in the mood for payback against Black. According to Douglas, "It was very evident in almost all our conferences that Bob Jackson thoroughly disliked Hugo Black and was out to destroy him. . . . A lot of that carried over to me also but Black, I think, was his primary target."[30]

Black and Douglas also drove Felix Frankfurter to distraction, although his animus came from a different source. A former Harvard Law School professor and celebrated civil libertarian, Frankfurter disappointed his liberal supporters on the Court by embracing a strenuous vision of judicial restraint. He considered himself the heir to Holmes and Brandeis, both of whom had been his mentors and friends, and he honorably followed the path that Holmes had marked out, deferring to Congress and the states in all but the most exceptional circumstances. But although Black and Douglas were initially inclined to follow Frankfurter in civil liberties cases because of their respect for his liberal credentials, they soon changed their minds and deserted him. This, understandably, infuriated Frankfurter, who assailed his former allies as politicians rather than judges. Writing to his friend Learned Hand, Frankfurter declared, "Hugo is a self-righteous, self-deluded part fanatic, part demagogue, who really disbelieves in Law." As for Douglas, Frankfurter called him one of the "two most completely evil men I have ever met" and disparaged him as "the most cynical, shamelessly amoral character" he had known.[31] This sort of invective was not unusual for Frankfurter, who alternated between embarrassing flattery of those he idealized—most notably Roosevelt—and vicious, gossipy denunciations of those who fell short of his own patriotic ideals. At least Frankfurter respected Black's and Douglas's intelligence, in contrast to his condescending dismissal of most of his colleagues, whom he considered his intellectual inferiors and treated as if they were dull-witted students. Frankfurter's voluble personality, obviously, was not conducive to winning friends and influencing colleagues, and contributed to the fact that he lost most of the great jurisprudential battles he fought against Black and Douglas. In particular, the Court eventually forced the states to respect most of the guarantees of the Bill of Rights, at Black's urging and over Frankfurter's objection. But toward the end of their careers, Black and Frankfurter found common cause in their shared distress over some of the liberal excesses of the Warren Court, and they exchanged affectionate letters after Frankfurter's retirement in 1962. When Frankfurter died three years later, Black wept.[32]

In their early years on the Court, Black and Douglas were most sharply tested in cases involving the president's authority to abridge civil liberties during wartime. Here their record is mixed. In 1942, President Roosevelt issued an executive order authorizing the army to engage in mass evacuations and detentions, excluding people who posed security risks from areas of the country vulnerable to attack. General John DeWitt, whom Black and Douglas knew and admired, then designated a sprawling military zone up and down the Pacific Coast and declared that all people of Japanese descent living there should be placed under curfew and eventually evacuated. In the end, more than 120,000 people, including 70,000 of Japanese descent, were herded into assembly centers and banished to relocation camps throughout the West. DeWitt's order was supported by many moderate and liberal politicians, including California's governor Earl Warren, who declared in 1943, "We don't propose to have the Japs back in California during this war if there is any lawful means of preventing it." But writing his memoirs as chief justice years later, Warren recanted his support, and he later wept when recalling the images of Japanese children being separated from their parents.[33]

And so in *Hirabayashi v. United States* (1943), the Court unanimously upheld the military curfew. Douglas, who at the time was still hungering after the 1944 vice presidential nomination, initially drafted a concurrence arguing that each person affected by the order should have an individual opportunity to prove his loyalty.[34] But whether or not he was motivated by political ambition, as some believed, Douglas eventually issued a more tepid concurrence that began with a tub-thumping warning about how "after the disastrous bombing of Pearl Harbor . . . the threat of Japanese invasion of the west coast was not fanciful but real."

The following year, in the even more infamous *Korematsu* case, the Court upheld the exclusion of more than 100,000 people from their homes. In his 6–3 opinion for the Court, Justice Black rejected the argument that singling out citizens of Japanese descent was a form of unconstitutional racial discrimination, and he emphasized that Congress had endorsed the exclusion. Black was especially moved by the idea that civilian courts should not second-guess military judgments. Douglas was more troubled, and he circulated a four-page dissenting opinion questioning the constitutionality of uprooting Japanese-Americans without giving them an opportunity to leave the military zone voluntarily. But he later withdrew his dissent and joined Black's opinion after Black emphasized that the Court had already upheld the curfew and that "evacuation and detention in an Assembly Center were inseparable." The most powerful dissenting opinion was issued by Justice Jackson, who objected that the Court's decision to validate "the principle of racial discrimination in criminal procedure and of transplanting American citizens" would lie about "like a loaded weapon ready for the hand of any authority that can bring forward a plausible claim of an urgent need."

It is easy enough, with the benefit of hindsight, to criticize Black and Douglas for upholding the evacuation of Japanese-Americans. But on the same day that the Court handed down *Korematsu*, it issued another opinion, *Ex Parte Endo*, written by Douglas, which puts both justices in a better light. *Endo* involved a young woman, Mitsuye Endo, who did not speak or read Japanese, and whose loyalty was unquestioned. Douglas's opinion concluded that she should be "given her liberty" because the congressional law authorizing curfews and evacuations in military zones said nothing about detention. The detentions had been improvised by military officers on the West Coast in response to rumor-mongering and popular hysteria from communities that did not want to receive Japanese-Americans who had been evacuated from San Francisco. Douglas's insistence that the military deserved deference when it acted with congressional support but not when it was

151

freelancing showed a sensitivity to the need for political supervision of executive excesses, which he abandoned later in his career.

In a national security case in 1953, Douglas's performance was much more erratic. The question was whether Julius and Ethel Rosenberg could be executed after having been convicted of conspiring to commit espionage and passing nuclear secrets to the Soviet Union. Black was deeply troubled by the convictions and, alone among the justices, voted to review the case each of the nine times it came before the Supreme Court. ("I believe [the Rosenbergs] to have been guilty," he later wrote, "but the prosecution wasn't conducted under the right law.")[35] Douglas, by contrast, showed Hamlet-like indecision: he voted against hearing the case on three crucial occasions when his vote would have made the difference. And then, in June 1953, after the other justices had already dispersed for the summer, he unexpectedly issued a stay of execution and then started driving west for his annual vacation. While driving through Pennsylvania that evening, he heard on the radio that Chief Justice Vinson had convened a special session of the Court the following day to reverse his emergency order. Although Douglas turned around and returned to Washington in time for the session, the Court voted against him 6–3 and the Rosenbergs were electrocuted that evening. Even sympathetic historians have been critical of Douglas's flip-flops in the Rosenberg case as the grandstanding of a justice who was trying to maintain his political viability.[36]

It's impossible to know, of course, whether Douglas actually changed his votes for political reasons. But it's clear that Black and Douglas operated within the Court in dramatically different ways. Douglas was contemptuous of the norms of the Court and of colleagues he considered intellectually slow. He made no effort to persuade colleagues of his own position, devoting his energies instead to burnishing his own reputation and scribbling books, magazine articles, and opinions during arguments on the bench. He sometimes dashed off his dissents before the majority opinions had actually circulated, and once, when a colleague was having trouble drafting the opinion from which he planned to dissent, Douglas quickly produced a draft of the majority opinion as well. Douglas angered the rest of the Court by leaving the capital before the end of each term to spend the summer in the mountains of Goose Prairie, Washington, accessible only by an antiquated telephone at the general store, miles from his cabin. In the end, his contempt for collegiality, persuasion, and the ordinary norms of legal doctrine deprived him of the lasting influence he sought.

Black, by contrast, was an evangelizing persuader rather than a loner, and used all of the formidable political skills he had learned in the Senate to bring skeptical colleagues around to his point of view. Because he cared about making deals, he felt less free than Douglas to change a position after he made a commitment, but since Black was more pragmatic, he was willing to compromise or to add language to an opinion if he thought it would win him additional votes. Justice Harry Blackmun, who said that Douglas "never had a close friend on the Court," called Black a "canny, lovable manipulator . . . ever the politician, ever the U.S. Senator still."[37] Chief Justice Earl Warren, no slouch at lobbying himself, trusted Black's political skills so implicitly that during the years they served together, from 1953 to 1969, he would stop by Black's chambers after the justices' conference to discuss who should be assigned majority opinions.[38]

Black's pragmatic concern about the institutional prestige of the Court was vividly displayed during his encounters with Douglas in cases involving racial segregation, culminating in 1954 in *Brown v. Board of Education*. In the early 1950s, Black and Douglas were ahead of most of their colleagues in urging an end to segregated schools. Black had no hesitation about striking down segregation,

The Warren Court in 1955, after the arrival of John M. Harlan (standing at far right), the grandson and namesake of the great jurist. Seated at the far left is Felix Frankfurter, who often opposed Black and Douglas during their years on the Court. Black sits between Frankfurter and Chief Justice Warren, and Douglas is seated at the far right.

telling his son, "I agree with old Justice Harlan's dissent in *Plessy v. Ferguson.*"[39] But Black was the only justice who had grown up in the Deep South, and he alone predicted correctly that if the Court outlawed segregation, the South would react with riots. At the first conference in which the justices discussed *Brown,* in the fall of 1952, Black warned that the states, while pretending to obey the Court, would take violent and evasive action, including perhaps abolishing their public school systems. He also worried that district courts would have to issue injunctions against those who resisted segregation; and as a supporter of labor unions, he feared the illiberal uses of "law by injunction." Nevertheless, he had no doubt that the "basic purpose" of the Fourteenth Amendment was to protect African-Americans against racial discrimination, while the purpose of segregation was to discriminate on the basis of race. Therefore, Black announced that he "would vote . . . to end segregation," despite his doubts.[40] Black's confidence that segregation was unconstitutional is hard to explain, since neither the text nor original understanding of the Fourteenth Amendment unequivocally forbids it. But perhaps he was stung by the accusations of racism at his confirmation hearings and resolved, like Harlan, to prove his critics wrong with missionary zeal.

By contrast, Douglas, who had no history or firsthand experience with racial conflict, announced that "segregation is an easy problem" and the answer was "very simple." "No classifications on the basis of race can be made. . . . A negro can't be put by the state in one room because he's black and another put in the other room because he's white."[41] For Douglas, the immorality of segregation was enough to make it unconstitutional, and in this case at least, his tendency to simplify complicated legal issues may have served him well.[42]

A few days after the Court struck down school segregation in twenty-one states in May 1954, Black went to a dinner held by the publisher of *The New Republic*. Other guests congratulated him on helping to herald a color-blind society. "There's going to be trouble and people are going to die," Black replied, adding that "before the tree of liberalism could be renewed in the South, a few candidates must water it with their blood."[43]

Black's fears were soon vindicated. *Brown* was popular in the country as a whole, where more than 50 percent of the public supported the end of segregation, but in the South, the reaction was as violent as Black had predicted. In trying to choose a remedy for segregation, Black was especially concerned that the Supreme Court would issue orders that southern obstructionists would disobey. He insisted that the Court should "write a decree and quit. . . . The less we say, the better we are."[44] Therefore, he and Douglas alone insisted on immediate desegregation, but only for the Kansas schoolchildren who were seeking admission to a segregated school in the *Brown* case.[45] The other justices, led by Frankfurter, preferred a gradualist approach that Black only reluctantly accepted. The Court ultimately required segregation "with all deliberate speed"—an invitation for recalcitrance and delay that the South thoroughly exploited.

In the end, it was the civil rights movement and federal Civil Rights Act of 1964, not the *Brown* decision, that led to real desegregation in the South. Black and Douglas disagreed in some of the cases involving the arrest of civil rights protestors for sit-ins, which Black called "sit-downs." He feared mob rule and saw the sit-ins as a threat to private property, while Douglas, less of a literalist, viewed them as a form of political expression. In 1966, for example, Black wrote a 5–4 opinion for the Court upholding the trespass convictions of more than thirty University of Tallahassee students who had blocked the driveway of the local jail to protest the arrest of other students a day earlier for demonstrating on behalf of civil rights. Black viewed sit-ins as conduct, not speech, and announced that the Constitution "does not forbid a State to control the use of its own property for its own lawful nondiscriminatory purpose." Douglas, who viewed the right to protest far more expansively, wrote a blistering dissent comparing the jailhouse to the Bastille, adding, "When it houses political prisoners or those who many think are unjustly held, it is an obvious center for protest." He later suggested, with some plausibility, that Black had been traumatized by the experience of picketers circling his house after his Supreme Court appointment to protest his membership in the Ku Klux Klan.

To the end, Black was a desegregationist, rather than an integrationist, who believed in equality of opportunity, not equality of results.

He was fierce in uprooting obstacles to court-ordered desegregation, and when Mississippi, in 1969, continued to drag its feet, Black blamed the delay on the Court's approval of desegregation with "all deliberate speed." He would never join another opinion that included the phrase, he announced, and, as a result, the Court handed down a decision demanding immediate desegregation.[46] But this new focus on racially balanced results opened the door to court-ordered busing—a policy that Black (unlike Douglas) opposed because the word *bus*, as one colleague suggested, was not in the Constitution. In fact, Black's suspicion was driven by his long-standing opposition to rule by judicial injunction, and to his conviction—once again accurate as it turned out—that busing would provoke massive southern opposition.

It pained Black greatly that Alabama shunned him after *Brown* came down. The state legislature passed a resolution declaring that he couldn't be buried in the state; his son had to abandon a planned run for Congress from Birmingham; and Black couldn't visit the state for more than a decade without wearing a bulletproof vest provided by the Secret Service. But Black proved to be more prescient than all of his colleagues about the reaction to the decision on the ground, and in the end he cared more about the Court as an institution than about his own nostalgic attachment to the region he never stopped loving.

Another area of law that Black and Douglas transformed was the application of the Bill of Rights to the states. Once again, Black was the intellectual leader, taking up the crusade that Justice Harlan had begun in the early 1900s, when he insisted that the states, as well as the federal government, should be required to respect all of the fundamental guarantees in the Bill of Rights, not only free speech but also the right to be free from unreasonable searches and seizures and compelled self-incrimination. Black's leading opponent in this crusade was Felix Frankfurter, the acolyte of Justice Holmes's strenuous vision of judicial abstinence, who dismissed Harlan and Black's position as an "eccentric exception" to the general understanding that the states should have to obey only those guarantees that judges decided were fundamental. Frankfurter's position struck Black as an invitation to judicial subjectivity—why should judges pick and choose among the various guarantees of the Bill of Rights? In a 1947 case involving compelled self-incrimination, Black offered extensive historical evidence to support his conclusion that the framers of the Fourteenth Amendment intended the Bill of Rights to bind states. Frankfurter and his minions at Harvard Law School scorned Black's argument as the simplistic polemic of a self-taught bumpkin, but subsequent scholarship has vindicated Black and Harlan's broad historical claims as more sound than Frankfurter's.[47]

In the early 1960s, the Court finally accepted Black and Harlan's claims, but in piecemeal fashion. It eventually held that the states had to respect most of the guarantees of the Bill of Rights rather than picking and choosing among them. The most satisfying victories for Black involved cases incorporating the basic guarantees of fair criminal procedures, which, as he recalled from his days as a police court judge, were central to fair trials. In perhaps the most inspiring case of all, Black wrote the opinion for the Court in *Gideon v. Wainwright* (1963), which held for the first time that states had to provide court-appointed lawyers for all defendants in felony cases. The case was brought by a poor suspect who had been convicted of a barroom burglary he did not commit. From jail, he handwrote his own petition to the Supreme Court which eventually persuaded the justices to take the case. Black relished the opportunity to repudiate a 1942 decision, from which he had dissented, which held that judges should decide, on a case-by-case basis, whether lawyers were necessary.

When Black had explicit constitutional language on which to hang his hat, he was happy to force the states to respect it. He joined

Chief Justice Warren in the controversial decision in *Miranda v. Arizona* requiring police to inform suspects of their right to remain silent and their right to a court-appointed lawyer. He also joined *Mapp v. Ohio*, which held that illegally seized evidence had to be excluded from state trials—perhaps the most influential criminal procedure decision of the 1960s. But Black balked when it came to second-guessing the legality of police searches. He refused, for example, to join the Court's decision in 1967 to strike down wiretapping without a warrant as a violation of the Fourth Amendment's guarantee against unreasonable searches and seizures. Conversations cannot be "seized" within the ordinary meaning of language, he argued; the framers were aware of eavesdropping but did not believe the Fourth Amendment prohibited it. Douglas, by contrast, insisted that electronic surveillance posed a serious threat to privacy, and he objected to one justice's suggestion that the president might be able to engage in surveillance without a warrant in cases where he decided national security was threatened. (Douglas's statement might have seemed paranoid, except for the fact that FBI files later confirmed that he and Black had actually been under surveillance during the 1950s by J. Edgar Hoover. The request may have come from Chief Justice Vinson, who believed that Douglas was a subversive radical and encouraged clerks and the Supreme Court police to spy on him.)[48]

As Black and Douglas slowly drifted apart in cases involving civil rights and criminal procedure, the alignments on the Court were changing as well. President Eisenhower's four appointments in the 1950s—Earl Warren, John M. Harlan, William J. Brennan, and Potter Stewart—created two new leaders of the liberal and conservative blocks: Harlan for the conservatives and Brennan for the liberals. Harlan was the grandson of the first Justice Harlan, for whom he was named, although he used his middle initial rather than his full name to distinguish himself from his celebrated relative. An establishment Wall Street lawyer with the impeccable credentials that eluded

Douglas—including Princeton and the Rhodes Scholarship—he commended himself to Eisenhower as a lower court judge when he upheld the convictions of suspected Communists. Eisenhower chose Harlan to replace Robert Jackson, who died of a heart attack in 1954, but Harlan proved more temperamentally effective than either the defensive Jackson or the arrogant Frankfurter in building ideological bridges. An instinctive patrician with beautiful manners, he wrote vigorous defenses of the right to privacy, moved by the sensibility he shared with his fellow establishment lawyer, Franklin Roosevelt's secretary of war, Henry Stimson, who once disbanded a spying operation on the principle that "gentlemen don't read each other's mail." This led him to make common cause with Douglas (and against Black) in the late-1960s opinions recognizing the right of married couples to use contraceptives and the right of suspects to be free from unreasonable forms of electronic surveillance. Although Harlan's conception of privacy was more carefully defined than Douglas's, the unexpected alliance between the establishment conservative and the antiestablishment liberal helped to enshrine the right to privacy in the Constitution.

Harlan rejected Black's absolutist vision of free speech and his effort to apply the entire Bill of Rights to the states. He also dissented from the Warren Court's leading criminal procedure decisions— including *Miranda*—and insisted repeatedly that respect for states' rights (which he called "Our Federalism") could protect individual freedom more effectively than heavy-handed judicial interventions. But he and Black developed an increasingly warm friendship, beginning with their shared opposition to the Warren Court's protection of sit-ins by civil rights protesters. "Things are very troublesome at the Court," Harlan declared in 1963. "Justice Black has been a rock. He is saving the Court. Some men are institutional men, who care about the institution, and Black is one of them."[49] Black respected Harlan for his own devotion to the institution, and reciprocated Harlan's praise with his own highest compliment. "John Harlan," he declared, "is one of the few people who convince me that there is such a thing as a good Republican."[50] As the Court grew more liberal in the 1960s, Harlan often found himself in dissent, but his ability to win the respect of both Black and Douglas is a testament to the appeal of his gentle, aristocratic temperament. Today Harlan is lionized by moderate-minded judicial liberals and conservatives, who revere his respect for precedent, stability, and continuity: both Chief Justice John Roberts and Justice Ruth Bader Ginsburg, for example, have invoked him as their hero.

On the other side of the political spectrum, William Brennan emerged in the 1960s as leader of the liberal faction of the Court, as Black moved to the right and Douglas became even more of an individualistic maverick. Brennan, a former state assemblyman from New Jersey, had a politician's strategic gifts: "Hiya, pal" was his usual greeting to colleagues and clerks, and he liked to remark, "With five votes, you can do anything around here," holding out his hand, with his five fingers extended. "Five, count 'em, five!" Unlike Douglas, he was always willing to compromise, accepting what he called "half a loaf rather than a full loaf" in order to build a majority. Soon after Brennan joined the Court in 1956, Black recognized that his affable personality and political skills would make him a force to be reckoned with. "Bill is my heir," he declared.[51] And Brennan vindicated this prediction, taking over Black's role in roaming the hallways and lobbying in chambers in search of votes. As the 1960s progressed, Brennan replaced Black as the deputy on whom Chief Justice Warren most heavily relied, and it was Brennan who was responsible for turning many of Black's dissenting opinions into majority opinions, in cases concerning free speech and criminal rights. As Black moved away from Brennan and Douglas as the decade progressed, siding with Harlan in cases concerning voting rights and reapportionment, Brennan and Douglas lamented the loss of their former leader. "Hugo changed, the man changed, right in front of us," Brennan observed. "We talked about it much, the Chief and Bill Douglas probably more than anyone else. Bill especially was really hurt. We lost our fifth vote."[52]

Although Black moved away from the increasingly aggressive liberals in their efforts to extend civil rights, criminal procedure, and privacy, he was steadfast throughout most of his career in defense of the First Amendment guarantees of free expression, free press, and freedom of religion. Surprisingly enough, both Black and Douglas got off to a shaky start in First Amendment religion cases. In 1940, they joined Felix Frankfurter's decision to uphold the right of public schools to expel students who refused to salute the American flag. The suit was brought by children of Jehovah's Witnesses, who believed that pledging allegiance to the flag, rather than the Bible, threatened the supreme authority of scripture. After extensive hand-wringing, Frankfurter declared that mandatory flag salutes might be foolish, but they were not unconstitutional. A year later, however, after a Jehovah's Witness meeting hall was burned in Maine, Black and Douglas decided they had made a mistake. In 1942, both of them filed a dissenting opinion in a case requiring the Jehovah's Witnesses to pay a licensing fee to sell their religious publications. Then, the following year, they helped persuade a majority of the Court to overrule Frankfurter's opinion and strike down compulsory flag salutes.

From that moment onward, Black was fierce in his defense of the rights of religious conscience and his opposition to state-sponsored religious rituals or aid to religion of any kind. Part of Black's zealous insistence on the separation of church and state came from his Baptist upbringing, part from his First Amendment literalism, and part from his old anti-Catholicism, which made him especially wary of state aid to parochial schools. Indeed, Black's concern about religious diversity was fanned by the anti-Catholic screeds of the strict separationist Paul Blanshard, who warned that the predominance of the Catholic Church would lead other religions to be suppressed.[53] Douglas, by contrast, had abandoned the Presbyterianism of his father, scorning the hypocrisy of organized religion in the same way that he scorned all manifestations of "the Establishment." He enjoyed discomfiting the sensibilities of the pious, and—influenced by his international travels and fervent environmentalism—ended up embracing a kind of nonsectarian Jeffersonian vision of "nature's God" to explain the spiritual glories of the wilderness. All this, combined with his political ambition, made Douglas less sure-footed than Black in religion cases.

In the *Everson* case in 1947, for example, Black wrote a stirring opinion for the Court upholding a New Jersey law that allowed local public school districts to pay for the transportation of students to Catholic parochial schools as well as other private schools. Black rejected the claim that this amounted to unconstitutional aid to religion, since the money for transportation went to the parents, rather than to the schools, and they could choose to spend it at religious or secular private schools as they saw fit. Quoting Jefferson, he announced, "The First Amendment has erected a wall between church and state. That wall must be kept high and impregnable. We could not approve the slightest breach." (Justice Jackson, in a stylish dissent, said Black's performance brought to mind Lord Byron's Julia in *The Rape of the Lock,* who "whispering 'I will ne'er consent,'—consented.")

Douglas joined Black in striking down religious classes in public schools in 1948. But only four years later, Douglas changed his mind and wrote a 5–4 opinion for the Court holding that New York could allow students to leave school early to attend religious classes in their own churches and temples. "We are a religious people whose institutions presuppose a Supreme Being," Douglas intoned over Black's dissent. His colleagues thought Douglas was trying to position himself for the 1952 presidential nomination, and Justice Jackson, in a separate dissent, all but accused him of changing his position for political purposes. "Today's judgment will be more interesting to students of psychology and of the judicial processes than to students of constitutional law," he wrote insinuatingly.

By 1962, when Black wrote his most important religion opinion, *Engel v. Vitale*, which struck down state-sponsored prayer in schools, Douglas had abandoned his presidential ambitions. Although he had originally voted to uphold the prayer, Douglas now agreed with the Court that New York could not require public school students to recite a purportedly nondenominational prayer composed by the Board of Regents. Black wrote, "It is neither sacrilegious nor antireligious to say that each separate government in this country should stay out of the business of writing or sanctioning official prayers." In delivering the opinion from the bench, he spontaneously added, in a trembling voice, "The prayer of each man from his soul must be his and his alone."[54] Douglas ended up writing an emotional and inflammatory concurrence that went even further than Black did, calling into question even minor government support for religious expression, such as the Pledge of Allegiance and the words "In God We Trust" on the currency. Partly because of Douglas's concurrence, the decision was one of the most controversial the Warren Court ever handed down: the Court received more negative mail about the *Engel* case than any other, and one study found that no case has inspired more opposition.[55] Douglas's performance—first supporting the prayer and then voting to eradicate all traces of religion from public life—was characteristically erratic.

If Douglas and Black traveled different paths in religion cases, they were side by side more often in cases involving free speech and free press. Free speech absolutism was Black and Douglas's crowning joint achievement: Black famously insisted that the First Amendment's command that "Congress shall make no law . . . abridging the freedom of speech" should be taken literally. "No law," he insisted, meant "*no law*," and he opposed government efforts to punish libel and defamation as well as obscenity. He and Douglas wrote some of their most inspiring defenses of free speech during the McCarthy era of the 1950s, when it was genuinely under siege. Black attributed his absolutism to his hero, Jefferson, declaring, "I believe with Jefferson that it is time enough for government to step in to regulate people when they *do* something, not when they *say* something."[56] (Black also liked that Jefferson was "for rigid adherence to constitutional language," that he was willing to "construe Acts of Congress liberally, upon occasion," and that "he coupled a positive faith in human beings with a predominantly negative attitude toward political agencies and institutions.")[57]

Ultimately, Douglas was willing to protect free speech more broadly than any justice in history, although Black may have had more lasting influence. In their first important encounter with free speech, Black and Douglas refined Justice Holmes's famous observation that speech could be banned whenever it posed a "clear and present danger" of illegal activity. Black worried that this standard would allow the government to suppress critics who advocated resistance to the law, even if there was no immediate danger of anyone acting on their suggestions. Instead, Black and Douglas insisted in 1941 "that the substantive evil must be extremely serious and the degree of imminence extremely high before utterances can be punished."

This new and more demanding standard served Black and Douglas well in the many cases involving the McCarthyite hysteria of the 1950s. When the Court, in 1951, upheld the conviction of Communist Party leaders under the Smith Act of 1950, Black objected that they had been charged not with attempting to overthrow the government, or with saying anything designed to overthrow the government, but merely for agreeing to assemble, talk, and publish revolutionary ideas at some point in the future. Any connection between their conspiracy and future lawless action was too remote, Black insisted, to justify censorship of speech and the press. (In his scribbled comments on the margins of Chief Justice Vinson's illiberal majority opinion, Black made his disdain for the scare-mongering clear: "The goblin'll get you," he wrote of the dissidents. "Bad men! To jail with them!")[58] Douglas wrote one of his most eloquent and persuasive dissenting opinions, pointing out that there was absolutely no evidence that the advocacy of Soviet-style Communism was on the verge of succeeding, and that subversive advocacy could be suppressed "only when the provocateurs among us move from speech to action."

Throughout the witch-hunting excesses of the 1950s, Black and Douglas stood bravely together, originally in dissent, and then, as the Court under Chief Justice Warren grew more liberal, increasingly in the majority. They voted to protect people who were convicted for associating with suspected Communists, radicals who were punished for making pro-Communist speeches, and suspects who were forced to incriminate themselves by congressional investigating committees. Black's own zeal in the 1930s as the chair of a similarly intrusive Senate committee seems only to have increased his sensitivity to the dangers of legislative investigations. In June 1957, a day that congressional critics called "Red Monday," the Court handed down four incendiary decisions, with Black and Douglas in the majority, that limited the scope of state and federal legislative investigation and lectured Congress about the dangers of broad intrusions into citizens' private lives. Although the Court would retreat from some of these decisions three years later, in the face of virulent criticism from Congress, the constitutional principles for broad protection of dissident speech had been established.

In the 1960s and '70s, when the American public was in more of a mood to protect speech critical of the government, the Court was prepared to follow suit. In 1964, in *New York Times v. Sullivan,* the Court unanimously reversed a $500,000 libel verdict against the *New York Times* obtained by an Alabama police commissioner who objected to an ad placed by civil rights protesters that criticized police conduct during a demonstration. In a memorable opinion, Justice Brennan said that public debate should be "uninhibited, robust, and wide-open," and therefore public officials could not sue for libel unless the statement in question was made with "actual malice"—that is, with knowledge it was false or reckless disregard for whether it was true. In his concurring opinion, which Douglas joined, Black lamented that the Court had not gone far enough. The "actual malice" language was too vague, he objected, and both the states and federal government should have no power at all to impose damages for libel on the press in response to criticisms of public officials. Black ended by expressing regret that the Court had stopped short of recognizing the right of the press "to criticize officials and discuss public affairs with impunity."

Black and Douglas eventually diverged in free speech cases because of their different attitudes toward the constitutional text. Black was less willing than Douglas to protect forms of symbolic expression—like burning flags or draft cards in protest—that he viewed as conduct rather than speech. "I've never said that freedom of speech gives people the right to tramp up and down the streets by the thousands," he said in a television interview in 1968 that once again indirectly invoked his own experience of being picketed. "It doesn't have anything that protects a man's right to walk around and around my house, if he wants to, fasten my people, my family up into the house, make them afraid to go out of doors. . . . That's conduct."[59] The following year, Black dissented from a case protecting the right to wear armbands to protest the Vietnam War. He took an equally cramped view of political protest during the civil rights era; and he emasculated the First Amendment right to freedom of assembly by holding that protesters could not demonstrate on public property without the government's consent. The arbitrariness of Black's judgments—he insisted that communicating ideas by burning flags or wearing armbands is "conduct" while having sex on camera is "speech"—suggests that Black's choice of formal categories may not have been completely divorced from his personal convictions.

Nevertheless, Black and Douglas converged once again in the final great free speech case of their careers, united by a common antagonist, President Richard M. Nixon. In 1971, the Nixon administration wanted to prevent the *New York Times* and *Washington Post* from publishing the Pentagon Papers, and the Court rejected its arguments. Black stayed up late into the night to write one of his greatest opinions. "Only a free and unrestrained press can effectively expose deception in government," he wrote. "And paramount among the responsibilities of a free press is the duty to prevent any part of the government from deceiving the people and sending them off to distant lands to die of foreign fevers and foreign shot and shell." Black was paraphrasing an old Confederate ballad, "I Am a Good Old Rebel." Douglas added a less carefully crafted but still vigorous dissent insisting that the purpose of the First Amendment is to prevent the government from suppressing "material that is embarrassing to the powers-that-be." As Black walked through the red velvet curtains after the decision was announced, his wife, Elizabeth, said, "Honey, if this is your swan song, it's a good one."[60] Indeed, the *Pentagon Papers* case was a fitting swan song for both free speech compatriots, who had redefined the law of free expression over three decades.

Douglas took special pleasure in ruling against Nixon, because he had just fought off an impeachment inquiry that Nixon instigated the summer before the Pentagon Papers case came down. Representative Gerald Ford, famously declaring that an impeachable offense is whatever a majority of the House decides, assailed Douglas for a

Douglas and his fourth wife, Cathy Heffernan, whom he met when she was a twenty-year-old waitress and college student, after their wedding in 1966.

variety of improprieties. He had, for example, written an article on folksinging for a pornographic magazine whose libel dispute was before the Court and, in another erotic magazine, had called for America's youth to rebel against the establishment the way the colonists rebelled against King George.[61] There were also charges that Douglas had accepted money from a foundation run by a Las Vegas casino operator, but no concrete wrongdoing emerged. FBI surveillance and other reports observed that Douglas was prone to binge drinking, attendance at left-wing meetings, and lunging at stewardesses whom he invited to visit him at the Court. Black expressed disappointment in Douglas's self-destructive behavior, incessant womanizing, and shoddy opinions, lamenting that Douglas, with all his talents, did not accomplish more. "What a waste," he said. "The guy has the best mind on the Court. He could have been the greatest justice ever. It's a shame Bill is so lazy. [If he] worked harder, we'd be in better shape."[62] Still, Black and Douglas sustained strong sentimental ties, and during the impeachment threats, Black passed Douglas a note on the bench that read: "Dear Bill: If they try to impeach you, I'll resign and be your lawyer. I have one more hard trial left in me. Hugo."[63]

After the *Pentagon Papers* case was announced, Black, who was eighty-five, declined rapidly. He checked into the hospital in July 1971 and was diagnosed with inflamed arteries. Although he yearned to break the longevity records held by John Marshall and Stephen Field, the only two justices who had served longer than he had, his failing health made that impossible. On September 17, 1971, having served on the Court for thirty-four years and one month—only four months short of Marshall—Black retired. A week later, he was dead.

Douglas held on for nearly four more years, but his behavior grew increasingly unpredictable. No longer bothering to pretend he was constrained by previous legal precedents or conventional legal arguments, he wrote a series of polemics on behalf of whatever political cause offended his sense of justice. "I'm ready to bend the law in favor of the environment and against the corporations," Douglas told a friend.[64] Convinced that the Vietnam War was unconstitutional, he issued an ill-written decision while on summer vacation ordering the government to halt the bombing in Cambodia. ("We know that someone is about to die. . . . I see no reason to . . . consider the harm to our foreign policy if one or a thousand more bombs do not drop.") All eight of his colleagues reversed the order by telephone only six hours later.[65] He wrote a passionate dissent in 1973 objecting to President Nixon's use of the army to spy on antiwar protesters, invoking a "tradition [that] goes back to the Declaration of Independence in which it was recited that the King 'has affected to render the Military independent of and superior to the Civil Power.'"[66]

And in *Roe v. Wade*, in 1973, he expanded his argument about "penumbras" and "emanations" from the right to privacy further than any other justice was willing to do. (Black, who scorned Douglas's whole idea of penumbras and emanations, had made clear that he opposed a constitutional right to abortion during discussions of a case two years earlier.) Douglas declared in a concurring opinion to *Roe* that the "Blessings of Liberty" protected by the Constitution included at least three sweeping categories of rights that were not explicitly mentioned in the Constitution itself: "First is the autonomous control over the development and expression of one's intellect, interests, tastes, and personality. . . . Second is freedom of choice in the basic decisions of one's life respecting marriage, divorce, procreation, contraception, and the education and upbringing of children. . . . Third is the freedom to care for one's health and person, freedom from bodily restraint or compulsion, freedom to walk, stroll, or loaf." The catalogue was either inspiring or risible, depending on one's views about judicial creativity, but all of it was derived not from conventional legal material but from Douglas's own romantic abstractions about justice.

Douglas's end was sad. Enfeebled by strokes, he refused to resign even though he had to be helped to the bench in a wheelchair and his attention would wander for long stretches of arguments. He drafted the second volume of his autobiography, so self-aggrandizing and indiscreet in its gossipy score-settling that it still makes the jaw drop. "This attitude toward 'enemies,' this use of 'threats' marked the essence of Nixon's *Mein Kampf*," Douglas wrote. "I personally thought his ascendancy to power marked the inquest of the Free Society which had been our boast since Jefferson and Madison."[67] Finally, his former clerks convinced Douglas that he could no longer continue. On November 12, 1975, he resigned, having served thirty-six years on the Court, longer than any other justice in history. He was wheeled into the justices' conference room, struggled to raise his arm, and exclaimed, "Keep the faith!"—his favorite slogan. A little more than four years later, he died.

In a polarized age, Douglas's legacy is hard neutrally to assess. Douglas had a ready answer to critics who charged that his opinions were hastily drafted, lacking in legal craftsmanship, and focused on results rather than legal reasoning. "For those who liked the result, it was scholarship," he observed shrewdly.[68] And perhaps he was right. There are many today who admire Douglas for his passionate defense of liberal ideals and are willing to overlook his personal and professional shortcomings. For Douglas's admirers, his recklessness and his passion went hand in hand and allowed him to pierce through legal technicalities in the interest of serving the cause of justice.

But there are other, less ideological liberals who acknowledge that Douglas's lack of interest in conventional legal arguments, and in the Supreme Court as an institution, ultimately harmed the cause of liberalism rather than helping it. "Few have seen Douglas as a model judge, and almost no one can be found to defend seriously the written part of his judicial career," writes Douglas's former clerk Lucas A. Powe, now a law professor at the University of Texas. "His opinions were not models; they appear too hastily written; and they are easy to ignore. For those of us who think Douglas was correct in his results and instincts, this is too bad. . . . By wholly eschewing doctrine, he not only suffered a loss of professional esteem, he suffered a loss of influence. . . . Because Douglas was a genius, there is a feeling of loss from so wonderful a mind's eschewing the minimum formalities of the job."[69]

Douglas is perhaps the most dramatic example in the history of the Court of intelligence and ability being undermined by a self-destructive temperament. As a result, Douglas today has nothing like the influence even of Holmes, who shared Douglas's self-absorption, dislike for working with others, natural intelligence, and vision of law as essentially politics. At the end of his life, Douglas liked to describe what he hoped would be his own legacy by quoting Holmes, who wrote of "the secret isolated joy of the thinker, who knows that, a hundred years after he is dead and forgotten, men who never heard of him will be moving to the measure of his thought."[70] But Douglas, unlike Holmes, had a contempt for the legal establishment (and for all establishments) and less reverence for the Court as an institution. As a result, Holmes today is still revered, while Douglas is dismissed as something of a crank.

Douglas's most lasting legacy includes his achievements as a corporate law scholar and head of the SEC, his environmentalism and his Jeffersonian (or Thoreauvian) utopianism: he persuaded the *Washington Post* to crusade for the preservation of the C&O canal in Georgetown by challenging the editors to a long hike. And he proposed a second Bill of Rights that would protect nature lovers against government and corporate predators by creating a legal presumption that threats to natural resources were threats to the common good. "The wilderness is a refuge for automated man," Douglas wrote in a characteristic soliloquy, bringing "into one's drab life an endless wonder and excitement of nature's flair for individuality rather than conformity."[71] Like Jefferson, Douglas was a sentimental idealist who romanticized nature and whose beliefs were often more radical than his contemporary political allies. And like Jefferson, Douglas is more honored as a poetic philosopher than a constitutional thinker.

In the legal arena, however, Douglas came to personify the liberal excesses of the Warren Court and helped to trigger the conservative judicial movement that culminated, in the 1980s and 1990s, in the appointment of justices who resolved to repudiate Douglas's jurisprudence by any means necessary. It is not a coincidence that Justice Clarence Thomas has in his chambers a sign ridiculing Douglas's opinion in the *Griswold* contraceptives case: "Please don't emanate in the penumbras." The conservative promise to appoint "strict constructionist" judges who refused to invent rights not explicitly enumerated in the Constitution is a rebuke to the freewheeling judicial abstract expressionism represented most flamboyantly by Douglas.

Black's legacy, by contrast, is more secure: as a liberal textualist, he completed the post–New Deal judicial revolution and then managed to foreshadow the conservative counterrevolution. Black may have disappointed liberals at the end of his career with his rigid refusal to recognize a right to privacy and to protect symbolic speech, but his devotion to the institutional legitimacy of the Court impressed his conservative colleagues in the 1960s, such as Harlan and Frankfurter, who worried that the liberals were going too far. Although he never lost a shrewd politician's sensitivity to the facts of individual cases and the amenities of relations with his colleagues, Black behaved less like a politician on the bench than Douglas did, because he was more concerned about judicial legitimacy than about particular political results.

As a result, Black became the thoughtful conservatives' favorite liberal, and his view that judges should not invent new rights—and that judicial subjectivity could be constrained only if the Constitution was interpreted in light of its text and original understanding—came to define the essence of conservative strict constructionism a generation after he died. After Black left the Court, the three pillars of his liberal legacy remained unchallenged: his attempts to wean the Court from the doctrine of substantive due process; his uncompromising devotion to the First Amendment; and, most important of all, his intellectual leadership in applying the Bill of Rights against the states.

The only part of Black's legacy that his conservative successors questioned was his validation of the New Deal: they were less pragmatic than he was and far more willing to strike down federal laws they felt exceeded Congress's power to regulate interstate commerce. In this respect, despite his sentimental attachment to Jeffersonian populism, Black was much more the jurisprudential heir of the canny nationalists Marshall and Harlan, and he shared Harlan's proselytizing temperament as well. ("At heart, he was a Baptist preacher," Douglas said of Black after his death.)[72] By insisting that judges should enforce all the provisions of the Constitution without deciding whether they are wise or prudent, Black led the Court out of the wilderness of legal realism and answered the charge that all law is politics. For this reason, his legacy has spoken to conservatives as well as liberals for more than half a century. He ushered in a new liberal judicial era at the beginning of his career and a new conservative era at the end.

CHAPTER FOUR

TWO FACES

OF

CONSERVATISM

William H. Rehnquist

Antonin Scalia

For years, Chief Justice William H. Rehnquist and Justice Antonin Scalia shared a passionate dislike of the 1966 decision in *Miranda v. Arizona*, which requires police officers to read suspects their rights. Both justices spent more than a decade ridiculing the constitutional soundness of *Miranda* and calling on the Supreme Court to chip away at it. But in 2000, without any warning, Rehnquist voted unexpectedly to uphold *Miranda*. In his 7–2 opinion for the Court in *Dickerson v. United States*, Rehnquist observed, "Miranda has become embedded in routine police practice to the point where the warnings have become part of our national culture." Rehnquist's apostasy provoked one of Justice Scalia's most vitriolic dissenting opinions. Joined by Justice Clarence Thomas, Scalia declared, "Today's judgment converts *Miranda* from a milestone of judicial overreaching into the very Cheops' Pyramid (or perhaps the Sphinx would be a better analogue) of judicial arrogance."

Rehnquist's evolution from *Miranda*'s leading critic to its improbable savior infuriated conservatives and confused liberals, yet it turned out to be emblematic of his long tenure. Liberals always simplistically lumped Rehnquist with the other conservatives on the Court, while conservatives never fully embraced him as one of their own. Furthermore, liberals never understood how significantly and frequently Rehnquist departed from doctrinaire conservative ideology, and conservatives failed to grasp that his tactical flexibility was more effective than the rigid purity of justices like Scalia. In truth, Rehnquist often staked out a pragmatic middle ground between the Right and Left and showed that it was a very good place to be. With efficiency and amiability, he led a Court that put the brakes on some of the excesses of the Earl Warren era while keeping pace with the sentiments of a majority of the country—generally siding with economic conservatives and against cultural conservatives. He was far more devoted to preserving tradition and majority rule than the generation of fire-breathing conservatives who followed him, a group led by Scalia. And his administration of the Court was quietly effective, making him one of the most successful chief justices of the twentieth century.

Rehnquist's political sensibility and experience were central to his stewardship. By temperament and training he represented an older strain of conservatism that has come to be seen as milder than the ideology that became prominent during his chief justiceship. Having cut his political teeth in Arizona in the era of Barry Goldwater, he came to the Court with a less angry and embattled attitude toward American democracy than younger conservatives like Scalia and Thomas, who developed a strong suspicion of Congress while working for Republican presidents in the post-Watergate era. Unlike Scalia, Rehnquist never had an apocalyptic sense of having lost the culture wars, because he was never intensely committed to fighting them in the first place. It is impossible to imagine Rehnquist having written the

While Chief Justice William H. Rehnquist (left) was praised by liberal and conservative colleagues for his amiability and efficiency, Antonin Scalia alienated his ideological allies with his angry dissents and ad hominem attacks.

screeds in which Scalia routinely indulges about the direction of contemporary American culture. "The Court must be living in another world," Scalia declared in 1996. "Day by day, case by case, it is busy designing a Constitution for a country I do not recognize."

Because Rehnquist was never a doctrinaire conservative, he was never fully appreciated by the conservative faithful. Their hero and intellectual standard-bearer is Scalia, who insists that he alone on the Court has a consistent judicial philosophy. Like Hugo Black, Scalia has long denounced the idea of the "living Constitution," which holds that judges should interpret the Constitution to reflect the changing beliefs of an evolving society. Instead, Scalia insists that the document should be interpreted in light of its "original meaning." There is nothing objectionable about this methodology, which in the hands of Black was sometimes useful in reducing the scope of judicial discretion. (Indeed, Scalia was so successful in proselytizing on behalf of the democratic virtues of his "original meaning" approach to the Constitution that a leading liberal legal scholar conceded in a debate with Scalia that "we are all originalists now.")[1] But Scalia applied his originalism with a heavier hand than Black, and without his pragmatic sensitivity to political context. As a result, he often alienated his conservative colleagues with his willingness to overturn precedents that they considered settled. He also alienated his liberal colleagues, who were unimpressed by his protestations of ideological purity and judicial restraint; they concluded that he applied his "original meaning" philosophy inconsistently, often choosing among conflicting conservative principles in order to reach a conservative result. Finally, in Scalia's hands "original meaning" was hardly a recipe for judicial restraint. If judicial activism is defined by a judge's willingness to strike down federal or state laws, then Scalia and Thomas were among the more activist justices on the Rehnquist Court, surpassed only by Anthony Kennedy and Sandra Day O'Connor. By contrast, Rehnquist was tied with Stephen Breyer for the role of second-most restrained justice, after Ruth Bader Ginsburg.[2] While all the conservatives on the Rehnquist Court insisted publicly that the judiciary should occupy a modest role in American politics and should defer to the judgment of elected legislators, Rehnquist was the conservative justice who most consistently practiced what he preached.

But perhaps the main reason that Scalia was never as influential as Rehnquist involved not intellectual inconsistency but judicial temperament. Although his jurisprudential premises were unobjectionable, Scalia seemed, like Thomas Jefferson, to view every disagreement as a form of apostasy. As a result he had no volume knob. Every dissenting opinion predicted the apocalypse and every colleague who disagreed with him was denounced as a politician or a fool. For Scalia, temperament and ideology were intimately connected. He had a powerful need to bind himself in advance to rigid rules, but was so convinced of his own virtue that he demonized all who fell short of the standards he imposed on himself. He increasingly became a maverick and a loner, more interested in stirring up controversy outside the Court than building coalitions inside of it. In this sense, though Scalia's judicial philosophy resembled that of Hugo Black, his temperament was closer to that of William O. Douglas, and that proved to be his undoing.

The contrasting temperaments of Rehnquist and Scalia were shaped by their upbringings in very different conservative households. "I'm a strong believer in pluralism," Rehnquist told *The New York Times Magazine* in 1985, after fourteen years on the Court, the year before he was promoted to be chief justice. "Don't concentrate all the power in one place. . . . You don't want all the power in the Government as opposed to the people. You don't want all the power in the Federal Government as opposed to the states." When pressed about the source of these views, he joked, "It may have something to do with my childhood."[3]

Rehnquist's Robert Taft–style conservatism—built on a faith in local majorities and a suspicion of broad federal power—did indeed reflect his Midwestern upbringing. Born in 1924, he was raised, along with his sister, Jean, in Shorewood, Wisconsin, an affluent Milwaukee suburb known for its Republicanism. Rehnquist's father, the son of Swedish immigrants, was an enthusiastic Republican who never attended college and made his living selling paper wholesale. His mother, who had majored in French at the University of Wisconsin, was fluent in five foreign languages and worked as a translator for local export businesses.

Rehnquist's early years were suffused with old-fashioned patriotism. He enthusiastically supported U.S. intervention in World War II, and in 1941 he participated in a reenactment of America's founding called United States of Young Americans.[4] Rehnquist won a scholarship to Kenyon College, in Ohio, but dropped out after the first quarter because he found the atmosphere intellectually frivolous. He enlisted in the Army Air Corps and spent three years as a weather observer, ending up in Morocco and Egypt (where he was photographed on horseback in front of the Sphinx). Reluctant to return to the cold Milwaukee winters—"I wanted to find someplace like North Africa to go to school," he said—he enrolled on the GI Bill at Stanford, where he majored in political science.

While he was in the Army Air Corps, Rehnquist encountered a book that would prove to be crucial to the development of his judicial philosophy, Friedrich A. Hayek's *The Road to Serfdom.* "This book was an advocacy book trying to show that state planning and socialism and that sort of thing didn't work economically and were dangerous politically," Rehnquist once told Brian Lamb in a C-SPAN interview. "It made quite an impression on me."

Rehnquist graduated Phi Beta Kappa from Stanford in 1948 with a bachelor's and a master's degree, and then got a second master's degree in political science from Harvard, in the hope of becoming a professor of government. While at Harvard he started a thesis about the conservative British political philosopher Michael Oakeshott, whose insistence on the importance of continuity and tradition for social stability resonated strongly with Rehnquist. Oakeshott, like Hayek, called into question the centrally planned welfare state, as part of a larger warning against the concentration of power in the hands of government. But Oakeshott resisted Hayek's effort to construct a rigid libertarian ideology as the answer to collectivism. Instead, he argued that the best way to protect limited government was with a pragmatically conservative approach to politics, rather than with abstract theories about the true nature of the state.[5]

William Rehnquist in 1952 with Justice Robert Jackson, whom he served as a law clerk. The memos about upholding segregation that Rehnquist wrote when he was a clerk to Justice Jackson were the most controversial of his career.

After Harvard, Rehnquist attended Stanford Law School and graduated in 1952 at the top of an impressive class that included Sandra Day O'Connor. Based on his stellar academic record and genial personality, he won a Supreme Court clerkship with Justice Robert Jackson, who had been Franklin Roosevelt's attorney general and was committed to the principle of judicial deference to legislatures. During his clerkship, Rehnquist wrote two highly controversial memos to Jackson that would provoke firestorms during his own confirmation hearings when he was nominated as an associate justice in 1971 and as chief justice in 1986. In the memos, Rehnquist seemed to urge

Jackson to dissent in two historic civil rights cases: *Brown v. Board of Education*, which would strike down school segregation, and *Terry v. Adams*, which would block efforts to exclude blacks from the pre-primary selection of Texas Democrats. Rehnquist claimed during the hearings that he was expressing these views at Jackson's request—an assertion disputed by Jackson's secretary. Several legal scholars believe that Rehnquist probably lied in denying that the views were his.[6] He appears to have been the only Supreme Court clerk during the 1952 term who supported *Plessy v. Ferguson*, the case that upheld railroad segregation in 1896, but he supported it at a time when the country as a whole was evenly split over desegregation and when at least four justices were ready to sustain it.[7] Whether he was speaking for himself or for Jackson, the central position that Rehnquist laid out in the memos—stressing the importance of judicial deference to the will of the majority—succinctly summarized what would become his judicial philosophy throughout his career.

After his Supreme Court clerkship ended in 1953, Rehnquist moved to Phoenix, in search of warm weather and conservative politics. He joined a small law firm and became active in local Republican circles, which had been revitalized under the newly elected Senator Barry Goldwater. A decade later Rehnquist would write speeches for Goldwater's 1964 presidential campaign.[8] Although Goldwater denounced the Warren Court's liberal decisions on obscenity and school prayer, he had little patience for his party's growing moralistic forces, which insisted that Christian virtue, rather than liberty, should be the Republicans' highest calling.[9]

In 1957, after the Warren Court issued a series of controversial decisions protecting the rights of suspected Communists, Rehnquist, then a young lawyer, wrote an article in *U.S. News & World Report* criticizing the law clerks he had known for their predominantly "'liberal' point of view," which he defined as "extreme solicitude for the claims of Communists and other criminal defendants, expansion of federal power at the expense of State power, great sympathy toward any government regulation of business—in short, the political philosophy now espoused by the Court under Chief Justice Earl Warren."[10] Rehnquist also strongly disagreed with the Warren Court's prominent role in advancing the civil rights movement. Testifying as a private citizen before the Phoenix City Council in 1964, he opposed a local public accommodations law, charging later that it would summarily do away with "the historic right of the owner of a drug store, lunch counter, or theater to choose his own customers." During his 1971 confirmation hearings, Rehnquist said that he had changed his mind about public accommodations laws, acknowledging that he had not understood how strongly minorities felt about protecting their rights.[11]

Every political movement has its moral blind spots, and civil rights was certainly a moral blind spot for Goldwater Republicans. Rehnquist's insistence on deferring to the will of the people is hard to reconcile with his indifference to the emerging majority of Americans who supported the rights of black people. Goldwater and Rehnquist were never white supremacists, but they seemed unconcerned that their devotion to states' rights could lead to the enshrinement of racism. (Justice Byron White, a Kennedy Democrat of the same generation who shared Rehnquist's devotion to majority rule, did not make the same mistake.) But Rehnquist ultimately embraced the *Brown* decision, and after he joined the Court he made no attempt to dismantle the civil rights revolution, as political opponents feared he would. His change of position reflected not only his reverence for the Court as an institution but also his sense that once a majority has spoken, the decision has a legal force that must be obeyed.

When Richard Nixon was elected president in 1968, he appointed as deputy attorney general Richard Kleindienst, a Phoenix lawyer who had worked on his campaign. Kleindienst persuaded attorney general John Mitchell to hire his friend Rehnquist as head of the Justice Department's Office of Legal Counsel, which provides constitutional advice to the president. In that post, Rehnquist distinguished himself as a conservative intellectual and an enthusiastic defender of executive power in the face of widespread social unrest. The country, Rehnquist said in a Kiwanis Club speech in 1969, had to devote all its energies to countering "the danger posed by the new barbarians." Two years later he staunchly defended the mass arrest of Vietnam protesters.[12] That year, with Justices Hugo Black and John M. Harlan retiring, Nixon considered some three-dozen candidates to fill the two vacancies, including Vice President Spiro Agnew and Senator Howard Baker of Tennessee. In his entertaining memoir, *The Rehnquist Choice,* the former White House counsel John Dean claims the credit (and also the blame) for being the first to float Rehnquist's name, even though Rehnquist was in charge of screening the other Supreme Court candidates. When Nixon first met Rehnquist, who was given to the loud shirts and psychedelic ties of the era, he wondered aloud, "Who's the guy dressed like a clown?" Upon hearing Rehnquist's name, Nixon said, "Is he Jewish? He looks it."[13] But when the other candidates fell by the wayside, the man Nixon was prone to call "Renchburg" won him over with his conservative credentials and unquestioned ability.

Rehnquist's first confirmation hearings focused on whether he had been truthful when he denied having challenged black and Hispanic voters as an Arizona poll watcher and on his account of the pro-segregation memos he had written for Justice Jackson nineteen years earlier. Although Rehnquist was unanimously praised as an accomplished lawyer, he came under fire from a group of liberal Democrats on the Judiciary Committee, including Senator Edward Kennedy, who charged that his record "reveals a dangerous hostility to the great principles of individual freedom under the Bill of Rights and equal justice for all people."[14] Even so, the Senate confirmed Rehnquist as an associate justice by a vote of 68 to 26.

Antonin Scalia was born only twelve years after William Rehnquist, but his temperament and political sensibility were shaped by parents of a more openly religious conservative sensibility. Born in 1936 in Trenton, New Jersey, Scalia grew up as an only child in a devoutly Catholic home. His mother, Catherine Panaro Scalia, was a schoolteacher and his father, S. Eugene Scalia, was a Sicilian immigrant who became a professor of romance languages at Brooklyn College. Scalia idolized his father, whom he would later call "a much more scholarly and intellectual person than I am . . . he always had a book in front of his face."[15] (Two centuries earlier, John Marshall had idolized his own father in similar terms.) Scalia's father impressed on him the importance of language, and of communing directly with literary texts, rather than relying on translations.[16] After moving to the New York City borough of Queens at the age of five, Scalia attended a local public school, and he participated in the "release time" program that allowed public school students to take time off for religious training, which Justice William O. Douglas had upheld as constitutional in 1940. As Scalia later recalled in 2002, "You'd get Wednesday off if you had a note from your parents and you could go to religious instruction, skip out of school while your classmates who didn't have the notes had to put in another hour-and-a-half or so. It was a good deal." Scalia applauded Douglas for upholding the program and for Douglas's observation that "we are a religious people whose institutions presuppose a Supreme Being." He also lamented that the Court would soon change its mind and hold that religion could not be favored over secularism.[17]

For high school, Scalia commuted to Manhattan to attend St. Francis Xavier, a Jesuit all-boys military academy, where he distinguished himself in debate, the French horn, and amateur theatricals.

(A classmate who was embarrassed to be playing Lady Macbeth in an all-male production never forgot Scalia's kind reassurances that the boys who made fun of him were jealous of the good part.) Scalia's flair for attention-getting performances extended to TV and radio quiz shows, where he was recognized as a "whiz kid." Scalia flourished in the classroom with four years of Latin and three years of Greek, and was so enthusiastic in his denunciation of liberalizations in the Catholic Church that at the age of seventeen, according to a high school classmate, he "could have been a member of the Curia."[18] Scalia went on to Georgetown University, where he continued his interest in acting, his academic excellence, and his devotion to doctrinal purity. He graduated summa cum laude in history and, in his valedictory address, referred to himself and his classmates as the future "leaders of a real, a true, a Catholic intellectual life."

Scalia's traditional Catholic education may have influenced his later insistence, as a judge, on binding himself to follow the original meaning of the Constitution regardless of his personal inclinations. One commentator argues that Scalia came to approach the Constitution in the same way that Catholics before the Second Vatican Council were taught to approach the Latin Mass: they were to "move through it with intent fidelity, with legalistic care," subordinating their personal desires to codified rules.[19] Another influence may have been his law school education. Scalia graduated magna cum laude from Harvard Law School in 1960, during the heyday of what was known as the "Legal Process" school. This philosophy developed in response to claims by legal realists, such as Justice Douglas, that legal decisions should be viewed as opportunities for judges to enact their policy preferences into law. By contrast, the pioneers of Legal Process, such as the Harvard professors Henry Hart and Albert Sachs, insisted that government had become increasingly complex after the New Deal and that elected representatives were better qualified than judges to make policy decisions. Five of the justices on the Rehnquist Court—Scalia, Kennedy, Souter, Ginsburg, and Breyer—had taken Hart and Sach's Legal Process course while at Harvard, and most of them emerged far more pragmatic and deferential to legislatures than Scalia.[20] But Scalia seems to have been especially moved by Hart and Sachs's insistence that judges should follow strict procedural rules in order to constrain their own discretion. While Scalia was in law school, Herbert Wechsler of Columbia Law School delivered a Holmes Lecture at Harvard, where he famously argued that Supreme Court justices should base their decisions on "neutral principles," without consulting their own policy preferences. Only "sustained, disinterested, merciless examination" of the reasoning provided by litigants could prevent the Court from becoming a "naked power organ," Wechsler insisted.[21] The argument seemed to resonate with Scalia.

During law school, Scalia met Maureen McCarthy, an English major at Radcliffe, whom he married in 1960. They had nine children, one of whom became a priest and all of whom were raised in the traditional Catholic faith. After law school, Scalia worked in a law firm, became a law professor at the University of Virginia, and was nominated to head the Justice Department's Office of Legal Counsel (Rehnquist's old position) in 1974, just before Richard Nixon resigned. Staying on during the Ford administration, Scalia issued a legal opinion saying that Nixon was entitled to keep the tapes of his presidential meetings and phone calls—a position the Supreme Court later rejected. In the Justice Department, Scalia absorbed the suspicion of Congress and support for strong executive power shared by other conservatives of his era, including solicitor general Robert Bork, White House chief of staff Dick Cheney, and Secretary of Defense Donald Rumsfeld. At the end of the Ford administration, Scalia left government to teach at the University of Chicago; he also a cofounded *Regulation*, a magazine that might have more accurately

On June 17, 1986, President Ronald Reagan announced the retirement of Chief Justice Warren E. Burger and the nominations of William Rehnquist to be chief justice and Antonin Scalia to be an associate justice.

been called *Anti-Regulation*. (In a characteristic article, Scalia wrote that "no bureaucracy should be making basic social judgments.") Appointed by President Ronald Reagan to the U.S. Court of Appeals in 1982, he distinguished himself with his caustic wit and his vigorous advocacy of judicial deference to administrative agencies. Four years later, when Chief Justice Warren Burger retired, Reagan appointed Scalia to be an associate justice of the Supreme Court, at the same time that he promoted Rehnquist to be chief justice.

In his confirmation hearings, Scalia defended his judicial philosophy of "original meaning" along the same lines that Hugo Black had: as a way of ensuring that democratic majorities can enact their will into law. He emphasized that "if somebody should discover that the secret intent of the framers was quite different from what the words seem to connote, it would not make any difference." "A constitution has to have ultimately majoritarian underpinnings," he declared. "If the majority that adopted it did not believe this unspecified right, which is not reflected clearly in the language . . . I worry about my deciding that it exists."[22] Democratic senators focused their energies on opposing Rehnquist's promotion to chief justice, and the full Senate confirmed Scalia after less than five minutes of debate by a vote of 98 to 0. Rehnquist, by contrast, had a bumpier ride; his nomination as chief justice was confirmed by a closer vote of 65 to 33.

During Rehnquist's and Scalia's confirmation hearings, witnesses predicted that Rehnquist would be a loner as chief justice but that Scalia would be a masterful consensus builder because of his wit and charm. In fact, the opposite came to pass: Rehnquist moderated the ideological passions he had displayed during his first years on the Court and he was less interested in doctrinal consistency than in the legitimacy of the institution itself. By contrast, Scalia would focus more on defending his own ideological purity than on persuading skeptical colleagues, and would alienate them in the process.

As chief justice, Rehnquist proved to be a master tactician, unlike his inept and pompous predecessor, Warren Burger, who infuriated his colleagues by changing his votes in order to seize the best opinions for himself and then often losing his majorities. Rehnquist was essentially a pragmatist who believed in certain core conservative values—primarily states' rights and convicting criminals—but didn't fuss too much about how he achieved his aims.

One of Rehnquist's unique and abiding talents was for getting along with his ideological opponents. When he first joined the Court, at the age of forty-seven, he was taken under the wing of William O. Douglas, a fellow westerner who saw in the irreverent young conservative an incarnation of his youthful self.[23] Rehnquist's other liberal colleagues were similarly impressed by his fairness and good nature: Thurgood Marshall called Rehnquist "a great chief justice," and William Brennan described him as "the most all-around successful" chief he had known—including Earl Warren.[24]

Another hallmark of Rehnquist's rule was his unparalleled organizational skill: he got opinions out quickly and made the arguments run on time. When, in a television interview, Charlie Rose asked him how he would most like to be remembered, Rehnquist said as a good administrator; he had tried, he said, to run "a relatively smoothly functioning Court." He suggested that his ability to get along with a group of strong personalities reflected "a relatively passive nature," a "very high boiling point," and the ability to compromise. One former clerk remembered Rehnquist best for his sensitivity toward colleagues: "He was very concerned about hurt feelings among the justices, and he was very careful and observant of the way that certain memos or interactions would make other justices react or feel. He always avoided invective in his own memos, and smoothed over hurt feelings when other justices used it."

Certainly Rehnquist was a creature of habit. His daily routine in his chambers remained the same for more than thirty years. He would arrive between 8:30 and 9:00, say hello to his two secretaries, go through his mail, and smoke a cigarette (for years he was a two-cigarettes-a-day man—no more, no less). At exactly 9:30 he would call in his clerks, gently reminding them, if they were even a minute late, that "the doctor doesn't wait for you." A trivia buff, he loved to test the mettle of his clerks at the morning meeting, asking them, for example, to name the five largest states in order of their area. During the day he would often go to the University Club for a swim, to alleviate chronic back pain, and he usually left the office at 4:00. He was not known for taking work home with him. When he assigned the writing of an opinion to himself, he would set a deadline for the first draft ten days away and then start asking his clerks about it after a week. He was insistent that his fellow justices meet his exacting standards for punctuality, and would punish those who fell behind on their opinions (including the notoriously slow Harry Blackmun) by not assigning them new ones. He ran an especially tight ship during the justices' private conferences. Briskly going around the table, in order of seniority, to allow each justice to give his or her views, he refused to let discussion wander. Some colleagues complained that this format discouraged active debate, but Rehnquist argued that because most of the justices had already made up their minds, a protracted colloquy would be a waste of time.

Rehnquist's courtroom style was similarly unvarying. He would cut lawyers off in mid-sentence when the red light on the bench began to flash, indicating that their allotted time had expired. (Each side gets precisely thirty minutes.) While some lawyers grumbled about this rigidity, Rehnquist's clockwork discipline looked appealing in retrospect when Justice John Paul Stevens, who presided in the chief justice's place during his battle with thyroid cancer in the 2004 term, let one advocate have extra time and was then compelled to grant an extension to his opponent.

The two chief justices whom Rehnquist most admired, John Marshall and Charles Evans Hughes, were both former politicians who had a knack for bringing together colleagues of different minds. Rehnquist noted that Marshall had been a Virginia congressman and secretary of state. Hughes, who served from 1930 to 1941, had been the governor of New York, a Republican candidate for president, and secretary of state. As Rehnquist told the C-SPAN interviewer Brian Lamb in a *Booknotes* appearance in 1993, Marshall had "an ability to get along with other people and persuade them that stood him in good stead when he was chief justice." And in a 1976 article in the *Hastings*

Constitutional Law Quarterly, "Chief Justices I Never Knew," Rehnquist wrote that he especially admired Hughes's businesslike conduct of his private conferences, which lasted only six hours as opposed to two or three days under Hughes's successor, Harlan Fiske Stone. Rehnquist concluded, "Hughes's superiority to Stone in presiding over the conference has a definite connection to their different amount of exposure to active political life."[25]

Rehnquist's successes as chief justice provide an object lesson that having a judicious temperament is far more important than having a rigidly consistent judicial methodology. Rehnquist always understood the political demands of whatever role he was asked to play, and was careful not to transgress its boundaries. His performance in presiding over the impeachment trial of President Bill Clinton in 1999 was masterful because he refused to pontificate, confining his interventions to rulings on procedural motions, which he handed down with confidence and skill. Had he played his role in a more intrusive or partisan way, the trial might have turned into a political circus. (As a gesture of thanks, the majority and minority leaders of the Senate gave him a ceremonial cup.) By refusing as chief justice to give interviews except about his books on Supreme Court history, and by devoutly guarding his privacy, he helped maintain and enhance the Court's carefully cultivated aura of mystery and authority.

"I've always admired Robert E. Lee for his refusal to write his memoirs," Rehnquist told Brian Lamb. "If memoirs are going to be interesting, if they're not going to be saccharine, you have to say some people didn't measure up and others did. . . . I think of a memoir as saying, 'When I came on the Court there were eight other justices and three or four were quite smart, but a couple of the others were creepy.' I don't want to get into that."

As an appellate judge, Scalia seemed to take a similar circumspect attitude toward questions of personal exposure. "One of the reasons that courts are held in generally high esteem is that they are not in the public consciousness very often, and one doesn't see that, lo and behold, they're made up of frail human beings like every other governmental institution," Scalia told C-SPAN in 1986. "Judges ought to make an effort to avoid becoming public figures, because it's not their personalities or their particular viewpoints that they are supposed to be promoting."

On the Supreme Court, however, Scalia ignored his own advice. Lacking Rehnquist's aversion to the spotlight, he proved, like William O. Douglas, unable to restrain himself from broadcasting his views on topics unrelated to his judicial duties. By repeatedly inserting his own personality into the public debate, he called his impartiality into question. In 1996, for example, Scalia ridiculed the idea that the Constitution protects a right to die at a time when two cases on the question were pending before the Court. Seven years later, in a speech to the Knights of Columbus's religious freedom rally, he asserted that the nation's founders never meant to "exclude God from the public forums and from political life," adding that nondenominational acknowledgments of God by the government "reflect the true tradition of religious freedom in America—a tradition of neutrality among religious faiths." As a result, Scalia had to recuse himself from hearing a constitutional challenge to the Pledge of Allegiance's inclusion of the words "under God." In 2004, Scalia was asked to recuse himself in a case involving Vice President Dick Cheney, with whom he had recently gone duck hunting. He refused, plausibly enough, but in his memo justifying his refusal he ridiculed his critics, lashed out at the public, and vilified those who questioned his motives. In the process, he did more to undermine public confidence in his judicial temperament than did the duck-hunting trip itself. In 2006, just before the Court considered a challenge to the constitutionality of military tribunals for detainees at Guantánamo Bay, Scalia ridiculed the challenge during a speech in Switzerland. "Give me a break," he declared. "I had a son on that battlefield, and they were shooting at my son, and I'm not about to give this man who was captured in a war a full jury trial. I mean, it's crazy." The same year, when a Boston reporter asked whether his participation at a mass for Catholic lawyers might raise questions about his impartiality, Scalia fanned the fingers of his right hand under his chin. "That's Sicilian," he said, explaining that the gesture meant he "could not care less." When the gesture was widely misinterpreted as obscene, Scalia wrote a sarcastic letter to the *Boston Herald* declaring, "From watching too many episodes of *The Sopranos,* your staff seems to have acquired the belief that any Sicilian gesture is obscene—especially when made by an 'Italian jurist.' (I am, by the way, an American jurist.)"[26] By refusing to let the matter rest, Scalia called even more attention to himself, and succeeded in looking even less judicious.

Unlike Rehnquist (but like William O. Douglas), Scalia has made a habit of giving extracurricular lectures on highly charged political questions. In a speech on "the Common Christian Good" to the Gregorian University in Rome in 1996, he delivered an extended attack on the idea that left-leaning governments have a monopoly on Christian virtue. "I know of no country in which the Churches have grown fuller as the governments have moved to the left," he announced.[27] He went on to declare that "far from doing Christ's work, state provision of welfare positively impedes it" and that "capitalism is more dependent upon Christianity than socialism is" because it relies on "honesty, self-denial, and yes, even charity." Scalia concluded by insisting "not that a government of the right is more Christ-like, only that there is no reason to believe that a government of the left is."[28] The entire performance called to mind the defensive nobleman from Gilbert and Sullivan's *Iolanthe* who insists that the rich are just as capable of virtue as the poor. And by denouncing a straw man from

the 1940s—how many governments, even in Europe today, claim that Socialism has a monopoly on virtue?—Scalia seemed to be holding up as an alternative Justice Douglas's 1940s vision of America as a Christian nation. He left a similar impression in other speeches. At a prayer breakfast at the First Baptist Church in Jackson, Mississippi, that same year, he denounced secular society's hostility toward the devout. "To the worldly wise, everything from Easter morning to the Ascension had to be made up by the groveling enthusiasts as part of their plan to get themselves martyred." He continued: "To be honest about it, that is the view of Christians taken by modern society. We are fools for Christ's sake. We must pray for the courage to endure the scorn of the modern world."[29] The speech provoked widespread condemnation from secular critics, some of whom did not realize that Scalia had been quoting Corinthians, but who plausibly accused him of indulging in Christian victimology. Despite Scalia's repeated insistences that he never allows his religious beliefs to influence his jurisprudence, his palpable anger at what he perceives to be the hostility of cultural elites contrasts strongly with the far less embattled religiosity of Rehnquist, who kept his beliefs to himself.

The most dramatic contrast between the temperaments of Rehnquist and Scalia was expressed in their relationships with their colleagues. While Rehnquist had a knack for getting along with his ideological opponents, Scalia managed to alienate even his ideological sympathizers. His contemptuous attacks on the pragmatic jurisprudence of Justice O'Connor—he said of one of her abortion opinions that it "cannot be taken seriously"—clearly took a toll. "Sticks and stones will break my bones, but words will never hurt me," O'Connor replied when asked about civility on the Court, though she added, "That probably isn't true."[30] Some scholars argued that Scalia's relentless personal attacks on O'Connor and Kennedy dissuaded them from overturning *Roe v. Wade*.[31] Scalia's tendency to dominate oral

argument with aggressive questions and showy put-downs alienated several justices, including Rehnquist, who once shook his finger at Scalia for interrupting Kennedy during a death penalty case.[32]

To some degree, Scalia's know-it-all performances have been softened by his wit. One study concluded that Scalia has received more laughs in the courtroom than any other justice by a wide margin, but Scalia's jokes were often at the expense of the lawyers and his colleagues: as one lawyer rifled through his papers to answer a question, for example, Scalia exclaimed, "When you find it, say Bingo."[33] He also has a reputation as something of a sore loser who reads his dissenting opinions from the bench in aggrieved tones. For all these reasons, he has failed to inspire anything like the affection that Rehnquist attracted from both sides of the political spectrum. By contrast, Stephen Breyer, whom the study rated the second-funniest justice, has a gentler temperament and more intellectual humility: at oral arguments, he often summed up the strongest arguments on both sides of a case, candidly identified the issues on which he was still undecided, and invited the lawyers to try to persuade him through an energetic conversation. Off the Court, too, Breyer, proved to be just as witty as Scalia, but without the nasty edge. During a debate with Scalia about the legitimacy of citing international law in Supreme Court opinions, for example, Breyer introduced himself self-deprecatingly. "Out of the ten times somebody asks me, 'Are you on the Supreme Court?'" he said, "nine of them thought I was Justice Souter." The lighter touch helped Breyer win support in important cases from O'Connor, who shared his pragmatic judicial philosophy.

Scalia, by his own account, is unconcerned about his relative failure to win many converts on the Court to his jurisprudential cause. In a 1989 article, he praised Chief Justice William Howard Taft even though many of his opinions "ran counter to the ultimate sweep of history."[34] Responding to a critic who argued that Taft's chief justice-

ship might have been more constructive if he had had "a large vision of things to come," Scalia wrote, "This is presumably the school of history that assesses the greatness of a leader by his success in predicting where the men he is leading want to go. That is perhaps the way the world ultimately evaluates things—but one may think that Taft, having (as I have described) a more celestial view of the judge's function, had a quite accurate 'vision of things to come,' did not like them, and did his best, with consummate skill but ultimate lack of success, to alter the outcome."[35] Although happiest in the martyr's role of principled defeat, Scalia might have been describing himself. "The worst thing about the Living Constitution is that it will destroy the Constitution," he declared in a typical jeremiad.[36] "The whole purpose of the Constitution is to prevent a future society from doing what it wants to do."[37]

Just as Black and Douglas voted together in most cases, so Scalia and Rehnquist were aligned more often than not. Between 1986 and 2003, Rehnquist agreed with Scalia in 79 percent of the cases that resulted in written opinions—a higher percentage than any other justice except for Clarence Thomas, who agreed with Scalia 86 percent of the time.[38] But between 1996 and 2003, Scalia wrote more dissenting opinions than any other conservative justice, and also was less likely than all the other conservative justices to vote with the majority of the Court.[39] Moreover, Scalia and Rehnquist diverged in important cases because Rehnquist was more willing to moderate his views out of concern for the legitimacy of the Court. And even in the many cases in which they agreed, Scalia and Rehnquist wrote strikingly different opinions that reflected their differing temperaments, sensibilities, and judicial philosophies.

Rehnquist in most cases simply voted to uphold federal and state laws. Reading his youthful and often solitary dissents, which earned him the nickname the Lone Ranger, it is hard not to be impressed by their energy, lack of pretense, and lack of anger. Rehnquist always respected the Court as an institution, even when he disagreed with the majority in particular cases. Instead of insisting on slavish adherence to the original meaning of the Constitution, or to judicial precedents, he focused instead on moving the law in a moderately conservative direction while trying to circumvent any potential roadblocks along the way. His clerks, past and present, reported that he would simply remove the reasoning from opinions if it got in the way of the result. "He took each case as it came," I was told by Michael K. Young, a former clerk who is now president of the University of Utah. "He thought that the Constitution was not designed to shape all of our behavior but to box in elected officials at the margins. . . . He didn't see the sky falling, the way Scalia sometimes does, and if you read his dissents, they're often pragmatic."

Typical of Rehnquist's early opinions was his 1973 dissent from *Roe v. Wade.* Without huffing and puffing or personal invective, Rehnquist made a straightforward but powerful case for majority rule. "The fact that a majority of the States, reflecting, after all, the majority sentiment in those States, have had restrictions on abortion for at least a century is a strong indication, it seems to me, that the asserted right to an abortion is not so rooted in the traditions and conscience of our people as to be ranked as fundamental," Rehnquist observed. It is striking to compare his even-tempered dissent with Scalia's wrathful and apocalyptic dissent nearly twenty years later in *Planned Parenthood v. Casey,* the case that reaffirmed *Roe.* In *Casey,* Scalia equated abortion with slavery—both of them issues "involving life and death, freedom and subjugation"—and predicted that the Court's decision would detonate a culture war in the same way that *Dred Scott,* in 1857, precipitated the Civil War. Scalia's dissent displayed his fine polemical gift, and his ability to puncture the pretensions of his colleagues with a sentence or a phrase. ("To portray *Roe* as the statesmanlike 'settlement' of a divisive issue, a jurisprudential Peace of Westphalia that is worth preserving, is nothing less than Orwellian," he wrote.) But Scalia's characteristic warnings that the sky was falling gave the impression that he viewed the decision as both a moral and a constitutional disaster. Rehnquist, by contrast, was less emotional, making it clear that he was willing to have legislatures decide the abortion question either way.

Rehnquist's moderate religious views—he was a quietly observant Lutheran—may have contributed to his relative equanimity about abortion and other questions involving the culture wars. Rehnquist read broadly and avidly but, unlike Scalia, never lorded his intelligence over his colleagues. ("What's a smart guy like me doing in a place this this?" Scalia once asked his clerks—smugness impossible to imagine from Rehnquist.) While Scalia scathingly criticized popular culture, Rehnquist loved to rent movies—both new and old—and also went to movie theaters by himself to see them. (His wife, Natalie, died in 1991 after a long struggle with ovarian cancer.) He never denounced the Court for taking sides in the culture wars, as Scalia routinely does.

Temperament and religious sensibility may go a long way toward explaining differences in approach—between Rehnquist, on the one hand, and Scalia and Thomas, on the other. But another part of the explanation has to do with the reaction to *Roe v. Wade* within the legal community. Because of *Roe,* a conservative judicial movement arose in the 1980s that was determined to curtail judicial discretion at all costs. *Roe* galvanized the religious Right and unleashed far more conservative outrage against the Court than Earl Warren ever did. After he became president in 1981, Ronald Reagan declared that he wanted to avoid what he saw as Nixon's mistakes in picking moderate justices like Harry Blackmun and Lewis Powell, and directed his Justice Department to find more reliable ways of identifying doctrinaire strict constructionists. A turning point for this movement came in 1985, when attorney general Edwin Meese delivered a speech to the American Bar Association denouncing the Burger Court for its "jurisprudence of idiosyncrasy." Meese asserted, "It has been and will continue to be the policy of this administration to press for a jurisprudence of Original Intention," which he defined as an "endeavor to resurrect the original meaning of constitutional provisions and statutes as the only reliable guide for judgment."

Despite the claims of Meese and Scalia, originalism has not been the prevailing mode of judicial discourse for most of America's constitutional history. It has come into fashion episodically, usually as a reaction against more freewheeling eras of judicial policymaking when the courts have become politically controversial and judges are eager to take refuge in the greater objectivities of text and history. In the early nineteenth century, for example, American judges modeled themselves on English common law courts, making law incrementally from case to case and deriving legal principles from legal precedents, rather than resorting to the original meaning of the Constitution as a matter of course. But then Thomas Jefferson and his followers claimed that John Marshall had abused his power by using the common law method to establish the Supreme Court as the final interpreter of the Constitution. To reduce the discretion of judges, Jefferson proposed the following canon of constitutional interpretation: "On every question of construction [we should] carry ourselves back to the time when the Constitution was adopted, recollect the spirit manifested in the debates, and instead of trying [to find] what meaning may be squeezed out of the text, or invented against it, conform to the probable one in which it was passed."[40] Replying sharply to Jefferson in 1833, Marshall's disciple Joseph Story stressed in his *Commentaries on the Constitution* that judges should follow "the fair meaning of the words of the text," rather than the "'probable meaning' of persons, whom they never knew, and whose opinions, and means of information, may be no better than their own."[41] But Story also suggested that judges should restrain themselves by following fixed and objective "rules of interpretation." One of Story's nineteen rules conceded that "much . . . may be gathered from contemporary history, and contemporary interpretation" of the original Constitution. But Story emphasized, like Scalia, that "nothing but the text itself was adopted by the people."[42]

The same political and hermeneutical drama was played out one hundred years later, around the turn of the twentieth century. Judges, faithfully applying the common law method, struck down economic regulations passed by progressive state legislatures, including maximum hours and minimum wage laws. Progressive critics, such as Hugo Black and Felix Frankfurter, accused the Court of enforcing arbitrary principles whose connection to the text of the Constitution was hard to discern. When Frankfurter was appointed to the Court, he and his fellow Roosevelt nominee Hugo Black had violent debates about who was the more faithful originalist.

Then the wheel turned once more. In the 1960s and '70s, the Court, led by Earl Warren and Warren Burger, was attacked by citizens and scholars alike for the aggressiveness of its excursions into social policy, and for a weakness for manufacturing opinions that even its friends found constitutionally unconvincing. In the 1980s, conservative judges and scholars, led most prominently by Scalia, challenged the Court to restore its democratic and intellectual legitimacy by abandoning the common law constitutionalism of the Warren era and tying itself once more to the originalist mast. Although Rehnquist's opinions referred intermittently to this doctrine of "originalism" (most notably in cases involving the separation of church and state), he invoked constitutional history when it was convenient and otherwise ignored it. Scalia, by contrast, has taken a very different approach. From his first days on the Court, he has insisted on the importance of construing each constitutional provision according to its presumed original meaning, no matter how disruptive the consequences might be.

During his tenure, Rehnquist voted most frequently not with Scalia but with Sandra Day O'Connor, a western pragmatist who was more interested in the practical realities of government than in doctrinal purity. O'Connor's approach to her job reflected her background as an Arizona state legislator in the 1970s, where she mediated between Democrats and Republicans with moderation and aplomb. Starting in the mid-1990s, Rehnquist and O'Connor were increasingly joined by Justice Breyer, a more liberal pragmatist who privately referred to Rehnquist and O'Connor as "the grown-ups" and contrasted their concern for the Court as an institution with the fire-breathing radicalism of Scalia and Thomas. Breyer's pragmatism and his sunny view of legislatures reflected his own experiences in and around government. His father was a lawyer for the San Francisco school board who emphasized the importance of participating in the political life of the city. Breyer took this lesson to heart as chief counsel to the Judiciary Committee under Senator Edward Kennedy from 1979 to 1980, where he worked on airline deregulation and federal sentencing reform. Each morning Breyer would meet for breakfast with his Republican counterpart, the chief counsel for Senator Strom Thurmond, and that experience convinced him that when legislative staff meets, both sides often try to achieve practical results that will help the country, rather than being prisoners of ideology. While recognizing that Congress wasn't perfect, Breyer concluded that it worked pretty well, and he left the job even more optimistic about the possibilities of bipartisan legislative cooperation than when he began.

On the Rehnquist Court, the conflict between the legalistic Scalia and the pragmatic Rehnquist, O'Connor, and Breyer sometimes created unusual alliances in cases involving privacy, religion, federalism, terrorism, crime, and executive authority. The pragmatists, led by Rehnquist or O'Connor, generally advocated deference to the president and Congress, interpreting laws broadly to give the government the flexibility to respond to important national problems. The legalists, led by Scalia, preferred to interpret laws and the Constitution strictly and were perfectly happy to rule against Congress without worrying about the practical consequences.

Consider the right to die. In 1990 and again in 1997, Rehnquist wrote important opinions for the Court holding that all people have a constitutionally protected interest in refusing unwanted medical treatment, even if the decision would hasten death. But Rehnquist also held that states could require clear evidence of the wishes of terminally ill people in a persistent vegetative state, and could refuse automatically to accept the claims of their parents that they would have wanted to die if given the choice. This moderate conclusion was too adventurous for Scalia, who insisted—as Hugo Black used to do—that the "due process" clause of the Constitution protected no substantive liberties at all. "The point at which life becomes 'worthless,' and the point at which the means necessary to preserve it become 'extraordinary' or 'inappropriate,' are neither set forth in the Constitution nor known to the nine Justices of this Court any better than they are known to nine people picked at random from the Kansas City telephone directory," Scalia wrote acidly. In the same spirit, Scalia dissented from a 2000 decision that Rehnquist joined, reaffirming the constitutional right of parents to rear their children as they think best. Rehnquist and his colleagues struck down a state law allowing courts to overrule the wishes of parents and to allow grandparents, for example, to visit their grandchildren if a judge decided it would be in the best interest of the child. Scalia objected that although the right of parents to direct the upbringing of the children was, in his view, one of the natural rights protected by the

Declaration of Independence, it was not protected by the U.S. Constitution.

Scalia and Rehnquist also diverged in important cases involving gender discrimination. In 2003, Rehnquist wrote a majority opinion holding that Congress could allow state government employees to sue their states for violating the federal Family and Medical Leave Act; Scalia and Thomas argued that this violated states' rights. And in 1996, Rehnquist concurred in a 7–1 majority opinion by Justice Ruth Bader Ginsburg striking down the Virginia Military Institute's long-standing all-male admissions policy. (Virginia had created a separate military institute for women, but Rehnquist noted that it was not plausibly equal to VMI.) Scalia filed a solitary and fierce dissenting opinion criticizing "this most illiberal Court, which has embarked on a course of inscribing one after another of the current preferences of the society . . . into our Basic Law." Focusing on tradition, Scalia criticized Justice Ginsburg for ignoring "the long tradition, enduring down to the present, of men's military colleges supported by both States and the Federal Government," and he reaffirmed his view that long-standing traditions should be preserved when they are not "expressly prohibited" by the text of the Bill of Rights. But Scalia did not explain why he believed that the text of the Constitution "expressly prohibits" the tradition of racial segregation in public schools but does not "expressly prohibit" the tradition of gender segregation in public schools. Moreover, traditionalism is hardly the same thing as originalism or textualism, the two methodologies on which Scalia has planted his flag. There was, after all, a long-standing tradition of segregated schools in 1954, but Scalia insists that *Brown v. Board of Education* was correct to uproot this tradition.

Originalist arguments helped Scalia little more than textualist ones. It is clear from congressional debates in 1866 that the Fourteenth Amendment was originally understood to permit gender segregation in public schools, but it is hard to make the case that it was originally understood to prohibit racial segregation in public schools. Even if the right to attend public schools is considered a fundamental civil right today, in a way that it was not in the mid-nineteenth century, this means that all citizens have to be given the right to attend the same schools on equal terms—and so gender segregation is just as impermissible as racial segregation. The Constitution makes no distinction between women and African-Americans. Scalia's opinion left the impression that he was choosing among competing constitutional philosophies—traditionalism, originalism, and textualism—in order to reach a conservative result. Rehnquist, who came from an older and more pragmatic conservative tradition, was less theoretical, more willing to look beyond text and history, and did not claim to apply a consistent methodology across the board.

Scalia did not always reach more conservative results than Rehnquist. On the contrary, his legalistic devotion to constitutional text and history led him to side against the government in some important civil liberties cases in which Rehnquist preferred to defer to state authority. Scalia took justifiable pride, for example, in his vote with a 5–4 majority in 1989 to hold that the First Amendment protects the right to burn the flag. For Scalia, his willingness to subordinate his personal dislike for flag burners to the commands of the Constitution was a sign of devotion to neutral principles. As Scalia put it (oddly using the third person), "Scalia did not like to vote that way. He does not like sandal-wearing bearded weirdos who go around burning flags. He is a very conservative fellow." He added, "I came down to breakfast the next morning, and my wife—she's a very conservative woman—she was scrambling eggs and humming 'It's a Grand Old Flag.' That's a true story. I don't need that! A living-Constitution judge never has to suffer that way."[43] By contrast, Rehnquist produced an emotional dissenting opinion in the flag-burning case, quoting John Greenleaf Whittier's

Civil War poem "Barbara Frietchie":" 'Shoot, if you must, this old gray head, / But spare your country's flag; she said."

Similarly, in cases involving unreasonable searches and seizures under the Fourth Amendment, Rehnquist rarely confronted a police search he wasn't happy to uphold. Scalia, by contrast, wrote important opinions attempting to translate constitutional values into the modern world. In one of his most impressive majority opinions, Scalia held in *Kyllo v. United States* (2001) that the police could not use thermal imaging devices without a warrant to search for unusual amounts of heat inside a house. By aiming one of these devices at the house of a drug suspect at three in the morning, the police concluded that he was using heat lamps to grow marijuana; they then got a warrant to search his house and found the drugs. In his opinion for a 5–4 Court, Scalia held that although the framers of the Fourth Amendment could not have anticipated thermal-imaging devices, they were determined to protect the privacy of the home. In order to protect the same amount of privacy in the twentieth-first century that citizens took for granted in the eighteenth, Scalia said, the Court would demand a warrant for the use of any cutting-edge technology that might reveal information about the inside of a home that would otherwise require a physical intrusion. To uphold the search, Scalia observed, would "allow technology to shrink the realm of guaranteed privacy." Rehnquist, by contrast, joined the dissenting opinion, which held unpersuasively that homeowners put out their heat waves the same way that they put out the trash, and therefore have abandoned any expectations that the privacy of their heat waves will be respected by the police.

The conflict between legalists and pragmatists on the Rehnquist Court was most intense in cases involving the power of the president in fighting crime and terrorism. The conflict first emerged in *Morrison v. Olson,* the 1988 case that upheld a federal law that created independent counsels who could investigate high government officials for alleged crimes. Rehnquist's opinion for the Court held that although the independent counsel was appointed by a special court, rather than by the president, his appointment did not violate the constitutional separation of powers because the president had the ability to fire the independent counsel for "good cause." Taking a pragmatic and flexible approach to executive power, Rehnquist emphasized that the independent counsel did not interfere too much with the president's constitutional power, and was not a covert attempt by Congress to expand its own power. In his blistering and solitary dissenting opinion, Scalia ridiculed this claim, insisting (as Hugo Black had insisted in the 1952 steel seizure case) that the Constitution entrusts all executive power to the president, and does not allow Congress to encroach on this power by tying the president's hands in any way. In a dramatic and prescient peroration, Scalia imagined the political consequences of independent counsels free to fish for executive malfeasance, unconstrained by politics or budgets. "How frightening it must be to have your own independent counsel and staff appointed, with nothing else to do but to investigate you until investigation is no longer worthwhile—with whether it is worthwhile not depending upon what such judgments usually hinge on, competing responsibilities," he wrote. "Even if it were entirely evident that unfairness was in fact the result—the judges hostile to the administration, the independent counsel an old foe of the President, the staff refugees from the recently defeated administration—there would be no one accountable to the public to whom the blame could be assigned." A decade later, Scalia's fears were vindicated by the ever-expanding inquisition of Kenneth Starr, whose initial appointment to investigate financial improprieties by President Clinton morphed into a prurient fishing expedition for embarrassing sexual behavior. Public outrage over the Starr investigation finally persuaded Congress to allow the independent counsel law to expire.

Scalia was not always alone in his insistence on rigid adherence to the constitutional text. For example, in *United States. v. Booker* (2005) and *Blakeley v. Washington* (2004), Scalia and Thomas joined three liberals on the Court in voting to strike down federal and state sentencing guidelines and in attempting to impose a sweeping new requirement that would have compelled juries to vote on each fact used to increase a sentence. Rehnquist, by contrast, sided with the more pragmatically minded justices—Breyer, O'Connor, and Kennedy—in arguing that sentencing guidelines should be upheld, although as advisory rather than mandatory restraints on judicial discretion.

The same conflict between the pragmatists and the legalists emerged in an important terrorism case in 2004, *Hamdi v. Rumsfeld.* The four most pragmatic justices—Rehnquist, O'Connor, Breyer, and Kennedy—concluded that the detention of Yaser Hamdi, an American citizen seized in Afghanistan, was permitted by the congressional resolution authorizing the president to use force against the perpetrators of the September 11 attacks. The language of the resolution was ambiguous, but the pragmatists read it in a way that avoided a potential constitutional conflict with the White House over the president's powers as commander in chief. But while the pragmatic plurality concluded that Congress had authorized Hamdi's detention, it went on to hold that Hamdi was entitled to access to lawyers and independent courts to review the legitimacy of his designation as an enemy combatant. The pragmatists then ordered lower courts to balance Hamdi's interest in liberty against the national interest in security. They said judges should not only provide Hamdi with a lawyer but also craft novel procedures that would ensure him a fair opportunity to contest his status without hampering the executive's interest in prosecuting the war on terrorism.

In one of his most surprising and impressive opinions, Scalia criticized the pragmatic plurality for creating criminal procedure by judicial fiat. Scalia lambasted the Court's "Mr. Fix-it Mentality," in which the pragmatic justices made up procedures that would ensure the constitutionality of the detentions, rather than insisting that Congress had not authorized them and forcing the executive to go back to the drawing board. Unless Congress has suspended habeas corpus, Scalia insisted legalistically, any American citizen must be tried as a criminal or released. "By repeatedly doing what it thinks the political branches ought to do, [the Court] encourages their lassitude and saps the vitality of government by the people," Scalia concluded. Scalia's prediction once again turned out to be prescient: because the Court beat Congress to the punch, Congress declined to pass a comprehensive preventive detention law regulating the president's conduct in the war on terror, and the president asserted his unilateral authority to set up military commissions and engage in domestic surveillance without explicit congressional approval.

Faced with assertions of unilateral presidential authority, however, the legalistic conservatives, including Scalia and Thomas, proved more willing to support the idea of an unchecked executive than the pragmatic conservatives, including Rehnquist, O'Connor, and Kennedy. In the case of *Hamdan v. Rumsfeld* (2006), Kennedy joined a divided opinion striking down the Bush administration's attempt to try suspected terrorists in military tribunals. Scalia, Thomas, and Samuel Alito filed passionate dissents suggesting that the president should be able to act decisively in the war on terror without congressional authorization. Once again, the debate between the legalistic and pragmatic conservative justices recapitulated an internal debate among conservatives about the scope of presidential power that began under Ronald Reagan and came to define the administration of George W. Bush. Kennedy and Rehnquist represented an older generation of states' rights conservatives who associated the presidency with the liberal nationalizing excesses of the New Deal and the

Great Society. By contrast, Scalia, Thomas, and Alito represented a younger generation of strong executive conservatives whose political sensibility was shaped in the Reagan and first Bush administrations, and who came to see a vigorous president as the only way of defending conservative ideals of limited government from the encroachments of the Democrat-controlled Congress. How a vision of presidential power that began as a defense of limited government transformed itself into a defense of unlimited government is one of the paradoxes of recent American political history.

Rehnquist, however, was not always a restrained pragmatist, willing to defer to decisions of democratic majorities. He was consistently willing to question federal power in cases involving states' rights. During his first decade on the bench, the most important states' rights case for which Rehnquist wrote the majority opinion was *National League of Cities v. Usery*, in 1976; that case heralded the beginning of the so-called federalism revolution, which imposed meaningful limits on congressional power for the first time since the New Deal. In his opinion, Rehnquist argued for limiting the federal government's ability to regulate the wages and hours of state and local government employees. The Tenth Amendment, he said, prevents Congress from acting in a way that "impairs the States' integrity or their ability to function effectively in a federal system." Although Rehnquist had mixed success maintaining majorities for this principle in the 1970s and '80s, by the 1990s he had found at least four reliable allies—Scalia, Thomas, Kennedy, and O'Connor. By not consistently deferring to Congress, both Rehnquist and Scalia failed to fulfill their oft-stated commitment to judicial restraint; under Rehnquist's leadership the Court indulged in an overconfident rhetoric of judicial supremacy and struck down thirty federal laws in one seven-year period—a higher rate than in any other Court in history.[44]

Scalia and Rehnquist showed a similar lack of restraint in one of the most controversial cases of their tenure together, *Bush v. Gore.* The case resulted from the closely contested presidential election of 2000. After the Florida Supreme Court ordered a manual recount of the undervotes (that is, punch card ballots on which no vote was recorded), Bush appealed to the U.S. Supreme Court, which halted the recount by a 5–4 vote. In a separate statement to the Court's opinion, Scalia predicted that there was a "substantial probability" that Bush would succeed in his challenge, and therefore the recount ordered by the Florida Court would "cast a cloud upon what [Bush] claims to be the legitimacy of his election." As it turned out, Scalia's prediction was wrong—a definitive manual recount conducted by the media after the election suggested that the counting standard Gore asked for would have elected Bush, not Gore, increasing rather than undermining Bush's legitimacy. (And, in any event, Bush's legitimacy was affected less by the Court than by the September 11 attacks eight months after he took office.) Nevertheless, Scalia, who made a career of ridiculing pragmatic arguments, justified the Court's decision to intervene in essentially pragmatic terms. "The Court's reputation" should not be considered as "some shiny piece of trophy armor," he announced in a speech after the election. "It's working armor and meant to be used and sometimes dented in the service of the public." Rehnquist, who had more standing to make pragmatic arguments, also defended the Court's intervention in *Bush v. Gore* on practical grounds. "There is a national crisis, and only you can avert it," he said in a speech discussing the Supreme Court's similar intervention in the contested election of 1876. "It may be very hard to say no." After the fact, however, both Rehnquist and Scalia's defense of *Bush v. Gore* was undermined by the revelation that Bush would have won the election by almost any conceivable scenario. Both Congress and the Florida state legislature were poised to reverse the Florida Supreme Court if given the chance, and according to the federal law passed to avoid a repeat of the chaos that followed the election of 1876, Congress, controlled by the Republicans, was the body authorized to resolve electoral disputes. Moreover, the decision in *Bush v. Gore* was hard to reconcile with the original understanding of the Constitution that Scalia embraces as his touchstone. As Justice Stephen Breyer noted in his powerful dissent, James Madison believed that allowing the judiciary to choose the presidential electors "was out of the question." Because the opinion was hard to justify according to any of the methodologies that Scalia and Rehnquist ordinarily applied, it might be viewed as an outlier, a reminder of the truism that the most politically contested cases tend to unsettle the judgment of judges and litigants.

In his *Bush v. Gore* dissent, Breyer insisted that, rather than casting themselves as saviors for a polarized nation, unelected judges should instead consider the institutional costs that result when they presume to short-circuit political battles. Afterward, Breyer set out to provide a broader defense of the pragmatic philosophy he shared, in some cases, with Rehnquist and O'Connor. In his 2005 book *Active Liberty,* Breyer argued that judges in constitutional cases should focus on the practical consequences of their decisions—in particular on the likelihood that a particular decision will promote political participation, rather than discourage it. "Courts should take a greater account of the Constitution's democratic nature when they interpret constitutional and statutory texts," he wrote.[45]

An emphasis on democratic participation is often associated with liberal scholars who take an unrealistic view of the people's deliberative abilities. Breyer took a far more modest view of judicial power. He argued for the resurrection of the liberal position of judicial restraint associated with judges such as Oliver Wendell Holmes, although Breyer's view of democracy was far more optimistic than Holmes's. Arguing for judicial humility, Breyer insisted that increased judicial

216

deference to democratic outcomes "will yield better law—law that helps a community of individuals democratically find practical solutions to important contemporary social problems."[46] In addition to defending judicial deference, Breyer also criticized Scalia's jurisprudence of original understanding. Since the framers of the Constitution did not want their own intentions to bind future generations of judges, Breyer argued, Scalia's literalistic originalism can only be defended in practical terms, as an effective way of controlling judicial subjectivity. But, in fact, Breyer insisted, pragmatic judges were even less subjective than their originalist opponents, because they were more cautious, more incrementalist, more concerned about the effects of their decisions on the institutions of government, and because they understood that "too radical, too frequent legal change has, as a consequence, a tendency to undercut . . . human needs."[47]

It was not only liberals like Breyer who accused Scalia and Rehnquist of ignoring the original meaning of the Constitution in cases where they had strong personal convictions; some conservatives raised the same questions. For example, the scholarship of one of the most respected conservative judges in the country, Michael McConnell of the U.S. Court of Appeals for the Tenth Circuit, suggests that Scalia and Rehnquist's efforts to strike down affirmative action, resurrect school prayer, and prevent Congress from construing the Bill of Rights more broadly than the courts could not easily be reconciled with the text or original understanding of the Constitution.[48] Their refusal to respond to these scholarly criticisms convinced skeptics that their devotion to constitutional history was opportunistic rather than principled. But because Rehnquist never claimed to be a high priest of original meaning, his reputation suffered less from the criticism than Scalia's did. In the end, Rehnquist claimed to care most about deferring to democratically elected officials, and as the most restrained and deferential conservative justice, he generally lived up to his word. Scalia deserves respect for asking to be judged by his adherence to a consistent judicial philosophy, but he has exposed himself to criticism when his application of that philosophy has appeared to be inconsistent.

During nearly two decades together on the Court, Rehnquist and Scalia were often perceived as close because they voted together in the high-profile cases involving the culture wars. Together, they voted to strike down affirmative action, to uphold sodomy laws and anti-gay rights initiatives, and to allow the display of the Ten Commandments. In each of these cases, they were in the minority, often because they were deserted by Justice O'Connor, who provided the fifth or sixth vote to create a majority for the liberal side. But even when Rehnquist voted with Scalia, he refused to indulge in the apocalyptic language that Scalia routinely employed. Objecting to the Court's 6–3 decision to strike down a Colorado anti-gay rights initiative in 1996, for example, Scalia complained, "The Court has mistaken a Kulturkampf for a fit of spite." In his dissent from a 5–4 decision to uphold affirmative action in law school admissions in 2003, Scalia thundered, "The Constitution proscribes government discrimination on the basis of race, and state-provided education is no exception." Criticizing a 5–4 decision to strike down one display of the Ten Commandments in 2005, he declared, "Nothing stands behind the Court's assertion that governmental affirmation of the society's belief in God is unconstitutional except the Court's own say-so." In all of these cases, Rehnquist either remained silent or expressed himself in far less aggrieved terms, suggesting that Scalia, unlike Rehnquist, took his culture war defeats personally.

It is too soon to be certain about Scalia's legacy. But at the end of the Rehnquist era, even conservative admirers concede that Scalia is more likely to make his mark outside the Court than inside of it. Unable to persuade his colleagues, Scalia has confessed that he writes with "verve and panache" to ensure that his opinions are quoted by the editors of legal textbooks, so they can influence future generations of lawyers and scholars.[49] In this ambition, Scalia has been successful: the leading constitutional law casebooks include more opinions by Scalia than any other justice, and more academic articles contain his name in the title than that of any other justice on the Rehnquist Court.[50] But many of these articles are critical of his methodology, and Scalia himself acknowledges that most of the academic community rejects his vision of "original meaning," or believes that he applies it inconsistently. In the long run, Scalia's influence may be limited not only by his temperament but by his insensitivity to political context. After all, Hugo Black, like Scalia, believed that judges should enforce the original meaning of the constitutional text—nothing more and nothing less. But Black did not interpret the text in a vacuum. While he cared about language and history, he also understood the need to preserve the Court's legitimacy as an institution of democracy. He joined opinions that Scalia later criticized as inconsistent with the original understanding of the Constitution—such as those requiring the state to pay for lawyers for poor defendants and requiring the police to read suspects their *Miranda* rights—because he felt they were plausibly consistent with the text of the Constitution and would help to restrain police excesses in an age when police powers had expanded in ways that the eighteenth-century framers could not have imagined. Black also insisted that the First Amendment required the government to be neutral between religion and secularism—not merely among religions, as Scalia has maintained. In addition to being a historically plausible account of the views of the American framers, Black's views were informed by his vast readings in European and American history, which convinced him that the broad intent of the American framers was to put the religious wars of Europe behind them and to keep religion and government in separate spheres. In this sense, Black's background as a politician served him well, whereas Scalia's isolation as a law professor has given his opinions an academic quality that may limit his ultimate influence.

In his presidential campaigns, George W. Bush promised to appoint justices in the mold of Scalia and Clarence Thomas. But when it came time to choose a successor to William Rehnquist in 2005, Bush chose a justice in the mold of Rehnquist. John Roberts, a former clerk to Rehnquist, appears to share many of the former chief's qualities of temperament and jurisprudence. He has a knack for getting along with ideological opponents and has been celebrated for his even temper, good humor, and lack of anger. He has no trace of conservative victimology and, as the most distinguished Supreme Court advocate of his generation, has a knack for persuading judges of very different orientations. Most important, Roberts, like Rehnquist, has refused to embrace originalism as the only touchstone of constitutional fidelity, and instead has styled himself a "bottom-up" judge rather than a "top-down" judge. Bottom-up judges, like Roberts and Rehnquist, are engaged by the facts of each case and are willing to follow the relevant legal precedents in whatever direction they happen to lead. Top-down judges, like Scalia, Thomas, and William O. Douglas, start with well-developed ideological commitments and impose them on each case, regardless of the facts. It was Rehnquist's suspicion of "top-down" approaches that made him one of the more successful chief justices in history. The fact that he was replaced by a chief justice in his own image is perhaps the greatest testament to his success.

The Future
of Temperament

———

Throughout the history of the Supreme Court, judicial temperament has helped to define the success or failure of individual
justices and of the Court as a whole. But it is not clear that this pattern will necessarily hold in the future, as the public demands more
details about the behind-the-scenes dramas on the Court and as the
justices face new pressures and new opportunities to promote themselves as individuals.

The responsibility for leading an increasingly individualistic
group of justices has fallen on Chief Justice John G. Roberts, Jr., who
took office in 2005. Based on the early impression he made in his
confirmation hearings and in his first year on the Court, Roberts has
displayed a temperament that suggests he has many of the personal
gifts and talents of the most successful justices, such as John Marshall, John Marshall Harlan, Hugo Black, and William H. Rehnquist.
As the leading Supreme Court advocate of his generation, Roberts appeared before the Court dozens of times, representing clients on both

sides of the political spectrum. Roberts's work as an advocate earned him a reputation for fair-mindedness. He was widely respected as a legal craftsman who did not come to cases with preconceived grand theories but instead took positions based on the arguments and legal materials in each case. Personally as well as jurisprudentially modest, Roberts prefers baseball analogies to showy displays of his formidable intellect. He treats litigants with even-handed courtesy and sends gifts to acquaintances with newborn children or notes to those whose family members are sick. Because of his appealing personality and personal thoughtfulness, it's easy when talking to him to forget that you are talking to the chief justice of the United States.

In July 2006, just after the end of his first term as chief justice, Roberts shared some reflections about the importance of temperament on the Supreme Court. The term had begun with more unanimous opinions in a row than at any point in the Court's modern history and ended with a series of divided opinions that provoked passionate charges and countercharges by the justices in the majority and in dissent. "It's sobering to think of the seventeen chief justices, certainly a solid majority of them have to be characterized as failures," he said with a rueful smile. "The successful ones are hard to number."[1] Roberts observed that the least successful chiefs had approached their jobs as law professors rather than as leaders of a collegial Court. Harlan Fiske Stone, a former dean of Columbia Law School, was a case in point. "I understand [Stone] was a failure as chief, because of his misperception of what a chief justice is supposed to be," Roberts said, gesturing to the justices' private conference room through an open door of his chambers. "It's his desk out there that is separate from the conference table, and he kind of sat at his desk, and the others were at the table, and he almost called on them and critiqued their performances. They hated that." Roberts laughed. "As a result, he was a failure as a chief justice."

Roberts attributed this record of failure not only to a misunderstanding of the job of chief justice but also to its circumscribed powers. "A chief justice's authority is really quite limited and the dynamic among all the justices is going to affect whether he can accomplish much or not," he said. "There is this convention of referring to the Taney Court, the Marshall Court, the Fuller Court, but a chief justice has the same vote that everyone else has." As a result, "the chief's ability to get the Court to do something is really quite restrained."

Roberts had been thinking a great deal about John Marshall, one of the few of his predecessors to have been an unequivocal success in the job. In Roberts's view, Marshall's success was a reflection of his temperament. "He gave everyone the benefit of the doubt, he approached everyone as a friend, the assumption was that this is someone I'm going to like unless proven otherwise," Roberts said of Marshall. "He was convivial, he took great pride in sharing his Madeira with his colleagues. . . . nothing about the artificial glad-hander type, it was just in his nature to get along with people. I think that had to play an important role in his ability to bring the Court together, to change the whole way judicial decisions were arrived at, to really create the notion that we are a Court, not simply an assemblage of individual justices, which of course had been the English model. It was the force of his personality." The fact that his fellow justices trusted Marshall, in particular, allowed him to bring the Court together. "That lack of pretense, that openness and general trustworthiness were very important personality traits in Marshall's success," Roberts observed.

Roberts contrasted Marshall's temperament with that of Thomas Jefferson, his archrival. "Jefferson certainly did not have the common touch," he emphasized. "To some extent, maybe affected, and perhaps I'm being unfair to Jefferson but more of, almost like a *philosophe*'s attachment to the ideas." Roberts shook his head. "It's sort of a cottage industry these days to downplay Jefferson, but when you look at him side by side with Marshall, Marshall comes across as a more substantial character, certainly more likable. Yes, I think they'd both invite you to share their table and pour you a drink, but you kind of think you'd have a very academic discussion with Jefferson and you'd have a good time with Marshall."

Although he hadn't had much time to think about the job before joining the Court, Roberts said he decided to embrace Marshall as a model during his first term. "Once you're here you don't immediately think you've got to be like Oliver Ellsworth," he said, laughing. (Ellsworth, chief justice from 1796 to 1800, was one of Marshall's obscure and forgotten predecessors.) "If you're going to start out as a competitive bicyclist, you're going to wonder how Lance Armstrong did it. You're not going to pick somebody else."

Roberts said his decision to embrace Marshall's vision was "a reaction to the personalization of judicial politics." He lamented that the unanimity of the Marshall Court had deteriorated over time. "There weren't a lot of concurring opinions in the thirty years when Marshall was the chief justice. There weren't a lot of dissents. And nowadays, you take a look at some of our opinions and you wonder if we're reverting back to the English model where everybody has to have their say. It's more being concerned with the jurisprudence of the individual rather than working toward a jurisprudence of the Court." Roberts praised justices who were willing to put the good of the Court above their own ideological agendas. "A justice is not like a law professor, who might say, 'This is my theory of this, and this is what I'm going to be faithful to and consistent with, and in twenty years we'll look back and say, I had a consistent theory of the First Amendment as applied to a particular area,'" he explained. Instead of nine justices moving in nine separate directions, Roberts said, "I

Chief Justice John Roberts decided, during his first term in 2005–6, to resurrect Chief Justice Marshall's vision of unanimity and collegiality. Under
his leadership, the Court produced more unanimous opinions in a row than
at any other time in its modern history.

do think it would be good to have a commitment on the part of the
Court to acting as a Court, rather than being more concerned about
the consistency and coherency of an individual judicial record."

Roberts seemed especially frustrated by the focus, in the media
and in the public at large, on the number of 5–4 decisions and the
shifting coalitions that determined them. "There was a question from
one of these groups that come in here: 'How do you decide who's going to be the swing vote?'" Roberts said, shaking his head. "I don't
know, we rotate. That has to undermine, that's a steady wasting away
of the notion of the rule of law, a personalization of it." He acknowledged that he was "kind of put out by some of the articles" at the
end of term emphasizing the divisions on the Court. "We had more
unanimous opinions announced in a row than ever before. There's

some limit on this statistic—in the modern Court, or in the modern era—but in the first 5–4 decision, people are writing, 'So much for unanimity.'" He said it was a bad thing that, at the end of each term, commentators published graphs about who on the Court agreed most often with whom. "It is such an egotistical analysis of the Court." He sighed. "The whole notion that it's functioning as a Court doesn't seem to appeal to anyone. . . . I think it's bad, long-term, if people identify the rule of law with how individual justices vote."

After years of "the personalization of judicial politics," Roberts acknowledged that it would not be an easy task to promote unanimity. He said that he had to emphasize the benefits of unanimity for individual justices, in order to effect what he called the team dynamic. "You do have to put people in a situation where they will appreciate, from their own point of view, having the Court acquire more legitimacy, credibility, that they will benefit from the shared commitment to unanimity in a way that they wouldn't otherwise," he said. To some degree, Roberts considered himself in an ideal situation, overseeing a Court that was evenly divided on important issues. "You do need some fluidity in the middle to develop a commitment to a different way of deciding things." In other words, on a divided Court when neither camp can be confident that it will win in the most controversial cases, both sides have an incentive to work toward unanimity—a kind of bilateral disarmament.

Marshall's example had taught him, Roberts said, that personal trust in the chief justice's lack of an ideological agenda was very important. "If I'm sitting there telling people, 'We should decide the case on this basis,' and if you, another justice, think, 'That's just Roberts trying to push some agenda again, and if it were more a different result that he did not like that he wouldn't be saying it,' they're not likely to listen very often," he observed. Roberts said he was inspired by Marshall's ability to win this kind of trust. "He could easily have got on the Court and said, 'I'm the last hope of the Federalists; we're out of Congress; we're out of the White House; and I'm going to pursue that agenda here.' And he would have not only damaged the Court but could have smothered it in the cradle. But instead he said, 'No, this is my home now, this is the Court, and we're going to operate as a Court, and that's important to me,' and as a result he made the Court the institution that it has become. So it's worth trying, and maybe it's worth trying for a little while, and if it becomes hopeless, then you can go back and not view that as a major effort."

Roberts said he was often struck by how people focus on controversial cases, like "*Brown* and the failure to achieve unanimity in *Bush v. Gore*. And the other justices say we need to act as a Court. Well, it's not just on the tough cases. And it's easier to do it if you get into the habit of doing it as a matter of routine. It's hard to shift gears." So Roberts had tried, in the less visible cases of the term, to develop "a culture and an ethos that says 'It's good when we're all together.'" He added that little cases, too, can provoke fierce initial disagreements. "Just because a case ends up unanimous doesn't mean that's how it started," he emphasized. "The vote may be divided in conference, and yet if you think it's valuable to have consensus on it, you can get it, and it's a little case, but once you do it in a little case, you can move on. And there were bigger cases as well."

Roberts said he intended to use his assignment power to achieve as broad a consensus as possible. "It's not my greatest power, it's my only power," he said, laughing. "Say someone is committed to broad consensus and somebody else is just dead set on 'my way or the highway. And I've got five votes and that's all I need.' Well, you assign that one to the other person, and it gives you a much better chance out of the box of getting some kind of consensus." He acknowledged that this approach might be perceived on the Court as a more controversial use of the assignment power than Chief Justice Rehnquist's stated policy of punishing only those justices who were slow in producing opinions. His colleagues were likely to understand a neutral policy of not getting assignments when they were late with opinions, he said, but they might well object if they felt that those justices who agreed with the chief were being rewarded with plum assignments. Instead, Roberts wanted to make clear that the rewards would go to those who wrote opinions in ways that might attract more votes, regardless of their ideological orientation.

Rehnquist was also famous for running a briskly efficient conference, but Roberts said that sometimes his vision of unanimity required longer discussions. "There's a lot less flexibility once something is in writing," he said. According to tradition, each justice speaks once, in order of seniority, before anyone can speak twice, but as the moderator, Roberts has the ability to shape the discussion by initially framing the issues in a case, inviting responses to particular points. "What I regard as the hardest work of my work month is how you present a case and what you say it's about," he said. Preparation for oral argument was easier, because "you can ask stupid questions and nobody seems to mind. I prepare enough, but the hard part is then I have a short amount of time for sometimes very tough cases to figure out how to present this that will make it most useful to the conference." In trying to frame a case so that as many justices as possible can converge around a common result, Roberts often finds it useful to define the principle in question as narrowly as possible. "In most cases, I think the narrower the better, because people will be less concerned about it," he said.

Roberts emphasized that Marshall's temperament and worldview came from his experiences as a soldier at Valley Forge, where he developed a commitment to the success of the nation. "Some have speculated that the real root of Marshall's ill feeling to Jefferson was that Jefferson was not at Valley Forge, was not in the fight, and had what Marshall might regard as a somewhat precious attachment to

ideas for the sake of ideas, while Marshall was more personally invested in the success of the American experiment."

Roberts said he had not thought about the sources of his own interest in unity and consensus and bringing people together or whether
there was anything in his upbringing that might account for it, similar
to Marshall's experiences as the oldest of an unruly group of fifteen
siblings. But he was willing to engage the question, recalling that his
father, an executive at Bethlehem Steel, "was most known for his willingness to work with unions at a time there was a lot of enmity—
between management and the unions." John Roberts, Sr., his son
recalled, would "show up unexpectedly at the union hall, buy a round
of drinks for the people in the union." In the 1960s and '70s, when
the Japanese were the great economic threat to the steel business,
Roberts's father insisted that union leaders accompany management
executives on a trip to Japan, so that both sides could personally evaluate the competition. "I would say that's a general view of bringing a
broader degree of consensus about a solution to a particular problem
than his peers might have adopted," Roberts recalled.

Roberts was known in high school for his leadership skills, as
captain of the football team, and for his academic ability, which he
cultivated with a light touch. His high school principal recalled that
he was "an outstanding student, but very quiet, low-key, never lorded
his intelligence over others."[2] Roberts, however, downplays the idea
that he learned leadership skills there: "It's kind of an unusual situation where there are twenty-five people in the class." He acknowledges that his undergraduate thesis at Harvard about the failure of
the British Liberal Party in the Edwardian era may have reflected his
early suspicion of the politics of personality. "My central thesis with
respect to the Liberal Party was that they made a fatal mistake in in-
vesting too heavily in the personalities of Lloyd George and Churchill,
as opposed to adopting a more broad-based reaction to the rise of

Labour, that they were steadily fixated on the personalities." But his most formative experiences, Roberts insisted, were as a Supreme Court advocate and as an appellate judge.

"You're always trying to persuade people, obviously, as an advocate," he said. "And I do find, and did find, that you can be generally more successful in persuading people, in arguing a case, if you go with something that you think has the possibility of getting seven votes rather than five. You don't like going in thinking, 'Here's my pitch and I'm honing it to get five votes.' That's a risky strategy." He laughed. As an advocate, Roberts prided himself for having represented both sides of an issue—liberals and conservatives, government and industry—and this increased his belief in the importance of a bipartisan vision of law. "I do think it's extremely valuable for people to be on both sides, and I mean being in private practice and being in government, arguing against the government and for the government," he said. "It does give you a perspective that you just can't get any other way, in terms of what the concerns of the other side really are. And it also gives you an added credibility, and that's very, very important."

Roberts says the most important source of his decision to resurrect Marshall's vision of unanimity was his brief experience as an appellate judge on the U.S. Court of Appeals for the District of Columbia Circuit. "For whatever reason, it is firmly embedded as part of the function of that court that you function as a court," he said. "It is part of a pushback against the higher degree of politicization of the appointment process there." In reaction to this politicization, judges on the D.C. Circuit have agreed, in Roberts's words, that "we're not politicians; we're judges; we're a court; and we're going to work real hard to be a court—partly because we don't like people thinking we're not, and partly because some of us had experience in the bitter period where we weren't." Roberts served on the D.C. Circuit for only two years, but the experience of working to achieve consensus impressed him. "That was my first experience as a judge, and I liked the way it worked," he said. On the D.C. Circuit, the convention was that the most junior judge spoke first in the private conference for each three-judge panel. On the Supreme Court, the chief speaks first. "So I always spoke first," Roberts noted with a laugh. "And what it means was that I kind of had to be prepared, almost like law school, to state the case from the very beginning."

Roberts sounded frustrated that consensus was more elusive on the Supreme Court than on the appellate court. "It's so much harder, first of all, with nine people than with three. You sit around with three people and ask, 'Where's the common ground?' and it's easy. With nine, it's much harder. It is, whatever else, a fascinating personal psychology dynamic to get nine different people with nine different views. It's going to take some time." Some justices prefer arguments in writing, others are more receptive to personal appeals, and all react badly to heavy-handed orders. To lead such an unruly group requires the skills of an orchestra conductor, as Felix Frankfurter used to say, or those of the extremely subtle and observant Supreme Court advocate that Roberts used to be.

Roberts acknowledged that chief justices are more likely to sublimate their personal views for the good of the Court than associate justices are, citing the example of his former boss, William Rehnquist. "I think there's no doubt that he changed; as associate justice and chief, he became naturally more concerned about the function of the institution," Roberts said. "He had settled views on *Miranda*, yet he's the one who appreciates that it had become part of the law, that it would do more harm to uproot it, and he wrote that opinion as chief for the good of the institution."

He added that Rehnquist was also a successful chief because of his temperament—namely, that he knew who he was and had no inclination to change his views simply to court popularity. "That Scandinavian austerity and sense of fate and complication," in Roberts's words, was an important part of Rehnquist's character, as was Rehnquist's Lutheran faith: "It's a significant and purposeful mode of worship to get up in the morning to do your job as best you can, to go to bed at night, and not to worry too much about whether the best that you can do is good enough or not. And he did not—once a case was decided, it was decided, and if every editorial page in the country was going to trash it, he didn't care. And it was on to the next one, he'd done his best, that was the way it was going to be." Roberts said he associated Rehnquist with a midwestern stubbornness. "Anyone who clerked for him was familiar with him intoning the phrase, 'Well, I'm just not going to do it.'" Here Roberts did a spot-on impersonation of Rehnquist's deadpan drawl. "That meant that was the end of it, no matter how much you were going to try to persuade him. It wasn't going to happen."

Roberts added that Rehnquist, like John Marshall, was noted for his lack of concern about dress and lack of pretense or false modesty. Just as Marshall was mistaken as an ordinary traveler on a stagecoach, so Rehnquist often traveled without being recognized as the chief justice. "When Rehnquist was in New Orleans at a judicial convention, he went to the local Lutheran church; they have a tradition of strangers introducing themselves. He stands up; he's asked what do you do. And he says, "I'm a government lawyer." There's not the slightest bit of contrivance to that. There's not an element of, 'This will show how modest I am.' It's how he thought of himself." If Rehnquist had spent his life in a two-man law practice in Phoenix, Roberts said, he would have been the same person. "His character in dealing with people, everything, would be the same. Someone like that is someone people are going to feel comfortable with even if they disagree very strongly. He knew where to draw the line and say, I guess we're just not going to agree on that, and let it go at that. And he was perfectly comfortable having a cigarette and a Miller's Lite, as he put it, and watching the ball game, with anyone, regardless of their views."

In the end, Roberts said, Rehnquist cared somewhat about building consensus, but not all that much: for example, he was willing to join opinions with which he disagreed as the sixth vote, but not the fifth. "I don't remember [promoting unanimity] as a feature that Rehnquist stressed much," Roberts recalled.

Roberts acknowledged that he had set himself a daunting task in trying to resist the polarization of the judiciary, but he viewed it also as a "special opportunity," especially in our intensely polarized age. "Politics are closely divided," he observed. "The same with the Congress. There ought to be some sense of some stability [in the Court] if the government is not going to polarize completely. It's a high priority to keep any kind of partisan divide out of the judiciary as well."

Much of Roberts's success or failure will be determined by his colleagues and their readiness to embrace his vision. "To the extent that my colleagues share that concern, we should be able to make some progress," he agreed. During his first term, Roberts was surprised that some justices talked openly about how to protect the legitimacy of the Court. "People are concerned about having new justices on the Court," he said. "People don't want the Court to seem to be lurching around because of changes in personnel. That certainly is a concern." He felt that his success in achieving an unusually high number of unanimous opinions was due to the other justices' eagerness to be helpful to a newcomer, much like a fiancé meeting his future in-laws for the first time at Thanksgiving. "I do think people were being particularly helpful and accommodating in the first term," he said. "Maybe they won't feel the same way the second. We'll see."

But even if Roberts's honeymoon were to last a little longer, he would confront a daunting series of challenges that Marshall never faced. In an age when the public demands that public officials turn themselves into personalities, and insists on evaluating their actions in personal terms, even the most savvy chief justice would face an uphill battle in persuading his colleagues to resist the relentless pressure to pursue the spotlight. Offering up homey autobiographical anecdotes to build political support has become a familiar strategy among Supreme Court nominees in confirmation hearings—Judge Samuel Alito, for example, talked frequently about his father, an Italian immigrant. But now personal exposure is becoming a strategy for the justices to connect to the public once on the bench: Clarence Thomas has received a $1.5 million advance for a memoir, with the working title *From Pin Point to Points After,* which promises to describe his rise from obscurity, including his personal impressions of his "emotionally overwhelming" confirmation battle, in which he was accused of sexual harassment by Anita Hill. Thomas is often silent on the bench but emotionally candid in his autobiographical speeches to African-American students, in which he identifies openly with their struggles and offers his own experiences as an inspirational tale. But exercises in personal revelation may make him an even more polarizing figure to a public that is already sharply divided about his jurisprudence. Promoted by conservative commentators to conservative readers, Thomas's book could make it even harder for him to disappoint his base in his judicial opinions, if he were even inclined to do so. And like William O. Douglas, Thomas may inadvertently harm his judicial reputation (which is, at the moment, unfairly underrated) by revealing more than he intends.

The focus on justices as personalities—demanded by the public and cultivated by some justices—is a direct challenge to Roberts's view that justice itself should be impersonal. "What you're trying to establish—wearing black robes and, in earlier times, wigs," he said, is "that it's not the person, it's the law." To persuade indi-

An early portrait of the Roberts Court in the fall of 2005. On January 31, 2006, Justice Sandra Day O'Connor retired from the Court and was succeeded by Justice Samuel A. Alito.

vidual justices to resist the pressures to promote themselves rather than the interests of the Court as a whole, he will have to appeal, in different ways, to their self-interest and to a broader understanding of their judicial role. Roberts understandably declined to criticize his colleagues by name. But when he objected to justices who act more like law professors than members of a collegial court, it was hard not to think of Scalia and Thomas, who are more interested in writing the equivalent of law review articles to demonstrate their jurisprudential consistency than in finding common ground with their colleagues.

Roberts could, in theory, appeal to justices like Scalia and Thomas—and their counterparts on the liberal wing of the court—in the following terms: in important cases, the Court is evenly divided between four liberals and four conservatives, and neither block can be confident, in any particular high-profile case, that it will prevail. Surely it would be in the best interest of each side if it could win in 50 percent of the cases by a unanimous vote, rather than gambling on the possibility of winning slightly more often by a 5–4 vote, since a unanimous victory would be harder, in the future, to overturn. Of course, the justice who would be most resistant to this kind of bargain would be the swing justice—at the moment, Anthony Kennedy, who naturally enjoys his unique opportunity to determine the outcome of the most controversial cases on his own. When the swing justice is as self-dramatizing as Kennedy, even the most skillful appeals to the Court's common interests may fall on deaf ears. But Kennedy, like most of the justices, also cares deeply about his reputation and the reputation of the Court as a whole, so perhaps the best way for Roberts to appeal to him and to his colleagues is by invoking the lessons of history.

If the pairings of judicial temperaments in this book suggest anything, it is that courting attention and partisan approval in the short term is no guarantee of judicial respect in the long term. In each of the pairings, there have been consistent tropes. The brilliant academic is less appealing, over time, than the collegial pragmatist. The self-centered loner is less effective than the convivial team player. The resentful braggarts wear less well than the secure justices who know who they are. The narcissist wields judicial power less sure-handedly than the judge who shows personal as well as judicial humility. The loose cannons shoot themselves in the foot, while those who know when to hold their tongues appear more judicious. (On the Court, a justice often achieves more by saying less.) The ideological purists are marginalized, while those who understand when not to take each principle to its logical extreme are vindicated by history. Those who view cases in purely philosophical terms are less sure-footed than those who are aware of the cases' practical effects. Those with the common touch win broader support than those who live entirely in abstractions.

Emphasizing the relationship between judicial temperament and judicial success is not meant to minimize the many ways that legal precedents and principles constrain and guide individual justices, constraints that have nothing to do with character. A degree of philosophical consistency, moreover, remains an important virtue: as Antonin Scalia argues at every opportunity, a judge who decides each case based on sympathy for the results rather than a coherent approach to constitutional interpretation would be lawless. Nevertheless, as Scalia also sometimes shows, justices who demand to be judged entirely by their adherence to consistent principles are especially vulnerable to the charge of philosophical inconsistency.

It is hard not to be struck by the fact that two of the most ambitious constitutional philosophers in American history—Thomas Jefferson and Oliver Wendell Holmes, Jr.—achieved greatness in political life because of, not in spite of, their philosophical inconsistencies. Jefferson was a relatively successful president because he was willing to abandon his strict constructionist ideals and to approve the Louisiana Purchase. He understood that the future of America depended on it. Holmes's contemporary reputation as a liberal and libertarian hero depends in large measure on his belated abandonment of the judicial abstinence on which he had staked his career and his embrace of judicial activism in cases involving free speech. The examples of Jefferson and Holmes suggest that a judicial philosophy is important, but so is a degree of judicial flexibility.

Marshall, after all, had a strong philosophy of his own, rooted in vigorous protections for national power and property rights, but he was willing not to press his philosophy in cases he knew he couldn't win. (Remember his axiom: "I am not fond of butting against a wall in sport.") Despite the charge of High Federalists that he was too fond of popularity, Marshall was not noted for his willingness to compromise on the Court. But he was able to articulate his principles in ways that his opponents could accept. As Roberts said, Marshall "was not in any sense—and this was part of what made him trustworthy—he was not a dealmaker, not a broker. That's not how he facilitated consensus. He had strongly felt principles, principles for which he had risked his life. . . . But he was willing to explain, to talk it out with people and he had a prodigious intellect, but he didn't scare people off with it. . . . He was friendly, open, people trusted him, and the force of his intellect carried the day and was able to bring people along." As for Marshall's willingness to disappoint his ideological supporters, Roberts says that even if Marshall had the votes to push the Federalist agenda harder than he did, "it was better to proceed in a way that he wasn't going to alienate people on the Court and turn the Court into another battleground."

In many ways, of course, judicial success has nothing to do with either judicial temperament or judicial philosophy, it simply reflects a justice's success in predicting the future. Oliver Wendell Holmes is admired today because his championing of judicial restraint in economic cases was vindicated by the New Deal; John Marshall Harlan is admired because his lonely embrace of racial equality was vindicated by the civil rights movement; and Hugo Black is admired because of his free speech libertarianism and insistence (with Harlan) that the Bill of Rights restrained the states—both positions vindicated in the Warren era. The blind spots of all three men (Holmes's radical majoritarianism on race and eugenics; Harlan's nativism; Black's Klan membership) are forgiven, if not forgotten, because each of them was on the right side of at least one big issue that future generations would care intensely about. By contrast, William O. Douglas's low reputation today is due not only to his self-indulgent behavior and lack of judicial craft but to his aggressively unapologetic style of liberal judicial activism—a style that has been, for more than a generation, politically out of fashion. Playing to any ideological base has its dangers since that base will almost certainly disappear at some point in the future. This is another reason why justices who can moderate their ideological passions for the good of the Court may serve themselves in the long run.

Each of these pairings has a type and antitype of a successful judicial temperament, but judicial temperament is not the only virtue. Jefferson and Holmes are among the greatest men in American history, and both represent important and admirable strains in American political thought that continue to inspire people today. Both appear indeed to have been geniuses, and genius always deserves admiration, whatever its secondary effects. The self-discipline and intellectual focus that Jefferson and Holmes displayed to cultivate their gifts are exhilarating to behold. Douglas was an important historical figure, regardless of his personal shortcomings—one of the finest chairmen of the Securities and Exchange Commission and a liberal icon of the first rank. Scalia is too close to us to be judged impartially, but his wit, intelligence, and methodological ambition make him among the most impressive of the current justices, and he writes like a dream. Indeed, reading Jefferson, Holmes, or Scalia, in different ways, is a literary pleasure, and literary pleasures are rare enough in the American constitutional tradition that they should not be taken for granted.

This has been an attempt to tell the story of the Supreme Court with accounts of some of the temperaments that shaped it. From that vantage point, Chief Justice Roberts is surely correct that the Court has best served itself and the nation when the individual justices have been willing to subordinate their own interests and agendas in the interest of building judicial consensus and institutional legitimacy. Whether Roberts will be able to achieve his goal of resurrecting John

Marshall's vision in a polarized, unbuttoned, and personality-driven age remains to be seen. But his ultimate success will depend not only on his colleagues but also on his own temperament and character. Roberts approvingly quoted the observation of Chief Justice Charles Evans Hughes that "Marshall's preeminence was due to the fact that he was John Marshall." If Roberts succeeds, his success will be due to the fact that he is John Roberts. Judicial temperament alone does not determine the path of the law, which tends to reflect the broader values of society over time. But temperament influences how and whether the Supreme Court manages to express constitutional values that are recognized by the American people as fundamental or whether it attempts in vain to impose contested values on an unwilling nation. Although the trajectory of the Roberts Court is impossible, at this early stage, to predict, the temperaments of the nine justices who compose it will continue to define the Supreme Court's role in American life.

Cases Cited

Abrams v. United States, 250 U.S. 616 (1919).

Adderley v. Florida, 385 U.S. 39 (1966).

Bailey v. Alabama, 211 U.S. 452 (1908).

Bailey v. Alabama, 219 U.S. 219, 228 (1911).

Berea College v. Kentucky, 211 U.S. 45, 69 (1908).

Blakely v. Washington, 542 U.S. 296 (2004).

Brown v. Board of Education, 347 U.S. 483 (1954).

Buchanan v. Warley, 245 U.S. 60 (1917).

Buck v. Bell, 274 U.S. 200 (1927).

Bush v. Gore, 531 U.S. 98 (2000).

Cheney v. United States Dist. Court, 541 U.S. 913 (2004).

Cheney v. United States Dist. Court, 542 U.S. 367 (2004).

Cohens v. Virginia, 19 U.S. 264, 413 (1821).

Cruzan v. Director, Missouri Department of Health, 497 U.S. 261 (1990).

Debs v. United States, 249 U.S. 211 (1919).

Dennis v. United States, 341 U.S. 494 (1951).

Dickerson v. United States, 530 U.S. 428 (2000).

Elk Grove Unified School Dist. v. Newdow, 542 U.S. 1 (2004).

Engel v. Vitale, 370 U.S. 421 (1962).

Everson v. Board of Education, 330 U.S. 1 (1947).

Ex parte Mitsuye Endo, 323 U.S. 283 (1944).

Fairfax's Devisee v. Hunter's Lessee, 11 U.S. 603 (1812).

Fletcher v. Peck, 10 U.S. 87 (1810).

Foster v. Illinois, 332 U.S. 134 (1947).

Frohwerk v. United States, 249 U.S. 204 (1919).

Gideon v. Wainwright, 372 U.S. 335 (1963).

Giles v. Harris, 189 U.S. 475 (1903).

Gitlow v. New York, 268 U.S. 652 (1925).

Griswold v. Connecticut, 381 U.S. 479 (1965).

Grutter v. Bollinger, 539 U.S. 306 (2003).

Gwin, White & Prince, Inc. v. Henneford, 305 U.S. 434, 455 (1939).

Hamdan v. Rumsfeld, 126 S. Ct. 2749 (2006).

Hamdi v. Rumsfeld, 542 U.S. 507 (2004).

Hammer v. Dagenhart, 247 U.S. 251 (1918).

Hawaii v. Mankichi, 190 U.S. 197 (1903).

Hirabayashi v. United States, 320 U.S. 81 (1943).

Holtzman v. Schlesinger, 414 U.S. 1316 (1973).

Jones v. Opelika, 316 U.S. 584 (1942).

Katz v. United States, 389 U.S. 347 (1967).

Korematsu v. United States, 323 U.S. 214 (1944).

Kyllo v. United States, 533 U.S. 27 (2001).

Laird v. Tatum, 408 U.S. 1 (1972).

Lochner v. New York, 198 U.S. 45 (1905).

Mapp v. Ohio, 367 U.S. 643 (1961).

Marbury v. Madison, 5 U.S. 137 (1803).

Martin v. Hunter's Lessee, 14 U.S. 304, 377 (1816).

McCabe v. Atchison, Topeka & Santa Fe Railway, 235 U.S. 151 (1914).

McCreary County v. ACLU, 125 S. Ct. 2722 (2005).

McCulloch v. Maryland, 17 U.S. 316 (1819).

Minersville School Dist. v. Gobitis, 310 U.S. 586 (1940).

Miranda v. Arizona, 384 U.S. 436 (1966).

Morrison v. Olson, 487 U.S. 654 (1988).

National League of Cities v. Usery, 426 U.S. 833 (1976).

New York Times Co. v. Sullivan, 376 U.S. 254 (1964).

New York Times Co. v. United States, 403 U.S. 713 (1971).

Nixon v. Herndon, 273 U.S. 536 (1927).

Northern Sec. Co. v. United States, 193 U.S. 197 (1904).

Patterson v. Colorado, 205 U.S. 454 (1907).

Planned Parenthood v. Casey, 510 U.S. 1309 (1994).

Plessy v. Ferguson, 163 U.S. 537 (1896).

Pollock v. Farmers' Loan & Trust Co., 158 U.S. 601 (1895).

Roe v. Wade, 410 U.S. 113 (1973).

Romer v. Evans, 517 U.S. 620 (1996).

Rosenberg v. United States, 346 U.S. 273 (1953).

Schenck v. United States, 249 U.S. 47 (1919).

Schlesinger v. Holtzman, 414 U.S. 1321 (1973).

Scott v. Sanford, 60 U.S. 393 (1857).

Slaughter-House Cases, 83 U.S. 36 (1873).

Standard Oil Co. v. United States, 221 U.S. 1 (1911).

Strauder v. W. Va., 100 U.S. 303 (1880).

Sweezy v. New Hampshire, 354 U.S. 234 (1957).

Talbot v. Seeman, 5 U.S. 1 (1801).

Terry v. Adams, 344 U.S. 883 (1952).

Texas v. Johnson, 491 U.S. 397 (1989).

Tinker v. Des Moines Independent Community School Dist.,
393 U.S. 503 (1969).

Troxel v. Granville, 530 U.S. 57 (2000).

United States v. Booker, 543 U.S. 220 (2005).

United States v. E. C. Knight Co., 156 U.S. 1 (1895).

United States v. Stanley, 109 U.S. 3 (1883).

United States v. Virginia, 518 U.S. 515 (1996).

Vegelahn v. Guntner, 167 Mass. 92 (1896).

Washington v. Glucksberg, 521 U.S. 702 (1997).

Watkins v. United States, 354 U.S. 178 (1957).

West Coast Hotel Co. v. Parrish, 300 U.S. 379 (1937).

West Virginia State Bd. of Educ. v. Barnette, 319 U.S. 624 (1943).

Whitney v. California, 274 U.S. 357 (1927).

Williamson v. Lee Optical of Oklahoma, Inc., 348 U.S. 483, 491 (1955).

Worcester v. Georgia, 31 U.S. 515 (1832).

Yates v. United States, 354 U.S. 298 (1957).

Youngstown Sheet & Tube Co. v. Sawyer, 343 U.S. 579 (1952).

Zorach v. Clauson, 343 U.S. 306 (1952).

Notes

INTRODUCTION
A QUESTION OF TEMPERAMENT

1. David G. McCullough, *Truman* (New York: Simon & Schuster, 1992), p. 901.

2. Howard Ball and Phillip J. Cooper, *Of Power and Right: Hugo Black, William O. Douglas, and America's Constitutional Revolution* (New York: Oxford University Press, 1992), p. 19.

3. Ken Foskett, *Judging Thomas: The Life and Times of Clarence Thomas* (New York: HarperCollins, 2004), pp. 281–82.

4. Chief Justice John Roberts, interview with the author, July 11, 2006.

5. Michael J. Klarman, *From Jim Crow to Civil Rights: The Supreme Court and the Struggle for Racial Equality* (New York: Oxford University Press, 2004), p. 298.

6. Ibid., p. 302.

7. Linda Greenhouse, *Becoming Justice Blackmun: Harry Blackmun's Supreme Court Journey* (New York: Times Books, 2005), p. 187.

8. Ibid., p. 60.

9. Ibid., p. 68.

10. Thomas M. Keck, *The Most Activist Supreme Court in History: The Road to Modern Judicial Conservatism* (Chicago: University of Chicago Press, 2004), p. 251.

ONE
THE VIRGINIA ARISTOCRATS
John Marshall and Thomas Jefferson

1. James F. Simon, *What Kind of Nation: Thomas Jefferson, John Marshall, and the Epic Struggle to Create a United States* (New York: Simon & Schuster, 2002), p. 137.

2. Leonard Baker, *John Marshall: A Life in Law* (New York: Macmillan, 1974), pp. 359–60.

3. Simon, *What Kind of Nation,* p. 35.

4. David McCulloch, *John Adams* (New York: Simon & Schuster, 2001), p. 582.

5. Merrill D. Peterson, *Thomas Jefferson and the New Nation* (London: Oxford University Press, 1970), pp. 668–69.

6. Letter from Thomas Jefferson to John Dickinson, 19 December 1801, in *The Writings of Thomas Jefferson,* vol. 10 (Washington, D.C.: Thomas Jefferson Memorial Association, 1904), p. 302.

7. Letter from Thomas Jefferson to Justice William Johnson, 12 June 1823, in Jefferson, *Writings* (New York: Library of America, 1984), p. 1474.

8. Frances Norton Mason, *My Dearest Polly: Letters of Chief Justice John Marshall to His Wife, and Their Background, Political and Domestic, 1179–1831* (Richmond, Va.: Garrett & Massie, 1961), p. 218.

9. John Marshall, *An Autobiographical Sketch* (Ann Arbor: University of Michigan Press, 1937), p. 3.

10. Jean Edward Smith, *John Marshall: Definer of a Nation* (New York: Henry Holt, 1996), p. 291.

11. James B. Thayer, *John Marshall* (Boston: Houghton, Mifflin, 1901), pp. 132–33.

12. R. Kent Newmyer, *John Marshall and the Heroic Age of the Supreme Court* (Baton Rouge: Louisiana State University Press, 2001), pp. 127–29.

13. Mortimer Schwartz and John Hogan, *Joseph Story* (New York: Oceana Publications, Inc., 1959), pp. 25–27.

14. Smith, *John Marshall: Definer of a Nation,* pp. 264–65.

15. Ibid., p. 12.

16. G. Edward White, *The Marshall Court and Cultural Change: 1815–1835* (New York: Oxford University Press, 1991), pp. 370–71.

17. Smith, *John Marshall: Definer of a Nation,* p. 466.

18. Letter from John Marshall to Joseph Story, 26 September 1823, in *The Papers of John Marshall,* vol. 9 (Chapel Hill: University of North Carolina Press, 1998), p. 338.

19. Joseph J. Ellis, *American Sphinx: The Character of Thomas Jefferson* (New York: Vintage Books, 1996), p. 139.

20. Newmyer, *John Marshall and the Heroic Age of the Supreme Court,* p. 149.

21. Peterson, *Thomas Jefferson and the New Nation,* p. 580.

22. Ellis, *American Sphinx: The Character of Thomas Jefferson,* p. 118.

23. Peterson, *Thomas Jefferson and the New Nation,* pp. 382, 384.

24. Leonard W. Levy, *Jefferson and Civil Liberties: The Darker Side* (Chicago: Elephant Paperbacks, 1989), p. 163.

25. Smith, *John Marshall, Definer of a Nation,* p. 26.

26. Marshall, *An Autobiographical Sketch,* p. 4.

27. Smith, *John Marshall: Definer of a Nation,* p. 36.

28. Newmyer, *John Marshall and the Heroic Age of the Supreme Court,* pp. 26–27.

29. Peterson, *Thomas Jefferson and the New Nation,* p. 7.

30. Ibid., p. 31.

31. Ibid., p. 18.

32. Ellis, *American Sphinx: The Character of Thomas Jefferson,* pp. 36–37.

33. Peterson, *Thomas Jefferson and the New Nation,* p. 246.

34. Ellis, *American Sphinx: The Character of Thomas Jefferson,* pp. 86–87.

35. Ibid., p. 367.

36. Peterson, *Thomas Jefferson and the New Nation,* p. 261.

37. David N. Mayer, *The Constitutional Thought of Thomas Jefferson* (Charlottesville, Va.: University Press of Virginia, 1994), pp. 58–59, 61.

38. Ibid., p. 257.

39. Ellis, *American Sphinx: The Character of Thomas Jefferson,* pp. 330–31.

40. Peterson, *Thomas Jefferson and the New Nation,* p. 601.

41. Geoffrey R. Stone, *Perilous Times: Free Speech in Wartime from the Sedition Act of 1798 to the War on Terrorism* (New York: W. W. Norton, 2004), pp. 46, 63.

42. Smith, *John Marshall: Definer of a Nation,* p. 236.

43. Baker, *John Marshall: A Life in Law,* pp. 304–5.

44. Newmyer, *John Marshall and the Heroic Age of the Supreme Court,* p. 127.

45. Peterson, *Thomas Jefferson and the New Nation,* p. 623.

46. William H. Rehnquist, *Grand Inquests: The Historic Impeachments of Justice Samuel Chase and President Andrew Johnson* (New York: William Morrow and Company, 1992), p. 22.

47. Baker, *John Marshall: A Life in Law*, p. 432.

48. Ellis, *American Sphinx: The Character of Thomas Jefferson*, pp. 263–64.

49. Smith, *John Marshall: Definer of a Nation*, p. 351.

50. Sandra F. VanBurkleo, "William Johnson," *The Oxford Companion to the Supreme Court of the United States*, ed. Kermit L. Hall et al. (New York: Oxford University Press, 1992), p. 449.

51. Peterson, *Thomas Jefferson and the New Nation*, pp. 905–6.

52. Smith, *John Marshall: Definer of a Nation*, p. 293.

53. Letter from Thomas Jefferson to Justice William Johnson, 27 October 1822, in Jefferson, *Writings*, p. 1462.

54. G. Edward White, *The Marshall Court and Cultural Change 1815–1835*, p. 189.

55. Ibid., pp. 370–71.

56. Letter from Joseph Story to Mrs. Sarah Waldo Story, 5 March 1812, in *Life and Letters of Joseph Story*, vol. 1 (Boston: Little and Brown, 1851), p. 217.

57. Mayer, *The Constitutional Thought of Thomas Jefferson*, pp. 250–51.

58. Charles Warren, *The Supreme Court in United States History* (Boston: Little Brown, 1923), p. 515.

59. Mayer, *The Constitutional Thought of Thomas Jefferson*, p. 280.

60. Ibid., p. 282.

61. Ibid., pp. 280–81.

62. Smith, *John Marshall: Definer of a Nation*, p. 452.

63. Letter from Thomas Jefferson to Justice William Johnson, 12 June 1823, in Jefferson, *Writings*, p. 1476.

64. Merrill D. Peterson, *The Jeffersonian Image in the American Mind* (New York: Oxford University Press, 1962), p. 27.

65. Mayer, *The Constitutional Thought of Thomas Jefferson*, pp. 290–91.

66. Ellis, *American Sphinx: The Character of Thomas Jefferson*, pp. 333–34.

67. Smith, *John Marshall: Definer of a Nation*, p. 518.

68. Peterson, *The Jeffersonian Image in the American Mind*, pp. 56–57.

69. Smith, *John Marshall: Definer of a Nation*, pp. 519–20, 524.

70. Peterson, *The Jeffersonian Image in the American Mind*, p. 162.

TWO

THE LEGACY OF THE CIVIL WAR

John Marshall Harlan and Oliver Wendell Holmes, Jr.

1. Sheldon M. Novick, *Honorable Justice: The Life of Oliver Wendell Holmes* (Boston: Little, Brown, 1989), p. 254.

2. Loren P. Beth, *John Marshall Harlan: The Last Whig Justice* (Lexington: Kentucky University Press, 1992), p. 174.

3. Tinsley E. Yarbrough, *Judicial Enigma: The First Justice Harlan* (New York: Oxford University Press, 1995), p. 128.

4. Richard H. Pildes, "Keeping Legal History Meaningful," *Constitutional Commentary* 19 (2002): 645, 648–49.

5. Alan F. Westin, "John Marshall Harlan and the Constitutional Rights of Negroes: The Transformation of a Southerner," *Yale Law Journal* 66 (1957): 637, 687, n. 228.

6. Yarbrough, *Judicial Enigma*, p. 6.

7. Ibid., p. 34.

8. Ibid., p. 52.

9. Beth, *John Marshall Harlan*, p. 67.

10. G. Edward White, *Justice Oliver Wendell Holmes: Law and the Inner Self* (New York: Oxford University Press, 1993), p. 55.

11. Ibid., p. 57.

12. Gerald Caplan, "Searching for Holmes Among the Biographers," *George Washington Law Review* 70 (2002): 769, 804.

13. Louis Menand, *The Metaphysical Club* (New York: Farrar, Straus and Giroux, 2001), pp. 43–44.

14. Novick, *Honorable Justice*, p. 205.

15. Menand, *The Metaphysical Club*, p. 62.

16. Robert W. Gordon, "Law as a Vocation: Holmes on the Lawyer's Path," in *The Path of the Law and Its Influence: The Legacy of Oliver Wendell Holmes, Jr.*, ed. Steven J. Burton (New York: Cambridge University Press, 2000).

17. Liva Baker, *The Justice from Beacon Hill: The Life and Times of Oliver Wendell Holmes* (New York: HarperCollins, 1991), pp. 95–96.

18. Menand, *The Metaphysical Club*, p. 61.

19. Albert W. Alschuler, *Law Without Values: The Life, Work, and Legacy of Justice Holmes* (Chicago: University of Chicago Press, 2000), p. 63.

20. Ibid., pp. 58–59.

21. Novick, *Honorable Justice,* p. 141.

22. Oliver Wendell Holmes, *The Common Law* (Boston: Little, Brown, 1963), p. 5.

23. Oliver Wendell Holmes, "The Path of the Law," *Harvard Law Review* 10 (1897): 457, 461.

24. *Vegelahn v. Guntner,* 167 Mass. 92, 108 (1896).

25. Linda Przybyszewski, *The Republic According to John Marshall Harlan* (Chapel Hill: University of North Carolina Press, 1999), p. 38.

26. Ibid., p. 41.

27. Beth, *John Marshall Harlan,* p. 93.

28. Przybyszewski, *The Republic According to John Marshall Harlan,* p. 178.

29. Beth, *John Marshall Harlan,* p. 123.

30. Westin, "John Marshall Harlan and the Constitutional Rights of Negroes," pp. 637, 698–99.

31. Bernard Schwartz, *A History of the Supreme Court* (New York: Oxford University Press, 1993), p. 101.

32. Beth, *John Marshall Harlan,* p. 229.

33. Yarbrough, *Judicial Enigma,* p. 152.

34. Caplan, *Searching for Holmes Among the Biographers,* p. 796.

35. Baker, *The Justice from Beacon Hill,* pp. 474–75.

36. Ibid., pp. 498–99.

37. Beth, *John Marshall Harlan,* p. 160.

38. Przybyszewski, *The Republic According to John Marshall Harlan,* pp. 44–45.

39. Ibid., p. 47.

40. Ibid., p. 45.

41. Ibid., p. 71.

42. Baker, *The Justice from Beacon Hill,* p. 77.

43. Ibid., p. 268.

44. Novick, *Honorable Justice,* p. 152.

45. Ibid., p. 266.

46. Finley Peter Dunne, *Mr. Dooley on the Choice of Law* (Charlottesville, Va.: Michie, 1963), p. 52.

47. Przybyszewski, *The Republic According to John Marshall Harlan*, p. 145.

48. G. Edward White, *The American Judicial Tradition: Profiles of Leading American Judges* (New York: Oxford University Press, 1976), p. 137.

49. Yarbrough, *Judicial Enigma*, p. 173.

50. Alschuler, *Law Without Values*, p. 27.

51. Przybyszewski, *The Republic According to John Marshall Harlan*, p. 149.

52. Beth, *John Marshall Harlan*, p. 193.

53. Ibid., p. 199.

54. Yarbrough, *Judicial Enigma*, p. 220.

55. Ibid., p. 222.

56. Ibid., p. 224.

57. Alschuler, *Law Without Values*, p. 67.

58. Novick, *Honorable Justice*, p. 202.

59. Baker, *The Justice from Beacon Hill*, p. 623.

60. David M. Rabban, *Free Speech in Its Forgotten Years* (New York: Cambridge University Press, 1997), pp. 133–34.

61. Stone, pp. 192–98.

62. Baker, *The Justice from Beacon Hill*, p. 589.

63. Ibid., p. 641.

64. Novick, *Honorable Justice*, p. 217.

65. Baker, *The Justice from Beacon Hill*, p. 347.

66. Ibid., p. 428.

67. *New York Times*, May 23, 1954.

68. Yarbrough, *Judicial Enigma*, p. 227.

THREE

LIBERTY AND LICENSE

Hugo Black and William O. Douglas

1. David J. Garrow, *Liberty and Sexuality: The Right to Privacy and the Making of Roe v. Wade* (New York: Macmillan, 1994), pp. 241, 245.

2. Roger K. Newman, *Hugo Black: A Biography* (New York: Pantheon Books, 1994), p. 537.

3. Ibid., p. 557.

4. Merrill D. Peterson, *The Jefferson Image in the American Mind* (New York: Oxford University Press, 1960), p. 357.

5. Ibid., p. 355.

6. Howard Ball and Phillip J. Cooper, *Of Power and Right: Hugo Black, William O. Douglas, and America's Constitutional Revolution* (New York: Oxford University Press, 1992), p. 73.

7. Ibid., p. 7.

8. Hugo Black, Jr., *My Father: A Remembrance* (New York: Random House, 1975), p. 15.

9. Ball and Cooper, *Of Power and Right*, pp. 17–18.

10. Newman, *Hugo Black*, pp. 82–83.

11. Ibid., p. 94.

12. Ibid., p. 108.

13. Ibid., p. 116.

14. Ibid., p. 94.

15. Ibid., p. 100.

16. Ball and Cooper, *Of Power and Right*, p. 63.

17. *See* Randolph Paul, "Federal Taxation: Questions of Power and Propriety," in *Hugo Black and the Supreme Court: A Symposium*, ed. Stephen Parks Strickland (Indianapolis: Bobbs-Merrill, 1967), p. 169.

18. Newman, *Hugo Black*, pp. 210–11.

19. Ibid., p. 236.

20. Ibid., p. 283.

21. Bruce Allen Murphy, *Wild Bill: The Legend and Life of William O. Douglas* (New York: Random House, 2003), p. 218.

22. Ibid., pp. 109, 154.

23. William O. Douglas, *The Court Years, 1939–1975: The Autobiography of William O. Douglas* (New York: Random House, 1980), p. 3.

24. James F. Simon, *Independent Journey: The Life of William O. Douglas* (New York: Harper & Row, 1980), p. 274.

25. Murphy, *Wild Bill*, p. 349.

26. Ibid., p. 351.

27. Ibid., p. 378.

28. Hugo Lafayette Black, *A Constitutional Faith* (New York: Alfred A. Knopf, 1969), p. xv.

29. Ibid., pp. 8–9.

30. William Domnarski, *The Great Justices, 1941–54: Black, Douglas, Frankfurter and Jackson in Chambers* (Ann Arbor: University of Michigan Press, 2006), p. 41.

31. Ibid., p. 90.

32. James F. Simon, *The Antagonists: Hugo Black, Felix Frankfurter and Civil Liberties in Modern America* (New York: Simon & Schuster, 1989), p. 260.

33. Newman, *Hugo Black*, pp. 315–19.

34. Murphy, *Wild Bill*, p. 207.

35. Newman, *Hugo Black*, pp. 423–24 (alteration in original).

36. Ball and Cooper, *Of Power and Right*, p. 123.

37. Ibid., p. 78.

38. Newman, *Hugo Black*, p. 471.

39. Ball and Cooper, *Of Power and Right*, p. 175.

40. Michael J. Klarman, *From Jim Crow to Civil Rights: The Supreme Court and the Struggle for Racial Equality* (New York: Oxford University Press, 2004), p. 294.

41. Ibid., p. 296.

42. Ibid., p. 299.

43. Newman, *Hugo Black*, pp. 438–39.

44. Ibid., p. 439.

45. Klarman, *From Jim Crow to Civil Rights*, p. 316.

46. Newman, *Hugo Black*, p. 601.

47. See, for example, Akhil Reed Amar, "The Bill of Rights and the Fourteenth Amendment," *Yale Law Review* 101 (1992): 1193, 1227.

48. Ball and Cooper, *Of Power and Right*, p. 217; see also Newman, *Hugo Black*, pp. 422–23.

49. Newman, *Hugo Black*, pp. 543–44.

50. Ibid., p. 588.

51. Ibid., p. 508.

52. Ibid., p. 570.

53. Ibid., p. 521.

54. Ibid., p. 523.

55. Lucas A. Powe, *The Warren Court and American Politics* (Cambridge, Mass.: Belknap Press, 2000), p. 187.

56. Newman, *Hugo Black,* p. 513.

57. Ibid., p. 405.

58. Ibid., p. 403.

59. Ball and Cooper, *Of Power and Right,* p. 141.

60. Newman, *Hugo Black,* p. 619.

61. Murphy, *Wild Bill,* p. 433–34.

62. Ibid., p. 476.

63. Ibid., p. 601.

64. Murphy, *Wild Bill,* p. 455.

65. Ibid., pp. 463–64.

66. Ibid., pp. 456–57.

67. Douglas, *The Court Years, 1939–1975,* p. 352.

68. Dorothy J. Glancy, "Douglas's Right of Privacy: A Response to His Critics," in *He Shall Not Pass This Way Again: The Legacy of Justice William O. Douglas,* ed. Stephen L. Wasby (Pittsburgh: University of Pittsburgh Press, 1990), p. 162.

69. L. A. Powe, Jr., "Justice Douglas, the First Amendment, and the Protection of Rights," in *He Shall Not Pass This Way Again,* pp. 69, 76–77.

70. Glancy, "Douglas's Right of Privacy," p. 169.

71. Simon, *Independent Journey,* p. 332.

72. Ibid., p. 11.

FOUR

TWO FACES OF CONSERVATISM

William H. Rehnquist and Antonin Scalia

1. Laurence H. Tribe, "Comment," in Antonin Scalia, *A Matter of Interpretation: Federal Courts and the Law* (Princeton, N.J.: Princeton University Press, 1997), p. 67.

2. Thomas Keck, *The Most Activist Supreme Court in History: The Road to Modern Judicial Conservatism* (Chicago: University of Chicago Press, 2004), p. 251.

3. John A. Jenkins, "The Partisan," *The New York Times Magazine,* March 3, 1985.

4. George Lardner, Jr., and Saundra Saperstein, "A Chief Justice-

Designate with Big Ambitions: Even as a Boy Rehnquist Hoped to 'Change the Government,'" *Washington Post,* July 6, 1986.

5. Paul Franco, *Michael Oakeshott: An Introduction* (New Haven: Yale University Press, 2004), pp. 11–12.

6. Richard Kluger, "Simple Justice," repr. in *The Supreme Court of the United States: Hearings and Reports on Successful and Unsuccessful Nominations of Supreme Court Justices by the Senate Judiciary Committee, 1916–1986,* vol. 12, ed. Roy M. Mersky and J. Myron Jacobstein (Buffalo: William S. Hein, 1989), p. 639. See also Mark Tushnet, *A Court Divided: The Rehnquist Court and the Future of Constitutional Law* (New York: W. W. Norton, 2005), p. 20.

7. Michael J. Klarman, *From Jim Crow to Civil Rights: The Supreme Court and the Struggle for Racial Equality* (New York: Oxford University Press, 2004), p. 309.

8. Tushnet, *A Court Divided,* p. 24.

9. Keck, *The Most Activist Supreme Court in History,* pp. 94–95.

10. Mersky and Jacobstein, *The Supreme Court of the United States,* vol. 12, p. 625.

11. Ibid., p. 623.

12. Saundra Sauperstein and George Lardner, Jr., "Nixon's Long Shot for a 'Law and Order' Court; on the Bench, a Confirmed Lone Ranger," *Washington Post,* July 6, 1987.

13. John W. Dean, *The Rehnquist Choice: The Untold Story of the Nixon Appointment that Redefined the Supreme Court* (New York: Free Press, 2001), p. 86.

14. Mersky and Jacobstein, *The Supreme Court of the United States,* vol. 8, 92nd Cong., 1st Sess., "Executive Report Together with Individual Views: Nomination of William H. Rehnquist," p. 54.

15. Margaret Talbot, "Supreme Confidence: The Jurisprudence of Antonin Scalia," *The New Yorker,* March 28, 2005, 43.

16. George Kannar, "The Constitutional Catechism of Antonin Scalia," *Yale Law Journal* 99 (1990): 1297, 1316.

17. Antonin Scalia, address, Pew Forum's "Call for Reckoning" Conference, January 25, 2002, available at http://pewforum.org/deathpenalty/resources/transcript3.php3.

18. Kannar, "The Constitutional Catechism of Antonin Scalia," 1310, n. 61.

19. Ibid., p. 1314, citing G. Wills, *Bare Ruined Choirs: Doubt, Prophecy, and Radical Religion* (New York: Doubleday, 1972).

20. Ken I. Kersch, "Stephen G. Breyer," in *Rehnquist Justice: Understanding the Court Dynamic*, ed. Earl M. Maltz (Lawrence: University Press of Kansas, 2003), pp. 246–47.

21. Richard A. Brisbin, Jr., *Justice Antonin Scalia and the Conservative Revival* (Baltimore: Johns Hopkins University Press, 1997), p. 15.

22. *Nomination of Judge Antonin Scalia to be Associate Justice of the Supreme Court of the United States: Hearing Before the Committee on the Judiciary of the United States Senate*, 99th Cong. (1986), p. 89.

23. Donald E. Boles, *Mr. Justice Rehnquist, Judicial Activist: The Early Years* (Ames: Iowa State University Press, 1987), pp. 131–32.

24. Tushnet, *A Court Divided*, p. 33.

25. William Rehnquist, "Chief Justices I Never Knew," *Hastings Constitutional Law Quarterly* 3 (1976): 637, 645.

26. Antonin Scalia, "Scalia Calls for Justice; Jurist Fires Back," *Boston Herald*, March 29, 2006 (letter to the editor).

27. Antonin Scalia, address, "The Common Christian Good," Gregorian University, Rome, Italy, May 2, 1996, available at http://www.learnedhand.com/scalia.htm.

28. Ibid.

29. Michael Stokes Paulsen and Steffen N. Johnson, "Scalia's Sermonette," *Notre Dame Law Review* 72 (1997): 863, 864.

30. Joan Biskupic, *Sandra Day O'Connor: How the First Woman on the Supreme Court Became Its Most Influential Justice* (New York: HarperCollins, 2005), p. 277.

31. Christopher E. Smith, *Justice Antonin Scalia and the Supreme Court's Conservative Moment* (Westport, Conn.: Praeger, 1993), pp. 99–101.

32. Ibid., p. 71.

33. Jay D. Wexler, "Laugh Track," *The Green Bag* 9 (Autumn 2005): 59, 60.

34. Antonin Scalia, "Originalism: The Lesser Evil," *University of Cincinnati Law Review* 57 (1989): 849.

35. Ibid.

36. Antonin Scalia, address, "Constitutional Interpretation the Old Fashioned Way," Woodrow Wilson International Center for Scholars, March 14, 2005, available at http://www.cfif.org/htdocs/freedomline/current/guest_commentary/scalia-constitutional-speech.htm.

37. Antonin Scalia, address, "A Theory of Constitutional Interpretation," Catholic University of America, October 18, 1996, available at http://www.courttv.com/archive/legaldocs/rights/scalia.html.

38. Ralph A. Rossum, *Antonin Scalia's Jurisprudence: Text and Tradition* (Lawrence: University Press of Kansas, 2006), p. 199.

39. Ibid., pp. 201–3.

40. Letter from Thomas Jefferson to Judge William Johnson, 12 June 1823, in *The Writings of Thomas Jefferson,* vol. 15 (Washington, D.C.: Thomas Jefferson Memorial Association, 1904), pp. 439, 449.

41. Joseph Story, *Commentaries on the Constitution of the United States with a Preliminary Review of the Constitutional History of the Colonies and States Before the Adoption of the Constitution,* vol. 1 (Boston: Hilliard, Gray and Co., 1833), pp. 390–92, n.1.

42. Ibid., pp. 388–89.

43. Talbot, "Supreme Confidence," p. 43.

44. Keck, *The Most Activist Supreme Court in History,* p. 293.

45. Stephen Breyer, *Active Liberty: Interpreting Our Democratic Constitution* (New York: Alfred A. Knopf, 2005), p. 5.

46. Ibid,. p. 6.

47. Ibid., p. 119.

48. Michael W. McConnell, "Originalism and the Desegregation Decisions," *Virginia Law Review* 81 (1995): 947; "Religious Participation in Public Programs: Religious Freedom at a Crossroads," *University of Chicago Law Review* 59 (1992): 115, 135; "The Supreme Court, 1996 Term: Comment: Institutions and Interpretations: A Critique of *City of Boerne v. Flores,*" *Harvard Law Review* 111 (1997): 153, 163. See also Michael W. McConnell, "State Action and the Supreme Court's Emerging Consensus on the Line Between Establishment and Private Religious Expression," *Pepperdine Law Review* 28 (2001): 681.

49. Rossum, *Antonin Scalia's Jurisprudence,* p. 205.

50. Ibid., pp. 205–6.

CONCLUSION
THE FUTURE OF TEMPERAMENT

1. Chief Justice John Roberts, interview with the author, July 11, 2006.

2. Peter Grier, "Roberts Blends Low-Key Style, High Ambition," csmonitor.com, July 25, 2005, available at http://www.csmonitor.com/2005/ 0725/ p01s01-uspo.html.

Acknowledgments

—

This book would not have been written without the support and guidance of Paul Golob at Times Books, who was enthusiastic about the project from the very beginning; shaped and improved the argument at every stage with invaluable editorial suggestions—large and small; enforced a series of tight deadlines as a kindly taskmaster; and made the entire experience a pleasure, with excellent jokes and good judgment from beginning to end. I feel very fortunate to have had the chance to work with him.

I'm grateful to Jody Sheff, the executive producer of the PBS series *The Supreme Court*, and Susan Marchand at Thirteen/WNET New York for asking me to write the companion book to the series, and to Michael Carlisle at InkWell Management for finding the right publishing home for the book. I am also grateful to Mark Zwonitzer, the astute producer of the series, for becoming a friend as well as a colleague. My agent, Lynn Chu, defended my interests with the ferocity of a tiger and the legal acumen of my judicial heroes: she is a force of nature, and I'm glad she's on my side.

Dean Frederick Lawrence at the George Washington University Law School provided research support that made it possible to meet a daunting deadline, and he and his wonderful wife, Kathy, offered intellectual friendship as icing on the cake. My friend Ben Wittes, who has the most judicious temperament I know, read the manuscript and enhanced the structure of the argument, once again. Over the years, *The New Republic*, *The New York Times Magazine*, *The New Yorker*, and *The Atlantic Monthly* have provided ideal platforms for developing some of the arguments and portraits that were incorporated into this book—in particular, a profile of Chief Justice William Rehnquist that appeared in the April 2005 *Atlantic*. The students in my judicial temperaments seminar during the spring of 2006 enthusiastically embraced the experiment of reading judicial biographies at the same time I was, and their fine papers and suggestions in response to drafts of the chapters refined the arguments immeasurably. Many thanks to all of them: Joseph Christian Andersen, Geoffrey Alan David, Steven James Driscoll, Arline Duffy, Marty Kwedar, Anthony James Marcavage, Rachel McGuane, Guilherme Roschke, Rebecca Maya Ross, Laurie Jennifer Rubin, Mayur Prasad Saxena, Susan Schneider, Robert A. Sheffield, and Alessandro Terenzoni. After the seminar ended, Susan Schneider was a skillful line editor of the chapters, and Arline Duffy and Mayur Saxena were meticulous and valued research assistants, checking the footnotes, copyediting the manuscript, and, in Mayur's case, tracking down the pictures. Carmen Fernandez at Thirteen/WNET New York and David Wallace-Wells at Times Books also played key roles in securing the illustrations. In addition, Judy Coleman, just graduated from Yale Law School, read a draft of the manuscript as a pro bono project and offered much appreciated insights.

On the home front, Hugo and Sebastian Rosen were due at the same time as the manuscript, and thoughtfully arrived on time. My wife, Christine, always my closest intellectual companion, enriched the book with her matchless conversation and is now the mother of these two lucky boys. Marveling at her competence, organizational skills, and devotion to their every need during these early weeks reminds me daily of how lucky I am to be married to such a remarkable woman.

—JEFFREY ROSEN

The producers of the PBS series *The Supreme Court* would like to thank the following for their contributions to the project: Tamara E. Robinson, vice president and director of programming, Thirteen/WNET New York; William R. Grant, executive in charge, Thirteen/WNET New York; Mark Zwonitzer, series producer; and Thomas Lennon, series director.

We would like to thank New York Life Insurance Company, the sole corporate funder for *The Supreme Court,* for its generous financial contribution, which made the series possible, and for its ongoing commitment to quality public television.

We are also very grateful to The John D. and Catherine T. MacArthur Foundation, which provided additional funding.

—JODY SHEFF, executive producer, Thirteen/WNET New York

The PBS series *The Supreme Court* is produced by HiddenHill Productions for Thirteen/WNET New York and is copyright © 2007 Educational Broadcasting Corporation.

Illustration Credits

Index

Entries in *italics* refer to captions.

About the Author

JEFFREY ROSEN is a professor of law at George Washington University and the legal affairs editor of *The New Republic*. He is the author of *The Most Democratic Branch*, *The Naked Crowd*, and *The Unwanted Gaze*. His articles have appeared in many publications, including *The New York Times Magazine*, *The Atlantic Monthly*, and *The New Yorker*. He is a frequent contributor to National Public Radio and lives in Washington, D.C.